C000070326

SHORTLIST

London
2007

WHAT'S NEW | WHAT'S ON | WHAT'S NEXT

www.timeout.com/london

Contents

London by Area

Essentials

Published by Time Out Guides Ltd
Universal House
251 Tottenham Court Road
London W1T 7AB
Tel: + 44 (0)20 7813 3000
Fax: + 44 (0)20 7813 6001
Email: guides@timeout.com
www.timeout.com

Editorial/Managing Director Peter Fiennes
Series Editor Ruth Jarvis
Deputy Series Editor Lesley McCave
Business Manager Gareth Garner
Guides Co-ordinator Holly Pick
Accountant Kemi Olufuwa

Time Out Guides is a wholly owned subsidiary of Time Out Group Ltd.

© Time Out Group Ltd
Chairman Tony Elliott
Managing Director Mike Hardwick
Financial Director Richard Waterlow
Time Out Magazine Ltd MD David Pepper
Group General Manager/Director Nichola Coulthard
Time Out Communications Ltd MD David Pepper
Production Director Mark Lamond
Group Marketing Director John Luck
Group Art Director John Oakey
Group IT Director Simon Chappell

Time Out and the Time Out logo are trademarks of Time Out Group Ltd.

This edition first published in Great Britain in 2006 by Ebury Publishing

Ebury Publishing is a division of The Random House Group Ltd
Company information can be found on www.randomhouse.co.uk
10 9 8 7 6 5 4 3 2 1

Distributed in USA by Publishers Group West (www.pgw.com)
Distributed in Canada by Publishers Group Canada (www.pgcbooks.ca)
For further distribution details, see www.timeout.com

ISBN To 31 December 2006: 1-904978-69-X. From 1 January 2007: 9781904978695

A CIP catalogue record for this book is available from the British Library

Colour reprographics by Wyndeham Icon, 3 & 4 Maverton Road, London E3 2JE

Printed and bound in Germany by Appl

Papers used by Ebury Publishing are natural, recyclable products made from wood
grown in sustainable forests

London Shortlist

The **Time Out London Shortlist 2007** is one of a new series of annual guides that draws on Time Out's background as a magazine publisher to keep you current with everything that's going on in town. As well as London's classic sights and the best of its eating, drinking and entertainment, the guide picks out the most exciting venues to have opened in the last year, and gives a full calendar of events for September 2006 to December 2007. It also includes features on the important news, trends and openings, all compiled by locally based editors and writers. Whether you're visiting for the first time in your life or just the first time since 2006, you'll find the *Time Out London Shortlist 2007* contains everything you need to know, in a portable and easy-to-use format. When you get to town pick up a copy of *Time Out,* London's definitive weekly listings magazine, and you'll be impeccably informed.

The guide divides central London into four areas, each of which contains listings for Sights & museums, Eating & drinking, Shopping, Nightlife and Arts & leisure, along with maps pinpointing all their locations. At the front of the book are chapters rounding up each of these scenes city-wide, and giving a Shortlist of our overall picks in a variety of categories. We also include itineraries for point-to-point days out, and essentials including transport information and hotels.

Our listings use phone numbers as dialled locally from within London. To dial them from elsewhere in the UK, preface them with 020; from abroad, use your country's exit code followed by 44 (the country code for the UK), 20 and the number given. We have noted price categories by using one to four pound signs (£-££££), representing budget, moderate, expensive and luxury. Major credit cards are accepted unless otherwise stated. We also indicate when a venue is NEW, and give **Event highlights**.

All our listings are double-checked but businesses do sometimes close or change their hours or prices, so it's a good idea to call a venue before visiting. While every effort has been made to ensure accuracy, the publishers cannot accept responsibility for any errors this guide may contain.

Venues are marked on the maps using symbols numbered according to their order within the chapter and colour-coded according to the type of venue they represent:

❶ Sights & museums
❶ Eating & drinking
❶ Shopping
❶ Nightlife
❶ Arts & leisure

SHORTLIST
Online

The *Time Out London Shortlist 2007* is as up to date as it is possible for a printed guidebook to be. To keep it completely current, it has a regularly updated online companion, at **www.timeout.com/london**. Here you'll find news of the latest openings and exhibitions, as well as picks from visitors and residents – ideal for planning a trip. Time Out is the city specialist, so you'll also find travel information for more than 100 cities worldwide on our site, at www.timeout.com/travel.

Time Out London Shortlist 2007

EDITORIAL
Editor Ruth Jarvis
Copy Editors Simon Coppock, Sarah Thorowgood
Researchers Jill Emeny, Cathy Limb, Patrick Welch, David Jenkins
Proofreader Julian Richards

STUDIO
Art Director Scott Moore
Art Editor Pinelope Kourmouzoglou
Senior Designer Josephine Spencer
Graphic Designer Henry Elphick
Digital Imaging Dan Conway
Ad Make-up Jenni Prichard
Picture Editor Jael Marschner
Deputy Picture Editor Tracey Kerrigan
Picture Researcher Helen McFarland

ADVERTISING
Sales Director/Sponsorship Mark Phillips
Sales Manager Alison Wallen
Advertising Sales Ben Holt, Ali Lowry, Jason Trotman
Copy Controller Amy Nelson
Advertising Assistant Kate Staddon

MARKETING
Marketing Manager Yvonne Poon
Marketing & Publicity Manager, US Rosella Albanese
Marketing Designer Anthony Huggins

PRODUCTION
Production Manager Brendan McKeown
Production Co-ordinator Caroline Bradford

CONTRIBUTORS
Ismay Atkins, Simone Baird, Jonathan Derbyshire, Guy Dimond, Ruth Jarvis, Anna Norman, Natasha Polyviou, Lisa Ritchie, Fiona Shield. Thanks also to contributors to the *Time Out Guide to London* and *Time Out* magazine.

PHOTOGRAPHY
All photography by Heloise Bergman, Andrew Brackenbury, Tricia de Courcy Ling, Britta Jaschinski, Jonathan Perugia, Ming Tang Evans, Alys Tomlinson and Muir Vidler, except: pages 2, 7, 99 Haris Artemis; pages 3, 43, 112, 113 Anthony Webb; page 29 Michelle Brooks; page 33 Nick Hufton; page 36 Battersea Park; page 38 Chris Woodage; page 41 Lois Greenfield; pages 44, 48, 53 Piers Allardyce; page 50 Tony Gibson; page 62 Sean Gallagher; page 66 Michael Franke; page 81 Christina Theisen; page 96 Alberto Uderzo; page 136 London and Continental Railways; page 138 Kevin Nicholson; page 151 Martin Daly; page 169 London 2012; page 177 Angela Moore; page 189 RBG Kew; page 191 English Heritage Photo Library/Jonathan Bailey. The following images were supplied by the featured establishments/artists: pages 2, 3, 9, 11, 25, 30, 35, 42, 52, 100, 107, 159, 210. Cover photograph: London Eye. Credit: Andrew Brackenbury.

MAPS
JS Graphics (john@jsgraphics.co.uk).

About Time Out

Founded in 1968, Time Out has expanded from humble London beginnings into the leading resource for those wanting to know what's happening in the world's greatest cities. As well as our influential what's-on weeklies in London, New York and Chicago, we publish more than a dozen other listings magazines in cities as varied as Beijing, Beirut and Mumbai. The magazines established Time Out's trademark style: sharp writing, informed reviewing and bang up-to-date inside knowledge of every scene.

Time Out made the natural leap into travel guides in the 1980s with the City Guide series, which now extends to over 50 destinations around the world. Written and researched by expert local writers and generously illustrated with original photography, the full-size guides cover a larger area than our Shortlist guides and include many more venue reviews, along with additional background features and a full set of maps.

Throughout this rapid growth, the company has remained proudly independent, still owned by Tony Elliott nearly four decades after he started Time Out London as a single fold-out sheet of A5 paper. This independence extends to the editorial content of all our publications, this Shortlist included. No establishment has been featured because it has advertised, and no payment has influenced any of our reviews. And, for our critics, there's definitely no such thing as a free lunch: all restaurants and bars are visited and reviewed anonymously, and Time Out always picks up the bill. For more about the company, see www.timeout.com.

Don't Miss
2007

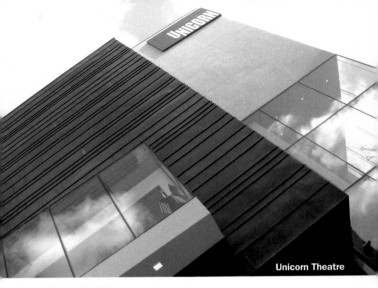

Unicorn Theatre

WHAT'S NEW
Sights & Museums

After its spate of millennial monumentalism, London has added few new buildings to its skyline or big hitters to its cultural roster. But it hasn't gone to sleep either. Despite fears of terrorism the city remains vital, forward-looking and full of visitors, a state of affairs likely to continue until the Olympics in 2012. And if there are no major public projects on the immediate drawing board, there are plenty of big-deal revamps (Tate Modern; National Gallery; Greenwich Observatory), reopenings (London's Transport Museum, p106; Museum of Childhood, p175) and small but excellent new museums (Benjamin Franklin House; Cartoon Museum; Museum of Brands, p185). Many of the major museums are now free,

and so receiving record numbers of visitors, which has stimulated city-wide involvement and a real sense of excitement.

Off the institutional circuit, London continues to be good at what it's always been good at. Despite a decade of left-leaning government, royal pomp and ceremony continue unabashed. A long history of immigration and a relatively tolerant attitude make this one of the most diverse cities in the world. And 'village' London continues to flourish, though there are fluctuations in the villages' fortunes. As property prices continue to rise, few ordinary people can afford to live in central London other than in the previously impoverished areas of

the old East End. You've probably heard that the Hoxton/Shoreditch arts and nightlife boom is old news, but in fact it's merely consolidating.

There are plans for several radical new skyscrapers that will dwarf the current London skyline, but none look like coming to fruition for several years. The most exciting structural projects are transport-related; first to complete, in late 2007, will be the St Pancras International station, a promising redevelopment of a beautiful Victorian landmark that will be the new terminus of the Eurostar passenger rail link to France. Otherwise, smaller but well-considered buildings and developments are the architectural news, such as the Unicorn Theatre (completed; p70) and Zaha Hadid's Architecture Foundation (originally due to complete in autumn 2006, but delayed), both on the South Bank.

We have to admit to thinking that London without its traditional

Conceived and designed by Marks Barfield Architects

Soar

above one of the world's
most extraordinary cities

+44(0)870 5000 600 or londoneye.com
⊖ Waterloo and Westminster

BRITISH AIRWAYS
London eye

Routemaster buses, withdrawn in late 2005, is like Paris without the Eiffel Tower, and it is also true that swift development and gentrification are stripping the capital of some of its individuality. But there's enough energy and creativity – and money – around to feel confident that new icons will emerge.

Neighbourhood

This book is divided by area. The **South Bank** primarily covers riverside Bankside, home of Tate Modern, and its characterful residential hinterland of Borough (with its market). The **City** takes in the once-walled Square Mile of the original city, compelling for its long and still-visible history, along with equally ancient Clerkenwell with its neighbourhood feel and interesting nightlife. The **West End** includes most of the central city. From east to west: the squares and Georgian terraces of literary Bloomsbury,

home of academia and the British Museum; Fitzrovia, its elegant streets speckled with inviting shops and restaurants; beneath them, Covent Garden, so popular with tourists it's easy to forget the charms of its boho boutique shopping, and Soho, storied nightlife centre whose sex industry refuses to be driven out. West of Soho is Mayfair, as expensive as its reputation but less daunting, with inviting backstreet mews and pubs, and, to its south and even posher, stately St James's (most famous resident: her Maj). North of Mayfair, across unlovely Oxford Street, is the elegant but still slightly raffish shopping district of Marylebone. **Westminster to Kensington** starts with the centre of UK politics (and history, but not a lot else) and moves west to swanky Knightsbridge, still-fashionable Chelsea and South Kensington's major Victorian museums.

Museum of Brands, Packaging & Advertising p9

National Gallery p148

Making the most of it

Some tips for getting the best out of London in 2007. Don't be scared of the transport system: invest in an Oyster travel smartcard (p215) and travel cashless through the city by bus and tube. Bus is best for getting a handle on London's topography. Some good routes to try just for their sightseeing opportunies are RV1 (riverside), 7, 8, 11 and 12, along with the 9 and 15 served by pensioned-off Routemasters (p81). Also, don't be afraid to wander at will: crime in central London is low, and walking can be the best way to appreciate its many character changes. No one thinks any the less of anyone consulting a map – so long as they dive out of the stream of pedestrian traffic. And most people will be happy to help with directions: Londoners' reputation for standoffishness is largely undeserved.

To avoid overcrowding follow the tips given in the text, and try to steer clear of the big draws at weekends and on late-opening nights, when the population turns out in force. Aim to hit exhibitions in the middle of their run – or prepare yourself for crowds (an audio tour at least helps screen out the chat). We've always tried to give last entry times, but don't turn up just before a place closes if you want to appreciate it fully. Some sights close at Christmas and Easter – ring ahead to confirm openings.

If time is short, start with a stroll along the South Bank, from Tower Bridge to Waterloo. Here's where you'll find 21st-century London's biggest draws, for both locals and visitors: Borough Market, the Tate Modern, the London Eye and the Millennium Bridge, along with the great photo-opportunities of Tower Bridge, the GLA building and the Houses of Parliament.

Roast

DON'T MISS
Eating & Drinking

London is now routinely mentioned in the same breath as such great restaurant cities as New York, Hong Kong, Paris, Singapore and Sydney. Of course, it wasn't always like this – and a lot of British cooking still does deserve to be the laughing stock of Europe. Yet in the last two decades there has been a revolution in London's catering, fuelled by greater affluence, increasingly discerning diners and not least by London's diversity – matched only by New York's – which has improved standards across the price range.

Every regional style of Indian food is well represented, from Kerala in the south (Rasa Samudra, p101) to Awadhi in the north (Moghul court cooking from Lucknow; Amaya, p154). Like everywhere else in the West, the Chinese food is mostly Cantonese (for dim sum, try New World, p122), but you can also find cooking from other parts of China, and some very innovative fusion Chinese dishes at restaurants such as Hakkasan (p98). Italian food is abundant; there are more French restaurants than there are *départements* of France, and virtually every other cuisine on the planet is represented too. Best of all, you no longer need to pay a fortune to eat – not unless, of course, you want to experience some of the most stunning restaurants you'll ever set foot in.

Which London has in spades. At the top end, this has become a very food-aware city, attracting scene-savvy chefs who have something to prove – even those of international renown such as Joël Robuchon. This is resulting in some strikingly creative and accomplished cooking – but it's largely at the top end. London's luxury hotels are home to an extremely talented kitchen cabal, including Jason Atherton at Maze (p138) and Gordon Ramsay at Claridge's (p138). In fact, Ramsay is so dominant – Atherton is a protégé – that the rest of the scene is a little subdued at the moment.

Ramsay is a bona fide celebrity chef – and then there are celebrity restaurants. The London scene is dominated by Caprice Holdings (www.caprice-holdings.co.uk), responsible for several places that reliably generate buzz and good, if safe, food – notably the Ivy (p111). By the time this guide is out, the group should have reopened Mayfair landmark Scott's. If anyone can restore the place to its former glamour, Caprice can: this could be one to watch.

But what of British food in the nation's capital? It has also been undergoing a renaissance. At the top end, Gordon Ramsay has done more than most to establish Britain's reputation for excellence in haute cuisine. Terence Conran has also been championing British food in the mid- and upper-price range of dining, though smaller operators such as St John (p88), Roast (p65) and the National Dining Rooms (p153) have tended to win more acclaim from Londoners. What we're most excited about, though, is the growth of affordable yet excellent British food. Gastropubs such as the Anchor & Hope (p65) or the Gun (p176) have done much to raise Londoners' expectations of pub grub (a mere decade ago most pub food orders

SHORTLIST

Best new
- Amaya (p154)
- The Ledbury (p186)
- Maze (p138)
- Roast (p65)

Best breakfast/brunch
- Baker & Spice (p156)
- Ladurée (p158)
- Smiths of Smithfield (p88)
- The Wolseley (p141)

Great value for money
- Canela (p110)
- Chowki (p118)
- Hummus Bros (p121)
- The Place Below (p79)

Most glamorous
- Hakkasan (p98)
- Les Trois Garçons (p178)
- Maze (p138)
- Sketch: The Gallery (p139)

Pubs with character
- The Cow (p185)
- Dog & Duck (p118)
- Jerusalem Tavern (p86)
- Lamb & Flag (p111)

Cocktail hour
- Blue Bar at the Berkeley (p154)
- LAB (p121)
- Loungelover (p178)
- Shochu Lounge (p103)
- Zuma (p160)

Something different
- Asadal (p120)
- Baltic (p65)
- Hunan (p154)
- Moro (p87)

Best of British
- Anchor & Hope (p65)
- Canteen (p175)
- Golden Hind (p130)
- National Dining Rooms (p153)
- St John (p88)
- Sweetings (p79)

wagamama

fast and fresh noodle and rice dishes from london's favourite noodle restaurant

wagamama.com

uk ı ireland ı holland ı australia ı dubai ı antwerp ı auckland ı copenhagen

were punctuated by the ping of a microwave). We're delighted too that one-time working-class staples such as pie and mash have been reclaimed and modernised (see box p66).

And those other British institutions – afternoon tea and the pub? We're sorry to report that afternoon tea has become something of a tourist trap, with most of the big 'name' hotels cashing in with charges of £30 per head or more for often lacklustre spreads and tepid settings. If you want something closer to the spirit of afternoon tea, we suggest you avoid the obvious places and instead go to French tea room Maison Bertaux (p121) in Soho; the Wolseley (p141) for a great British experience; or, if you're a true tea connoisseur, the sumptous Chinese tea room Yauatcha (p123) or the cheaper but no less sincere Postcard Teas (p139).

We'd like to pretend London's pubs are filled with grey-haired ladies sipping stout and old men reading the international pages of broadsheets, but unfortunately London suffers from the disease of binge-drinking that afflicts much of northern Europe. At 11pm on Friday night, you will see London at its worst, with more drunken rows, brawls and pavement pizzas than you would get in a year in a Mediterranean capital. The pubs and bars of the West End – Soho and Covent Garden, mainly – are the worst, and best avoided late in the evenings and at weekends unless your idea of fun is talking to yobs in football colours who think you've just spilled their pint.

However, there are still plenty of charming and historic pubs to be found even in the heart of London, and we've suggested a handful in our Shortlist. They all stock a fine selection of well-tended real ales.

There's one area where there can be little argument that New York outstrips London, and that is cocktail bars. But don't despair: London does have some great ones if you know where to look, and the bartenders are dab hands at using fresh fruit juices in ways that impress even New Yorkers. As for the bar scene, places such as the Blue Bar at the Berkeley (p154) and the bar at Zuma (p160) match anything you'll find in Manhattan – just make sure you book a table, unless you're prepared to be jostled out of your seat by a Russian oil magnate or an Estonian supermodel.

Neighbourhood watch

Covent Garden is full of mediocre, overpriced, chain-like bars and restaurants. Away from the main drag of Old Compton Street, adjacent **Soho** has a much better range of well-priced and interesting places to eat, including Busaba Eathai (p97), Hummus Bros (p121), Imli (p121) and Chowki (p118).

Mayfair is expense-account territory. If someone else offers to take you and pay, accept graciously. The **City** and **Westminster** are, generally speaking, not great areas for eating out, with restaurants there propped up by less discerning expense-accounters.

Knightsbridge and **South Kensington** are similarly overpriced, but if you're making the trip to Harrods, Ladurée (p158) is a good spot for a simple but entertaining lunch as well as a great place to marvel at the pâtisserie. On the **South Bank**, the Tate Modern has a couple of very decent brasseries, but if you need to escape their canteen-like surroundings, Baltic (p65) is good for splurge and the Anchor & Hope gastropub is worth the

osatsuma

MODERN JAPANESE DINING

6 Wardour Street, London, W1 020 7437 8338
www.osatsuma.com
→ PICCADILLY CIRCUS LEICESTER SQUARE
Open M-T 12-11 W-T 12-11.30 F-S 12-12 Sun 12-10.30

walk if you arrive early or late (bookings are not taken).

Shoreditch in east London is now the centre of London's bar and nightlife scene, but there's not a lot to choose between scores of trendy but identikit mediocre bars there. Loungelover (p178) is a notable exception, worth booking a seat at (incredibly, it's a cocktail bar with designated seating and fixed time slots). Next to Shoreditch, **Brick Lane** is also very nightlifey but it's not great for food and drink; the street's 50-plus curry houses might be legendary and can be cheap, but they're also not very good.

Serious curry pilgrims will be richly rewarded by a jaunt out of central London to **Tooting** for tons of cheap regional options; to Ealing Road in **Wembley** for Gujarati and Mumbai-style food; or to Southall, a Punjabi home from home. The numerous Turkish and restaurants of **Dalston** are thriving at the moment, as are Shoreditch's great-value Vietnamese cafés (on Old Street and Kingsland Road). It's hard to pick a dud.

Like everywhere else in the world, London has chain bars and restaurants, some of them surprisingly good, most with outposts right across town. Wagamama (www.wagamama.co.uk) has become a global brand because its sleek Asian canteen style is a winning formula. Family-friendly but generally likeable café chain Giraffe and mid-market Italian Carluccio's (p98) too have raised the bar on what multiples can achieve, and new-wave burger mini-chains using prime quality ingredients are now popping up everywhere. We're also hoping that an investor with deep pockets spots Mr Jerk (p122): we love its Caribbean food, and we'd like to see a lot more than just two branches in our city.

Dos & don'ts

Don't expect to be able to get a table at a buzz restaurant any day of the week without booking at least a week ahead. If you find yourself caught without a booking, try a gastropub, where at least you can wait indoors; head for one of the ethnic food neighbourhoods above; or be grateful for the trend towards walk-in business only (at Busaba Eathai, for example).

Many restaurants add a 10 per cent or 15 per cent service charge to the bill; check whether this is the case before leaving anything extra, and be wary of the sneaky and extremely common practice whereby a restaurant adds a service charge, then brings you your credit-card slip 'open' (with a space left for adding a further 'gratuity'). Although not illegal, this despicable practice tends to catch out visitors.

Note that from summer 2007, you will not be allowed to smoke in restaurants (or any other enclosed public place).

Shochu Lounge p15

Tracey Neuls p23

WHAT'S NEW
Shopping

Britain may not be a nation of shopkeepers for much longer. Supermarket supremacy at the cost of the traditional butcher, baker et al has become a hot topic in Parliament and local press, and the campaign to protect the character of London's shopping districts from creeping chainification continues. While many specialist shops are under threat, fashion boutiques are booming, a paradox fuelled by Londoners' ever-increasing obsession with designer labels and niche brands.

For now at least, the retail landscape is extraordinarily varied. Perhaps more than in any other city, London's strengths are twofold: the charm of the old and the shock of the new. In the very heart of this 21st-century megalopolis, you can still discover shops so traditional, that even the impeccably mannered, tail-coated staff seem plucked from an age when dinner conversation revolved around the latest instalment of *Bleak House*. Yet a glance at the catwalks during London Fashion Week – fed by a constant stream of talent from revered design college Central St Martins – confirms the city's style-makers as arguably the most mould-breaking on the international scene. Even our national chains interpret trends in innovative ways: a case in point is Topshop (p134), beloved by fashion stylists and teenagers alike, which recently made its first foray on the catwalk.

Fashion forward

Hot designers du jour include golden boy Giles Deacon, deconstructionist duo Preen – whose assured autumn/winter 2006-7 collection shows effortlessly sophisticated sex appeal – and promising newcomer Alice McCall.

Britain's colonial past and cosmopolitan present isn't just reflected in the exotic produce of its market stalls. That cultural richness is beginning to manifest itself in clothes created by a generation of designers drawing on their heritage; two of the most interesting are Indian Anamika Khanna and Duro Olowu, who grew up in Nigeria. Other great British names to look out for in boutiques include Eley Kishimoto and Emma Cook.

To find items by the bright young stars of tomorrow, you'll either need to head east, to the northerly section of Brick Lane and its offshoots (some shops open only in the latter part of the week to coincide with the Sunday market, p47), or west to Portobello Road, where they set up shop at Portobello Green market (under the Westway flyover) on Fridays and Saturdays. These are also good areas to hit if you're looking for vintage clothing, although retro mania means it's everywhere.

Market values

London's exuberant markets are great places to sample street life and pick up a few bargains in the process. One of the most central is on Berwick Street (p123), where stalls displaying fruit, veg and fish are surrounded by shops selling cheap fabrics, CDs and the less wholesome wares of Soho's red-light district. Borough Market (p68), from Thursday to Saturday, is the foodie's favourite. Even if

DON'T MISS: 2007

LETS FILL THIS TOWN WITH ARTISTS
BEST CHOICE TOP BRANDS LOW PRICES

EASELS

75% OFF

£12.95
WINSOR & NEWTON
DART SKETCHING
EASEL
RRP £39.99

£9.95
DALER-ROWNEY
EDINBURGH
TABLE BOX EASEL
RRP £29.50

70% OFF

70% OFF

£49.95
DALER-ROWNEY
SALISBURY EASEL
RRP £200

PAINTS

HALF PRICE

DALER-ROWNEY
SYSTEM 3
250ML ACRYLIC
ALL HALF PRICE

HALF PRICE

HALF PRICE

WINSOR & NEWTON 14ML ARTISTS
WATERCOLOUR ALL HALF PRICE
WINSOR & NEWTON ARTIST OIL 37ML
ALL HALF PRICE

BRUSHES

WINSOR & NEWTON ARTIST HOG BRUSH SET
RRP £26 NOW £12.95 HALF PRICE

HALF PRICE

CANVAS

70% OFF

WINSOR & NEWTON
ARTIST QUALITY CANVAS
UP TO 70% OFF

SETS & GIFTS

HALF PRICE

REMBRANDT PASTELS
MANY HALF PRICE SETS

HALF PRICE

£4.75
FABER-CASTELL 9000
12 ART PENCILS
8B-2H IN TIN RRP £9.50

£9.47
WINSOR & NEWTON 8X14ML
DRAWING INKS SET RRP £18.95

LESS THAN HALF PRICE

A4 - £3.50, A5 - £2.75
DALER-ROWNEY EBONY
HARDBACK SKETCH PAD
RRP (A4) £8.50, (A5) £6.25

HALF PRICE

PRESENTATION PORTFOLIOS
MANY HALF PRICE ITEMS

you aren't looking to buy a bunch of daffs or some begonia bulbs, head to East London's Columbia Road (p47) on a Sunday morning just to breathe the scented air of the lush flower market and wander into the interesting shops that open on the sidelines.

Antique roadshow

Boho Portobello Road Market (p188) is packed with more than 1,000 antique and bric-a-brac stalls on Saturdays but can get uncomfortably crowded. If you want to avoid the crush, smaller Alfie's (p133) in Marylebone houses high-quality dealers. Secreted behind Islington's Upper Street, Camden Passage (p171) is an atmospheric enclave of shops and arcades selling everything from Victorian games to vintage kitchen equipment (market open Wednesdays and Saturdays).

Culture club

London is known for its book and record stores, though lots of the independents have gone under recently. Bibliophiles are irresistibly drawn to Charing Cross Road, but even locals often overlook the discreet pedestrian lane Cecil Court with its line-up of small specialist antiquarian bookshops. Daunt Books in Marylebone (p133) has a beautiful Edwardian conservatory with travel books and related novels arranged by country.

Those looking for indie record stores should divide their time between Soho (around Berwick Street) and Notting Hill (around Portobello Road); the CD/DVD chains are on Oxford Street.

Neighbourhood watch

If you want a taste of retail past, **St James's Street** is lined with anachronistic specialist shops that are worth checking out in the same spirit as when visiting the British Museum. They include London's oldest hatter, a delightfully old-fashioned chemist and the royal shoemaker. In **Mayfair** the best (and best-known) of the royal arcades is Burlington Arcade, where you can pick up classy cashmere or an authentic Globe-Trotter suitcase (albeit at a price). Enter on Vigo Street, or Piccadilly just east of Old Bond Street. Stuffy **Savile Row** has been given a shake-up in recent years by a handful of tailoring upstarts with modern design sensibilities.

Bond Street remains the domain of British and European luxury labels, auctioneers and posh galleries. To the north, it's best to hurry across heaving thoroughfare **Oxford Street**, with its chains and department stores, and duck into **St Christopher's Place** – a picturesque café- and shop-lined alleyway that leads to the bottom of Marylebone. Hyped to the hilt and in danger of tipping over into a chi-chi village cliché, curving **Marylebone High Street** offers a varied selection of clothiers, perfumeries, gourmet food shops, design stores and jewellers, but it's in the meandering backstreet **Marylebone Lane** that more interesting newcomers, such as avant-garde shoemaker Tracey Neuls (p134), are rubbing shoulders with time-honoured residents such as century-old deli Paul Rothe & Son (No.35, 7935 6783), still run by white-coated Rothes.

A couple of London's most celebrated streets have recently been lifted out of decades in the chain-dominated doldrums. **Carnaby Street**, that emblem of 1960s cool, became prey to tacky souvenir shops and ersatz pop-culture emporiums, but has been salvaged by an influx of quality youth clothing brands and Kingly Court (p123), a small shopping centre housing interesting independent boutiques (including vintage). Tucked behind Carnaby, cobbled, car-free Newburgh Street has a further cache of one-off jewellery and clothes shops.

Once synonymous with the Swinging London of Mary Quant, Jean Shrimpton and Terence Stamp, and, later, punk pioneers Vivienne Westwood and the Sex Pistols, the **King's Road** in Chelsea has morphed into shopping-mall mediocrity, although Viv's first shop still survives 36 years on at World's End (430 King's Road, SW10, 7352 6551). Fittingly it's this end of the street that has been given a boost by a crop of hip stores, such as the Shop at Bluebird (p162).

Equally, **Covent Garden** shouldn't be written off as a tourist trap. North-west of the piazza, cobbled Floral Street and the offshoots of Seven Dials are fertile browsing ground. In the mix you'll find urban streetwear, arty erotica,

Space NK p21

niche cosmetics, quality coffee and British cheeses. Don't miss the sweet little square of **Neal's Yard**, with its funky wholefood cafés and organic herbalist.

Unless you're looking to flash your Platinum AmEx in the international designer salons of **Sloane Street** or marvel at the magnificent art nouveau food halls of Harrods (p162), there's little reason to visit **Knightsbridge**. To the south, however, pretty **Elizabeth Street** is one of central London's most overlooked gems, offering an interesting array of goods in its smart shopfronts, including cutting-edge footwear, rare perfumes, fine chocolate and artisan breads. For luxe designer labels without the crush, **Notting Hill** (especially around the intersection of Westbourne Grove and Ledbury Road) is overflowing with posh boutiques.

London is a conurbation that encompasses numerous villagey neighbourhoods. If you have time to venture further afield, **Primrose Hill**, **Islington** and Northcote Road in **Clapham** are pleasant places to browse.

Shop talk

Most goods are subject to value added tax (VAT) of 17.5 per cent, which is usually included in prices. Books, children's clothes and food are exempt. Some retailers operate a scheme that allows visitors from outside the EU to claim back VAT on goods over a certain amount – you'll need to obtain a form in-store and have it stamped at Customs when you leave the country. Shops in central London are open late (until 7pm or 8pm) one night a week (Thursday in the West End, Wednesday in Chelsea and Knightsbridge), although some department stores stay open late most nights.

The End p28

Nightlife

Given the amount of space 24-hour licensing received in our fire-breathing tabloids when it was introduced in late 2005, you'd have thought that London's youth would be drinking round the clock and living in gutters by now. Not quite. It's actually served to revitalise clubland, adding more and more variety, no matter the time or day – no longer must pubs stop serving at 11pm, nor clubs at 2am or so. See p50 24-Hour Party City for how to have fun round the clock.

Clubbing

London currently rules the world when it comes to clubbing. You name it, we've got a healthy scene

rockin' it. A 1,000-plus capacity venue like the three-room converted meat store Fabric (p90) still gets queues round the block, and this is where weekend tourists tend to head, but smaller, 200-capacity venues are doing a roaring trade for those in the know. Dance music – house, trance and techno – remains enormously popular, but we're still feeling the effects of the electroclash boom of 2002 (synths and electro are massive, with DJs expected to mash up different genres in their sets) and indie is on the up and up.

If there's been one explosion to name-check in the past year, it's been… well, we're yet to coin a

The Home of Funk

Carwash

"The Ace of Clubs" - Time Out

www.carwash.co.uk   0870 246 196

phrase for it. Part cabaret, part burlesque, part performance – all with a healthy sprinkling of DJs, live bands and quirky stuff. On the same bill you can expect roller girls serving tea or popcorn, and a silky crooner followed by a striptease artist elbowed off the stage by jumpin' 11-piece swing band. Looking very much like a small school hall, Bethnal Green Working Men's Club (p177) rules this particular scene. Whether it's at an early 1920s jazz soiree or a rock 'n' roll jivefest, the kids sure do know how to dress the part – top to toe, from coiffured hair and Brylcreem to seamed stockings and spats. And don't even try to get on the dancefloor unless you know your Lindy hop from your boogaloo.

The minimal scene (or ketamine music as non-fans sneer) has been both enormous and influential, and has taken Ibiza's lead: the best parties happen after hours around the East End. This bleepy, beepy, glitchy music is all about still dancing at 8am on Monday morning in Whitechapel warehouses, but the chances are that if you hit a dancefloor anywhere in London you'll hear some of it.

Forget paying £20 to see your favourite superstar DJ: recent months have seen many a bar-cum-club offer such talent for free. The bunker-esque T-Bar (p182) is one of those leading the way, and if you're visiting on a budget (and want to get off the tourist track) it's well worth checking to see what's coming up.

Doing it live

Every guy worth his skinny jeans and kohl eyeliner wants to be in a band, and every boozer now has up-coming bands thrashing cheap speaker stacks in its back room. London's live scene is more energetic and diverse than ever.

SHORTLIST

Best for designer posing
- Loungelover (p178)

Best for vintage dressing
- Bethnal Green Working Men's Club (p177)
- 333 (p181)

Best for sound systems
- The Key (p105)
- Ministry of Sound (p68)
- Plastic People (p181)

Best for all-night partying
- The Cross (p105)

Best for free DJing
- T-Bar (p182)

Best for sunny days
- Canvas (p105)

Best for comfy Sunday sessions
- Big Chill Bar (p180)

Best for mega-star DJs
- The End (p114)
- Fabric (p90)

Best for bands
- Barfly (p172)
- Carling Academy Brixton (p28)
- Luminaire (p173)

Best for gay clubbers
- Crash (p68)
- Heaven (p115)

Most welcome return
- Ronnie Scott's (p127)

Best folk/roots nights
- Soft Focus at the Three Kings of Clerkenwell (p88)
- Health & Happiness at the Social (p105)

Best for cocktails
- Floridita (p118)
- Glass (p121)
- Lab (p121)
- Opium (p123)
- Shochu Lounge (p103)

Promoters are putting grime MCs like Lethal Bizzle next to sets by punk kids the Horrors. Bands like the Klaxons refract their rock through the lens of hoover-powered rave music, and once-static indie kids are dancing to legions of electro outfits (New Young Pony Club), rockabilly yoofs (Vincent Vincent and the Villains) and groovesome nu-folk bands.

It's worth checking out the perfectly retro Luminaire (p173), Barfly (p172) and the beloved Carling Academy Brixton (211 Stockwell Road, SW9 9SL, www. brixton-academy.co.uk), whose great sound and atmosphere make it well worth a trip to the end of the Victoria line.

As the divide between guitar and dance music becomes ever more blurred, so too do club nights, now offering a heady mix of bands, DJs and those in between. The Barfly has several regular mosh-'em-up, mash-'em-up club nights, while Trash at the End (p114) – the West End club that's anything but – still sees the indie kids jump around to Erol Alkan's essential selection of guitars, pop and electronic fare every Monday.

A refurbished Ronnie Scott's (p127), Soho's most famous jazz club, reopened in the spring of 2006, much to the relief of jazz fans in town. A double relief, in fact, because Ronnie's had also sorted out the previously dire kitchen.

Gay disco

The clubs around the newly named 'Vauxhall village' are still the place to go, whether Friday night or Sunday lunchtime. Horse Meat Disco gets a perfect cross-section of freaks and uniques out to play every other Sunday afternoon at South Central (349 Kennington Lane, SE11 5QY, 7793 0903). The Ghetto in Soho (p126), tucked

behind the Astoria, gets long queues of straight kids and bent kids and those in between for NagNagNag, an electro synth fest with JoJodeFreq at the helm – plenty of European bands drop by to do the night live.

Just for laughs

London is the undisputed comedy capital of Europe. If you want sure-fire stand-up, the big hitters remain the basement Comedy Store (p125) and the Soho Theatre (p129), but it's also worth seeking out the smaller venues listed each week in *Time Out* magazine – and not just because they're miles cheaper.

Making the most of it

One piece of advice? Plan your weekend. During the summer, London sees a crop of outdoor parties and festivals that you'd kick yourself if you missed by just a few days. Over Christmas, New Year's Eve and the half dozen or so bank holidays, it really kicks off. In a good way. If you're hankering after some Secretsundaze secret party action, or are dying to find out whether the latest hot young band really is worth the hype, then you need to schedule your weekend carefully. Check **www.timeout.com/london** to coordinate your visit.

Now, unhelpfully, we're going to contradict ourselves: in London, there's always something going on, no matter the day, no matter the hour. Even long-in-the-tooth Londoners fall across brand new happenings just by taking the wrong street, and the best way to get a taste of 'real London', instead of the city every postcard-collecting tourist sees, is to go with the flow. Someone tells you about a great party? Check it out. You read about an exciting new band on the tube? Go and get a ticket.

You'll no doubt have some 'essentials' mapped out in your head, but, if you miss them this time, you can always come back.

Once here, be sure to get to grips with our transport system. Don't worry, it's not as daunting as you might think. The tube is self-evident, but, come midnight, it stops running. Black cabs are pricey and hard to find at night, but safe. There are also licensed minicabs; some bigger nightclubs run their own service, or you can summon one by phone. Beware illegal minicab touts. Far better to check out the excellent Night Bus system before you head out (try the handy Journey Planner at www.tfl.gov.uk). A couple of minutes working out which Night Bus gets you back before you go

out can save hours of blurry-visioned confusion later on. For more on the city's methods of transport, see p213 Getting Around.

In addition to *Time Out* magazine and its website, www.dontstayin.com is excellent for on-the-ground clubbing news, and record shops are an invaluable source of flyers, tickets and advice about what's going on when you're in town. City 16 in Shoreditch (1 Cheshire Street, E2 6ED, 7613 5604) is the most friendly. Indie fans should hit www.irlondon.co.uk for the latest talk.

If you're after comedy in late July or throughout August, bear in mind that most names head to Edinburgh for the Fringe Festival, and most comedy venues either close or run small bills. October, meanwhile, is great for fresh shows.

Luminaire

The Lord of the Rings p33

Arts & Leisure

The story of the arts in London in 2007 is all about renovation and renewal. Londoners have long enjoyed the presence of numerous world-class performing arts venues on their doorsteps, but now several of these are reopening with facilities improved beyond recognition. Nor is this just a tale of bricks and mortar: personnel changes at a number of key institutions are certain to shake things up still further.

Undoubtedly the biggest news of all is the redevelopment of London's foremost arts complex, the South Bank Centre. Work on this enormous project began in 2003 and it reaches a significant milestone in 2007 with the completion of substantial improvements to the Royal Festival Hall (p70). Concert-goers, in particular, will benefit, as the previously patchy acoustic in the main hall is being improved.

The board of the South Bank is promising an artistic programme to match the architectural transformation currently being wrought alongside the Thames. The person responsible for delivering this is new artistic director Jude Kelly, whose track record running first the Battersea Arts Centre and then the West Yorkshire Playhouse in Leeds, not to mention directing several award-winning West End productions, suggests she has the requisite vision and energy.

Also noteworthy is the extensive renovation of the Roundhouse (p173) in Camden Town. This former railway shed, which played a central role in the flowering of the 1960s counterculture in Britain, reopened in June 2006 with a performance of *Fuerzabruta*, an airborne spectacular from the creators of the hit *De La Guarda*. In the autumn the major Dance Umbrella festival (p36) opens at the Roundhouse with a performance, in the round, of Merce Cunningham's *Ocean*.

Elsewhere, the English National Opera prospers at the splendidly restored Coliseum (p115), while the new Lilian Baylis Theatre at Sadler's Wells (p173), which opened in 2003, is a sleekly welcoming home for the best in contemporary dance.

Film

A key part of the South Bank redevelopment is the building of the British Film Institute Centre next to the National Film Theatre (p70). The NFT continues to boast the most ambitious programming of any cinema in London, placing particular emphasis on new foreign films and exhaustive retrospective studies of the work of individual directors. It's also an important venue in the annual BFI London Film Festival (p36 & p42), which is Britain's largest public film event, screening more than 300 movies from 60 countries. The festival is held every autumn and celebrates its 50th anniversary in 2006. Among the major films that have been given an early airing at previous LFFs have been *Good Night, and Good Luck*, *Hidden*, *Vera Drake* and *Lost in Translation*.

SHORTLIST

Best new venue
- Rich Mix (p182)

Best revamped venue
- Roundhouse (p173)

Best for new plays
- Royal Court Theatre (p164)

Best for old plays
- Shakespeare's Globe (p61)

Cult musical most likely to succeed
- *Spamalot* (p128)

Most eagerly awaited cult musical
- *The Lord of the Rings* (p106)

Best for new movies
- London Film Festival (p36)

Best for old music
- Wigmore Hall (p134)

Best arthouse cinemas
- ICA Cinema (p147)
- Curzon Soho (p127)

Loveliest auditoriums
- The renewed Coliseum (p115)
- Lilian Baylis Theatre at Sadler's Wells (p173)

Best bargains
- Standby tickets at the Barbican (p82)
- Standing tickets for a fiver at the English National Opera (p115)
- Standing tickets in the stalls at the Proms (p41)

Best off-West End theatres
- Almeida (p173)
- Donmar Warehouse (p115)

Most innovative work
- London Sinfonietta, at the South Bank Centre (p70)
- Richard Alston Dance Company, at The Place (p106)

Aside from the Hollywood staples occupying screens in the West End, not to mention an extensive repertory and arthouse circuit, cinephiles visiting London have a range of smaller-scale annual festivals to choose from. Highlights include the Women's Film Festival at the ICA (p147) in March, the Children's Film Festival (p42) at the Barbican in November, and the Australian Film Festival at the Barbican in May.

Classical music & opera

In 2007 the Barbican arts centre (p82) reaches its 25th anniversary, a milestone marked by some significant changes at the top of one of its resident companies, the London Symphony Orchestra. Sir Colin Davis assumes the post of president of the LSO, only the sixth person to hold the job in the orchestra's century-long history. An important date in Davis's 2006/7 season is a performance of Elgar's *The Dream of Gerontius* in June, to coincide with the 150th anniversary of the great English composer's birth.

Sir Colin's successor as principal conductor will be Valery Gergiev, who picks up the baton in January. Apparently Gergiev will continue to fulfil conducting responsibilities in St Petersburg, Moscow and with the Met in New York. But the LSO is nevertheless confidently trumpeting 12 programmes a year with its new maestro. In the first half of 2007, these will include works by Stravinsky, Prokofiev and Debussy.

There's change afoot at English National Opera too, where Edward Gardner announces his arrival as musical director with a revival, in May 2007, of Mozart's *La clemenza di Tito*. Gardner's brief, together with artistic director John Berry, will be to consolidate ENO's reputation for celebrating English opera (especially Britten) and for promoting contemporary work, as well as paying attention to the core repertory that is the stock-in-trade of its less ambitious, more venerable neighbour in Covent Garden, the Royal Opera House (p116), itself the subject of thorough renovation in the late 1990s.

Meanwhile, the future of chamber music in the capital looks rosy after the news that the lease on the Wigmore Hall (p134) has been secured for another couple of hundred years. This is due in large part to the work of director John Gilhooly, whose combination of administrative flair and artistic sensitivity ensures that the Wigmore Hall retains its unrivalled international standing as a venue for chamber music and recitals.

Theatre

In 2006 the Royal Court Theatre (p165) completed five decades as Britain's leading venue for new playwriting, but a new chapter opens in January 2007 when Dominic Cooke takes over as artistic director, after Ian Rickson's successful eight-year stint in the job. Cooke promises to continue Rickson's emphasis on hard-hitting writing with a political edge, which has re-established the Royal Court as the home of theatrical radicalism in the UK.

Marianne Elliott, currently an associate director at the Royal Court, has been invited to join artistic director Nicholas Hytner's revolution at the National Theatre (p70). Elliott's 2005 production of Ibsen's *Pillars of the Community* was a critical success and as a consequence she's been invited back to direct an adaptation of Michael Morpurgo's novel *War Horse*.

Another 2005 success, Melly Still's production of *The Coram Boy*, returns to the National for an extended run in November 2006.

Hytner's vibrant regime, which kicked off with the controversial *Jerry Springer – the Musical*, makes that of his predecessor Trevor Nunn seem like a bad dream. Among other highlights in 2007, Hytner is promising a new work with music and lyrics by Blur frontman Damon Albarn and a production, previously staged on Broadway, of Tony Kushner's musical *Caroline, or Change*.

Three musicals also promise to be among the hottest West End tickets for 2007. Kevin Wallace's production of the stage adaptation of Tolkien's *The Lord of the Rings* is due to open at the Theatre Royal Drury Lane (p117) in May. Then there's Mike Nichols directing Simon Russell Beale and Tim Curry in Monty Python's *Spamalot* at the Palace. And the Broadway smash *Wicked*, which tells the untold story of the Witches of Oz, arrives at the Apollo Victoria with American director Joe Mantello.

Dance

London boasts a number of internationally recognised venues for contemporary dance, including Sadler's Wells, the Place (p106), home to the Richard Alston Dance Company, and the Barbican. One of the reasons London is able to attract the best international contemporary dance companies is the commitment of Dance Umbrella, a body whose annual autumn festival is drawing unprecedentedly large audiences for often quite challenging work. The 2006 festival will close in spectacular fashion at the Barbican with Michael Clark's *Mmm...*, the second part of his ongoing Stravinsky Project.

Contemporary dance in London has acquired a new venue. Spring 2006 saw the Siobhan Davies Dance Studios (www.sddc.org.uk) open in Southwark, in a building refurbished by architect Sarah Wigglesworth. The building will mostly be used for rehearsals and classes, but will host autumn's International Workshop Festival.

What's on

We have included in this guide long-running musicals that we think are likely to survive into 2007 and beyond. However, a new crop will inevitably open throughout the year, along with seasons at individual venues. *Time Out* magazine and www.timeout.com have the most informed and up-to-date listings.

ENO at the Coliseum

THE NATIONAL TRUST

LONDON'S BEST
KEPT SECRETS

HAM HOUSE

Escape to a green oasis of calm and tranquillity, just minutes away from central London

- Ham House in Richmond and Osterley Park & House in Isleworth are easily accessible by London Underground from central London.

- Outstanding and unique treasure houses, offering a glimpse of life in the 17th and 18th centuries.

OSTERLY PARK & HOUSE

Properties open April to end of October.
For opening times and further information call
Ham House (020 8940 1950) or Osterley Park (020 8232 5050)
or visit www.nationaltrust.org.uk

Calendar

Greenwich & Docklands International Festival p41

This is the pick of London events that had been announced as we went to press. To stay completely current, buy a copy of *Time Out* magazine, or check timeout.com/london (and look out for Shorlist events, posted three months in advance).

Dates of public holidays are picked out in **bold**.

September 2006

Until summer 2007 **Festival of Muslim Cultures**
Various locations
www.muslimcultures.org
See box p40.

Throughout month **Time Out London on Screen**
Various locations
www.timeout.com/londononscreen
Screenings, events, shorts and galas.

3 **Regent Street Festival**
www.regentstreetonline.com

10 **Brick Lane Festival**
www.bricklanefestival.com

10-11 **DMC World DJ Championships**
Hammersmith Palais
www.dmcworld.com

14-7 Jan 07 **Leonardo da Vinci**
Victoria & Albert Museum, p166

16 **Great River Race**
Thames, Richmond to Greenwich
www.greatriverrace.com
260-odd boats, over a 22-mile course.

16-17 **Mayor's Thames Festival**
Between Westminster & Blackfriars Bridges
www.thamesfestival.org

16-17 **Open House London**
Various locations
www.londonopenhouse.org
Free access to over 500 buildings.

17 **Alexandra Palace Antiques & Collectors Fair**
www.pigandwhistlepromotions.com

21-23 **100% Design**
Earls Court & Spitalfields
www.100percentdesign.co.uk
Interior design trade show.

21-4 Oct **Dance Umbrella**
Various locations
www.danceumbrella.co.uk
Stunning contemporary dance.

October 2006

Ongoing Festival of Muslim
Cultures (see Sept); Leonardo da
Vinci (see Sept); Dance Umbrella
(see Sept)

2 **Pearly Queens & Kings
Harvest Festival**
St Martin-in-the-Fields, p150
www.pearlysociety.co.uk
A 3pm service for the professional
Cockneys, in traditional outfits.

3-8 **Decorative Antiques
& Textiles Fair**
The Marquee, Battersea Park
www.decorativefair.com

3-15 **Chelsea Crafts Fair**
Chelsea Old Town Hall,
Kings Road
www.craftscouncil.org.uk

4-7 Jan 2007 **Cézanne in Britain**
National Gallery, p150

12-21 Jan 2007 **David Hockney**
National Portrait Gallery, p150

18-21 Jan 2007 **Velázquez**
National Gallery, p150

19-3 Nov **50th London Film
Festival**
National Film Theatre (p70) and
other venues.
www.lff.org.uk

3 Oct-21 Jan 2007 **Turner Prize
Exhibition**
Tate Britain, p150
www.tate.org.uk
An exhibition of the work of this year's
nominees: Tomma Abts, Phil Collins,
Mark Titchner and Rebecca Warren.

November 2006

Ongoing Festival of Muslim
Cultures (see Sept); Leonardo da

Bonfire Night

Vinci (see Sept); Cézanne in
Britain (see Oct); David Hockney
(see Oct); Turner Prize (see Oct);
Velázquez (see Oct); 50th London
Film Festival (see Oct); Turner
Prize Exhibition (see Oct)

5 **London to Brighton
Veteran Car Run**
From Hyde Park
www.lbvcr.com

5 **Bonfire Night**

10-19 **London Jazz Festival**
Various locations
www.serious.org.uk

11 **Lord Mayor's Show**
Various streets in the City
www.lordmayorsshow.org
An inauguration procession.

12 **Remembrance Sunday
Ceremony**
Cenotaph, Whitehall

Mid Nov **State Opening of
Parliament**
House of Lords, Westminster
www.parliament.uk
Limited public access but you can
watch the Queen arrive by coach.

17-19 **Battersea Contemporary Arts Fair**
www.bcaf.info

18-26 **Children's Film Festival**
Barbican Centre, p82
www.londonchildrenfilm.org.uk

Nov-Dec **Christmas Tree & Lights**
Covent Garden, Regent Street & Trafalgar Square
www.london.gov.uk/www.coventgarden market.co.uk/www.regent-street.co.uk

December 2006

Ongoing Festival of Muslim Cultures (see Sept); Leonardo da Vinci (see Sept); Cézanne in Britain (see Oct); David Hockney (see Oct); Turner Prize (see Oct); Velázquez (see Oct); Turner Prize Exhibition (see Oct); Christmas Tree & Lights (see Nov)

12-21 Dec **Spitalfields Festival**
Various locations
7377 1362/www.spitalfieldsfestival. org.uk
Classical music.

15-17 **Frost Fair**
Bankside Riverwalk
Three-day food and wine fair.

25 Christmas Day

26 Boxing Day

31 **New Year's Eve**
Trafalgar Square

January 2007

Ongoing Festival of Muslim Cultures (see Sept); Leonardo da Vinci (see Sept); Cézanne in Britain (see Oct); David Hockney (see Oct); Turner Prize (see Oct); Velázquez (see Oct); Turner Prize Exhibition (see Oct)

1 New Year's Day

5-14 **London Boat Show**
ExCeL, Royal Victoria Docks
www.londonboatshow.com.

12-28 **London International Mime Festival**

Various locations
7637 5661/www.mimefest.co.uk

Mid Jan **Russian Winter Festival**
Various locations
www.eventica.co.uk
An eclectic mix of Eastern European treats, particularly Russian folk acts.

17-21 **London Art Fair**
Business Design Centre, Islington
www.londonartfair.co.uk

February 2007

Ongoing Festival of Muslim Cultures (see Sept)

8-12 **Collect Arts & Craft Fair**
Victoria & Albert Museum
www.craftscouncil.org.uk

15-7 May **Gilbert & George**
Tate Modern, p63

18 (tbc) **Chinese New Year Festival**
Chinatown, Leicester Square & Trafalgar Square
www.chinatownchinese.com

March 2007

Ongoing Festival of Muslim Cultures (see Sept); Gilbert & George (see Feb)

Date (tbc) **Alternative Fashion Week**
New Spitalfields Traders Market
www.alternativearts.co.uk/events/

3 **Total eclipse of the moon**

3-4 **Start of Barbican 25th Anniversary celebrations**
See box p90.

17 **St Patrick's Day Parade & Festival**
Various locations
www.london.gov.uk
Irish music and dancing, arts and crafts.

Mid March **Human Rights Watch International Film Festival**
Various locations
08707 550062/www.hrw.org/iff.

Late March-mid Apr **London Lesbian & Gay Film Festival**

Sprite Urban Games

National Film Theatre, p70
7928 3232/www.llgff.org.

29 March-22 July **'Surreal Things'**
Victoria & Albert Museum, p166
See box p162.

April 2007

Ongoing Festival of Muslim
Cultures; Gilbert & George (see
Feb); London Lesbian & Gay Film
Festival (see March)

6 Good Friday

9 Easter Monday

7 **Oxford & Cambridge
Boat Race**
Thames, Putney to Mortlake
www.theboatrace.org

9 Easter Monday Bank Holiday

22 **London Marathon**
Greenwich Park to the Mall
www.londonmarathon.co.uk

May 2007

Ongoing Festival of Muslim
Cultures (see Sept); Gilbert &
George (see Feb)

7 Early May Bank Holiday

13 **Baishaki Mela (Bangladeshi
New Year Festival)**
Brick Lane
7539 3411/www.visitbricklane.com
Bengali arts, music and culture.

22-26 **Chelsea Flower Show**
Royal Hospital grounds, Chelsea
www.rhs.org.uk

26 May-9 Sept **Kew
Summer Festival**
Royal Botanic Gardens
www.kew.org

28 Spring Bank Holiday

May-July **Royal Academy
Summer Show**
Royal College of Art, Kensington Gore
www.rca.ac.uk
Graduate degree shows.

June 2007

Ongoing Festival of Muslim
Cultures (see Sept); Kew Summer
Festival (see May); Royal
Academy Summer Show
(see May)

June-Aug Coin Street Festival
Bernie Spain Gardens, South Bank
www.coinstreetfestival.org
Celebration of different communities.

June-Aug Opera Holland Park
*0845 230 9769/www.operaholland
park.com.*

Early June **Beating Retreat**
Horse Guards Parade, Whitehall
An evening of Cavalry drumming.

4-22 Spitalfields Festival
See above Dec 2006.

Mid June **Open Garden
Squares Weekend**
www.opensquares.org
Private squares opened to the public.

Mid June **Meltdown**
South Bank Centre, p70
www.rfh.org.uk
Festival of contemporary music.

Mid June **Taste of London**
Regent's Park
www.tasteoflondon.co.uk
Four days of outdoor cheffery.

Mid June **Trooping the Colour**
Horse Guards Parade
www.roy.gov.uk
The Queen's official birthday parade.

15-24 Architecture Week
Various locations
7973 5246/www.architectureweek.co.uk

Mid June-July **Pride London**
Hyde Park to Trafalgar Square
www.pridelondon.org

25 June-8 July **Wimbledon Lawn
Tennis Championships**
www.wimbledon.org

Weekend Late June
Sprite Urban Games
Clapham Common
www.spriteurbangames.com
Boarding, biking, music and more.

Late June-early July **City of
London Festival**
www.colf.org
A themed-festival of music and arts.

Late June-Aug **Kenwood
Lakeside Concerts**
7973 3427/www.picnicconcerts.com.

Party on

London never used to be great at music festivals. But the past couple of years have seen an explosion in outdoor parties, and it's Clapham Common that takes the crown.

Get Loaded in the Park has been drawing the party people for three sell-out years every August. It brings in big-hitter indie, breaks and electro bands and DJs to headline, and has a Comedy Store tent and a laughing-gas room. **Southwest Four** takes place over the August Bank Holiday weekend, and sees megastar house, techno and trance DJs rock the main stage, with oodles of smaller arenas. Bacardi's three-day **B-Live** in July adds a summery, Latin twist, with salsa bands joining soulful house DJs. Groove Armada's excellent **Lovebox** weekender started in Clapham but is now at Victoria Park. You don't get much more London than the **TDK Cross Central** festival in King's Cross Goods Yard. Inhabiting cobbled lanes and railway arches, and with mega-clubs like Canvas, the Cross, and the Key (all p105) participating, it marries the latest new bands, guitars and heavy eyeliner with electronic sounds of the underground.

Hyde Park is playing catch-up, too. Events in 2006 included the **O2 Wireless Festival** in June and, in July, **Hyde Park Calling**.

■ www.blivelondon.co.uk
■ www.crosscentral.co.uk
■ www.getloadedinthepark.com
■ www.loveboxlondon.com
■ www.hydeparkcalling.co.uk
■ www.southwestfour.com
■ www.wirelessfestival.co.uk

Festival of Muslim Cultures

Running from January 2006 until July 2007, the Festival of Muslim Cultures is a UK-wide series of cultural events. These include exhibitions, film screenings, performing arts and youth projects, designed to promote the best of the arts from the Muslim world. Organisers of the festival, who have been keen to avoid affiliation with any ideological or political movement, include academics, politicians and cultural figures (with the patron HRH the Prince of Wales).

Popular themes have been issues of identity and how the arts can be a positive force for societal change. The aim of the festival is to promote respect of Muslim cultures during a time of strained relations between the Muslim world and the West.

Events that have already taken place include a Pakistani film festival, a showcase of the work of Iraqi artist Issam El Said, a 'Bellini and the East' exhibition at the National Gallery and a tour by Islamic Relief, which seeks to provide aid to developing countries. Planned for late 2006 are 'Beyond the Page', contemporary art from Pakistan at Asia House (1 Sept-11 Nov), and 'Arabian Nights' (25 Nov), a day of storytelling, music and talks on at the Wallace Collection (p130). For future events, see the website.
■ www.muslimcultures.org).
■ Asia House, 63 New Cavendish Street, Marylebone, W1G 7LP (7307 5454/www.asiahouse.org).

July 2007

Ongoing **Kew Summer Festival** (see May); Royal Academy Summer Show (see May); Coin Street Festival (see June); Opera Holland Park (see June); Wimbledon Lawn Tennis Championships (see June)

July-Oct **Time Out Park Nights**
Serpentine Gallery, Hyde Park
www.timeout.com
Events and screenings.

3-8 **Hampton Court Palace Flower Show**
7649 1885/www.rhs.org.uk

6-8 **Tour de France, Grand Départ**
Trafalgar Square & central London.
7222 1234/www.tourdefrancelondon.com
See box p126.

7 **William Hill Greyhound Derby**
Wimbledon Stadium
www.wimbledonstadium.co.uk

July (tbc) **Greenwich & Docklands International Festival**
www.festival.org

July-Aug **Dance Al Fresco**
Regent's Park
www.dancealfresco.org
Social dancing outdoors.

Late July **Lovebox Weekender**
Victoria Park
www.loveboxweekender.co.uk
Weekend dance music festival.

July-Sept **BBC Sir Henry Wood Promenade Concerts**
Royal Albert Hall
www.bbc.co.uk/proms

End July-Aug **Rushes Soho Shorts Festival**
7851 6207/www.sohoshorts.com
Free screenings of short films.

August 2007

Ongoing **Kew Summer Festival** (see May); Coin Street Festival (see June); Opera Holland Park (see June); Dance Al Fresco (see July); Time Out Park Nights (see July); BBC Sir Henry Wood Promenade Concerts (see July);

Festival of Muslim Cultures

Rushes Soho Shorts Festival
(see July)

2-6 Jan 2008 **Lee Miller**
Victoria & Albert Museum, p166

1st weekend Aug **Fruitstock**
Regent's Park
www.dancealfresco.org
Live music and posh food stalls.

Early Aug **Carnaval del Pueblo**
Burgess Park, Camberwell
www.carnavaldelpueblo.co.uk
Latin American festival and parade.

Early Aug **Vibrations**
Burgess Park, Camberwell
www.southwark.gov.uk
African and Caribbean music.

26-**27 Notting Hill Carnival**
www.lnhc.org.uk
Europe's biggest street party.

31 **10th Anniversary of the death
of Diana, Princess of Wales**

September 2007

Ongoing Kew Summer Festival
(see May); BBC Sir Henry Wood
Promenade Concerts (see July);
Time Out Park Nights (see July);
Lee Miller (see Aug)

2nd Sun **Brick Lane Festival**
See above Sept 2006.

Mid Sept **Great River Race**
See above Sept 2006.

Mid Sept **London Fashion
Week & Weekend**
Natural History Museum
www.londonfashionweek.co.uk

22-23 **Mayor's Thames Festival**
See above Sept 2006.

Mid Sept **Open House London**
See above Sept 2006.

Mid Sept **Dance Umbrella**
See Sept 2006 above.

27-6 Jan 2008 **Golden Age
of Couture**
Victoria & Albert Museum, p166

October 2007

Ongoing Time Out Park Nights
(see July); Lee Miller (see
|Aug); Golden Age of Couture
(see Sept)

1-mid Nov **Ozmosis**
Barbican Centre, p82
Festival of all things Australian.

Fruitstock p41

2 **Pearly Queens & Kings Harvest Festival**
See above Oct 2006.

Early Oct **Raindance Film Festival**
Various locations
*7287 3833/www.raindance
filmfestival.org*

Mid Oct-Jan 2007 **Turner Prize**
See above Oct 2006.

19 Oct-3 Nov **London Film Festival**
See above Oct 2006.

November 2007

Ongoing Lee Miller (see Aug);
Golden Age of Couture (see
Sept); Ozmosis (see Oct); Turner
Prize (see Oct)

5 **London to Brighton Veteran Car Run**
See above Nov 2006.

5 **Bonfire Night**

11 **Lord Mayor's Show**
See above Nov 2006.

12 **Remembrance Sunday Ceremony**
See above Nov 2006.

Mid Nov **State Opening of Parliament**
See above Nov 2006.

Mid-late Nov **Children's Film Festival**
See above Nov 2006.

16-25 **London Jazz Festival**
See above Nov 2006.

Nov-Dec **Christmas Tree & Lights**
See above Nov 2006.

December 2007

Ongoing Lee Miller (see Aug);
Golden Age of Couture (see Sept);
Turner Prize (see Oct)

Mid Dec **Frost Fair**
See above Dec 2006.

12-21 **Spitalfields Festival**
See above Dec 2006.

25 **Christmas Day**

25 **Boxing Day**

31 **New Year's Eve**
See above Dec 2006.

Itineraries

The River Run

When author John Burns wrote 'The Thames is liquid history' in 1943, he wasn't wrong. The river is London's raison d'être and, for the two millennia since the Roman settlement of Londinium was founded on its banks, has been its main artery, its conduit to the rest of the world, its sewer, soul and inspiration. It has witnessed myriad defining events, launched Britain's naval might and borne royalty, ideas and commerce on its tides. But while it's no longer a working river, the Thames remains at the heart of London life and identity, its banks studded with modern monuments alongside the historic sites.

Our itinerary takes you into just two of the attractions en route, chosen because they relate to the river itself, but also acts as a sampler of places to which you might want to return. It lasts a full day and entails a fair amount of walking.

Our itinerary starts out east in **Greenwich**, a historic naval base and home to royalty. The best way to get there is by train from Charing Cross, a 15-minute journey (times on 7222 1234). Aim to arrive at 9am. From the station, turn left on to Greenwich High Road and continue for ten minutes until it joins Greenwich Church Street in the atmospheric heart of the riverside town.

Our itinerary allows for two hours in Greenwich. To stay within the theme, we suggest you spend them at the excellent **National Maritime Museum** (p182) and learn about Britain's seafaring history, but on a warm day, you may prefer to visit **Greenwich Park** instead. This is the oldest enclosed Royal Park, a huge expanse of green, with a deer park in one corner and the Greenwich World Heritage Site, home to the

ITINERARIES

Old Royal Observatory (p183), at its centre. From Thursday to Sunday shopping addicts will find the lure of Greenwich's covered **market** (p184) and its gifty/antiquey galleries irresistible.

By 11am you need to be at the **Greenwich Foot Tunnel** (8921 5493). The domed entrance tower is located on the riverfront alongside the *Cutty Sark* (p182), the famous 19th-century tea clipper. The tunnel, opened in 1902, takes you under the Thames. At both ends there are spiral staircases and lifts . As you pace out the ten-minute walk, you will feel an uneasy awareness of the river above you, but the sense of foreboding is quickly dispelled when you emerge into Island Gardens at the southern tip of the Isle of Dogs (the land enclosed in the Thames's pendulous loop). On a sunny day, Island Gardens is a little slice of paradise; take a seat on a bench and enjoy stunning views back towards Greenwich.

From here, follow signposts to Island Gardens station, then take the Docklands Light Railway to West India Quay, a short journey that offers views of the towers of Canary Wharf, London's City overspill that moved in as part of a 1980s regeneration scheme. Although London's docklands were in irreversible decline, the programme was brutal and controversial.

The story of their heyday is told at your next stop, the **Museum in Docklands** (p175). From West India Quay station walk past the *SS Robin Gallery* and the various bars and restaurants that overlook West India Dock North; at the end is the museum. Resident in an 1802 warehouse built to store sugar, rum and coffee from the Caribbean, it houses a comprehensive and interactive exhibition documenting the development of London around the Thames.

From here, take a relaxing but swift boat ride to the heart of the city. Ask museum staff for directions to Canary Wharf pier, a short walk away. Boats to Bankside, your destination, run about every 40 minutes. However, times change with the season, so if you want to avoid a wait, call ahead for departure times (0870 781 5049). Tickets cost £4.55.

As you speed along the serpentine river, make sure you glance up at the famous Victorian structure of **Tower Bridge**. On the right bank immediately afterwards is the **Tower of London** (p76), a fortification dating back to the first Roman settlement that has since served as an armoury, a zoo, a royal prison and a crown-jewel strongroom. Opposite is a more contemporary organ of govenment, the big glass blob of **City Hall**.

Disembark at Bankside, where you'll find yourself surrounded by an abundance of London's landmarks. Patience. We're coming back to them, but cross to the northern side of the Thames at Southwark Bridge, a little way back in the direction you came from. If this is a weekday, make a slight detour to your lunch spot (sorry, weekenders, you'll have to wait another quarter-hour). Southwark Street turns into Queen Street; on the corner with Queen Victoria Street is the time-capsule seafood restaurant **Sweetings** (p79). Knock back some potted prawns with a tankard of ale, eavesdrop on tales of the City and enjoy the elegant caff surroundings.

Return along Queen Street and resume your route by turning westwards down Upper Thames Street (coming from Sweetings, that's a right; coming direct from Southwark Bridge, it's a left) and following signs to the **Millennium**

Bridge. This was the first new pedestrian river crossing in central London for over a century, linking St Paul's Cathedral (p76) to the imposing Tate Modern (p 63). Famously unstable when it opened (and then immediately closed for 18 months and £5 million of renovation), the Millennium Bridge has been outdone in beauty by the even newer Hungerford pedestrian bridge upriver, but the perspectives it offers on the monuments at either end are unsurpassed.

Once you reach the other side of the Millennium Bridge, you'll be stationed in front of **Tate Modern** (p63), which is your weekend lunch stop. Inside you will find a café on Level 2 (p67) that commands impressive views of the river and provides delicious food for both the peckish and the starving.

Refreshed, you're ready for a 45-minute amble along the South Bank, heading upriver (that's left out of Tate Modern). After passing under Blackfriars Bridge you'll see the Art Deco OXO Tower on your

left. This 220-foot structure affords wonderful views over the river and its environs from its public viewing gallery. Climb the spiral staircase for one floor; round to the left are the lifts, which you take up to the eighth floor.

The next section winds its way past Gabriel's Wharf, a cluster of appealing but not very exciting shops and restaurants, then through the pretty surroundings of the Silver Jubilee path and past the various cultural institutions of the South Bank. Just after Waterloo Bridge, which you pass beneath, you'll reach Jubilee Gardens, which lie in the shadow of the 135-metre **British Airways London Eye** (p55). At its foot is Waterloo Pier, from where you can take the Tate-to-Tate Boat (p63). You should arrive here just in time to catch the 4.11pm service, the last of the day (if you've been haring along, you might make the 3.31pm). Your destination is Tate Britain.

While you're putting your feet up on this final boat journey, look out to the right at the neo-gothic architecture of the **Houses of Parliament** (p148). You can also check the accuracy of your watch by Big Ben's chimes and have a look to see whether there is a light shining above the clock face, which means that Parliament is in session. Not long to rest though, because the journey only takes seven minutes.

Tate Britain (free admission; p150) houses the national collection of British art and is particularly interesting to our tour because of the Joseph William Turner gallery. Turner himself explored the Thames by boat in 1805, and his oil paintings of the river are dotted around the exhibition. As you do, contemplate the differences between the Thames depicted by Turner and the Thames you've experienced today.

British Airways London Eye

Spitalfields Market p48

Market Heaven

From the Routemaster bus to the local boozer, traditional London is being usurped by modernity. All the more reason, then, to celebrate the dynamism of London's East End markets, where an ailing costermonger culture has been bolstered by independent shops and stalls serving the newer, artsy, middle-class residents of the area – often on the same street. On Sunday mornings half a dozen distinct markets disgorge into the streets north of Aldgate: strung together, they offer a window into London old and new.

At an average rate of stall-browsing and refreshment-taking, it will take four to five hours to cover the mile-and-a-half route. Though the history is interesting at any time, the walk really only works on a Sunday, when the markets are in full swing. If you start at 9am, you should arrive at Columbia Road in time to enjoy the final hour of the flower market.

Start off at Liverpool Street station; exit to the left on to Bishopsgate, then make a quick right up Petticoat Lane, or Middlesex Street, as the authorities and street signs have been trying unsuccessfully to rename it for 175 years. Old ways die hard here, and the trade in pound-store essentials, tourist tat and sardonic repartee is much the same, adjusted for century, as it was in 1903, when rusty locks, chipped china shepherdesses and basins of boiled peas were among the wares.

After Wentworth Street, take the second (unnamed) street on the left, past cheap chain-store fashions and a leather market that recall the area's rag-trade heritage. Go right at Goulston Street and you'll come to **Tubby Isaacs** (established 1919), one of London's

Columbia Road

last remaining seafood stalls. Get yourself a £2 seafood mix, sprinkle with chilli vinegar and gulp down a real piece of history.

Go left on Whitechapel High Street and you pass Aldgate East tube station. Aldgate itself was one of the City's original four gates, but everything on this walk is just outside the City boundaries: after the Great Fire of London, markets were exiled from the City for safety reasons and took to crowding its margins instead.

Take a left up Commercial Street. There's little to see here until you reach Nicholas Hawksmoor's recently restored **Christ Church**, built between 1715 and 1729 as part of a missionary initiative to 'civilise' (read: suppress) the wild East End. Nearby is the Ten Bells pub, famously patronised by Jack

the Ripper's prostitute victims – evidence, perhaps, that the civilising mission didn't work. Fournier Street, which separates church from pub, is the home of artists Gilbert and George, first among the creative migrants to move here.

Now go through the gateway on the west side of Commercial Street to enter the fine cast-iron Victorian structure of **Spitalfields Market**. Until the late 1980s this was a wholesale fruit, veg and flower market; when it moved out, an eclectic mix of stalls and local businesses took over. There's lots of interesting crafty stuff, from individual silk-screened T-shirts to hand-developed London photos, but, as you move further in, you won't fail to notice some boxy glass protrusions. The market has lately been targeted by deep-pocketed City developers: despite widespread protests, the 1930s western wing was demolished in 2005, and replaced by Norman Foster-designed office buildings and retail units. Successfully? Explore the new glass-covered Market Street, lined with chi-chi shops, before retiring to consider your verdict over coffee and crumpets at **Canteen** (2 Crispin Place, 0845 686 1122, p175). In one of the new units, it's a slick shared-table open-kitchen operation serving satisfying born-again British grub.

Leave Spitalfields through the handsome Lamb Street exit to the north, cross Commercial Street, carry on up Hanbury Street and dip straight into the **Sunday (Up)Market** on the left. Many refugees from Spitalfields have moved here lately, making it an edgy mix of decor ideas, own-design fashions and directional vintage.

Soon Hanbury Street meets **Brick Lane**. A sizeable Bengali population has led to this area being widely known as Banglatown. Look to the right and you'll see the Jamme Masjid mosque, originally a chapel for Huguenot silk weavers and later a synagogue, reflecting how the area has made itself a refuge for successive waves of immigrants. Racial tension still occasionally surfaces, but things are calmer here than they've been for decades.

On Sundays this is an international free-market zone. Part flea market, part hawker, part recycler of goods of dubious legality, Brick Lane is an ancient East End animal that spreads voraciously down neighbouring streets and alleys. Turn left and you'll see how the area's art and nightlife crowd contribute coffeehouses and quirky fashion and design shops; on the right,

heralded by a one-woman chocolate van doling out treats and charm (see box p74), is the **Art Market**, where hand-made fashions and good-value paintings are on sale.

Take a right on people-packed **Cheshire Street**, which holds shops and stalls both cute and conservative. At the one extreme is **Labour & Wait** (No.18, 7729 6253), purveyors of an small range of bijou garden tools; on the other is the unnamed, unreconstructed shoe lock-up selling old-school leather footwear. Past further stalls hawking individual shoes and label-less clothes, an indoor market sells things from the border between antique and second-hand: spoons, CDs, tellies and some covetable Roberts radios (DAB not generally included).

Turn left at St Matthew's Row and carry on over Bethnal Green Road on Turin Street to Gosset Street, through gradually gentrifying Bethnal Green. At Gosset, go right, then left up Barnet Grove. You'll pass some lovely Victorian terraces, spared by the Blitz bombings that peppered this area. A quick detour down Wellington Row takes you past a mural by guerrilla street artist Banksy.

Barnet Grove ends at **Columbia Road**, the garden centre of the East End. Punters move in both directions along the tiny road, trays of bedding plants and potted trees raised aloft. Before you join the fray, stop off at the **Royal Oak**, a classic pub-turned-gastropub where you can people-watch a cross-section of East Enders over a pint of proper ale and a £13 lunch. Then either join the market throng or peruse the gifty, gardeny shops on each side as you make your way to the other end of the market, where you should find a cab to take you home.

Opium

24-Hour Party City

Make no mistake: London is where it's at when it comes to nightlife. No other city in the world can touch our variety or quality. And now that pubs and clubs can serve right around the clock, it's not only possible to stay up for days on end, but you'll be swamped with choice. So pack your most comfortable dancing shoes and don't forget your sunglasses: you'll be putting your stamina to the test for our 24-hour Saturday night agenda.

Start off at Kilburn Park tube for some live band leap-around action. The **Luminaire** (p173) is a new gig venue that is adored by Londoners for its customer-friendly attitude and varied bills, which usually kick off at 8pm.

You should have worked up an appetite by 11pm, so hop on a tube to Piccadilly, pausing to take in the bright lights of Picadilly Circus before heading into Soho, which is once again buzzing after a slump in the cool stakes. For a taste of old-school Soho, grab a panini at the counter of 24-hour stalwart **Bar Italia** (22 Frith Street, 7437 4520), a six-decade-old nightcrawlers' institution.

Start to rev up your night with a cocktail (or three) at **Opium** (1A Dean Street, 7287 9608). It's not as wallet-bashingly expensive as other cocktail bars in the area, but with

ITINERARIES

low-lit, carved alcoves to recline in, you'd hardly know the difference.

Either hail a rickshaw (and pray!) or, for a real taste of West End London on a Saturday night, walk north to Oxford Street, turn right and keep going until it becomes New Oxford Street. West Central Street is on your right past the famous umbrella shop at at No.53.

Adding a whole lot of credible cool to the West End's usually pretty naff club culture, the **End** and attached bar **AKA** (p114) see a rotating selection of long-running, killer underground house, techno and electro parties on Saturday nights, so you'll be in for a treat whatever you fancy. AKA usually has house selections for a more chilled crowd, while the Lounge and main club down below jump until 7am. You only have till 2am, though,

before you have to grab your coat and take a licensed minicab outside (ask the bouncers to point you to one) to the Key in King's Cross. No time to spare: this will be your biggest splurge of the evening.

Down a cobbled lane in the revamped King's Cross Goods Yard, home to three of London's most favourite clubs: the **Cross** (p105), all Ibizan-styled palm trees and exposed brickwork; the enormous **Canvas** (p105), home to Roller Disco on Thursdays and Fridays; and the **Key** (p105), which is where you're heading. The disco-tastic lit dancefloor works whether the DJ throws down breaks cuts or minimal-electro heaven, and the recently opened Chandelier room off the side adds a bigger space to relax in after busting moves for hours on end. Again, resident clubs rotate weekly, but tend to veer towards seriously underground electro, deep house and twisted noises.

Come kicking-out time, most folk will grab the Sunday papers and make for somewhere quiet to recover. No such luck for you! Head out the front door and back towards the main road, where you'll turn right (away from King's Cross station). It's then a brisk few minutes' walk to **EGG** (200 York Way, N7 9AX, 7609 8364), home of London's most beloved afterparty, Jaded. Kicking off at 5am, the three floors are full of people intent on chasing the rave.

Around lunchtime, you'll probably have done enough clubbing, at least for a little bit. It's time to make tracks to the East End. Head down the hill to King's Cross station and get the Hammersmith & City or Circle line east to Liverpool Street, coming out at Bishopsgate. Make your way to Corbet Place; it's time for brunch. The **Big Chill** (corner of Dray Walk and Corbet Place, www.big chill.net) offers scrummy tapas-style bites, or full breakfasts if you can handle that amount of food, and plenty of squishy sofas to relax on.

Once your feet start tapping again, it's over to **93 Feet East** (p181) for you. The wrap-around courtyard sees Sunday parties that were made for carrying on, with big-name DJs heaving their record boxes through a friendly, international crowd. If and when your hunger kicks in again, **Brick Lane Beigel Bake** is the place. Cross the square and cut through Dray Walk, then turn left into Brick Lane. Walk a few blocks to the end where, on your left, is London's most famous bagel shop. Restore your energy levels – you've earned it. If you're still raring to go, T-Bar (p182) is just around the corner.

The End p51

London by Area

British Airways
London Eye

The South Bank

Historically, the South Bank was always an undesirable address. The real city and its grandeurs grew up north of the Thames, and not much at all developed south of the river until a couple of centuries back, certainly nothing you'd want to share with polite society.

Oh, how times change. In the past couple of decades, the South Bank has become central to London life. The big national institutions that comprise the **South Bank complex** have become increasingly dynamic, and the broad riverside walkway that takes you from Tower Bridge to Westminster Bridge (and further, if you care to go) has developed into one of the city's great pleasures, stringing together sights, historic insights, tourist diversions and outdoor events against a progression of awe-inspiring views. The clutch of buildings and bridges that were opened around the Millennium – including **Tate Modern**, the **British Airways London Eye** and the **Millennium** and **Hungerford Bridges** – add to both the skyline and the things-to-do list (though note that the Saatchi Gallery has moved out of County Hall and into Chelsea; p157). Revitalised **Borough Market**, foodie central, typifies the South Bank's appeal: visitors find it charming, but it's far from being solely a tourist attraction.

Away from the river, there's a taste of upbeat inner-city life – along, for example, The Cut, or Borough High Street – as well as the **Imperial War Museum**.

Sights & museums

Bramah Museum of Tea & Coffee

40 Southwark Street, Bankside, SE1 1UN (7403 5650/www.bramah museum.co.uk). London Bridge tube/rail. **Open** 10am-6pm daily. **Admission** £4; £3.50 reductions. **Map** p57 E2 ❶

Edward Bramah, a former tea taster, set up this museum and his regular tours, talks and teas are the best thing about it. Pots, maps, caddies and ancient coffee-makers are on display. Linger in the (naturally) well-stocked café, where a pianist usually tinkles away in the early afternoon.

British Airways London Eye

Riverside Building, next to County Hall, Westminster Bridge Road, South Bank, SE1 7PB (0870 500 0600/customer services 0870 990 8883/www.ba-londoneye.com). Westminster tube/Waterloo tube/rail. **Open** *Oct-May* 10am-8pm daily. *June-Sept* 10am-10pm daily. **Admission** £13; free-£10 reductions. **Map** p56 A3 ❷

The 450ft (137m) monster, whose 32 glass capsules each hold 25 people, commands superb views. You can take a gamble with the weather and book in advance, but it's usually possible to turn up and get a ticket on the day. 'Night flights' offer a more twinkly experience, and you can even get married in a pod.

Clink Prison Museum

1 Clink Street, Bankside, SE1 9DG (7403 0900/www.clink.co.uk). London Bridge tube/rail. **Open** *June-Sept* 10am-9pm daily. *Oct-May* 10am-6pm daily. **Admission** £5; £3.50 reductions. **Map** p57 E2 ❸

This small, grisly exhibition looks behind the bars of the hellish 12th- to 18th-century prison. On display for the 'hands-on' experience are torture devices and the fetters whose clanking gave the prison its name.

Dalí Universe

County Hall Gallery, County Hall, Riverside Building, Queen's Walk, South Bank, SE1 7PB (7620 2720/ www.daliuniverse.com). Westminster tube/Waterloo tube/rail. **Open** 10am-6.30pm daily. Last entry 5.30pm. **Admission** *Oct-Apr* £11; £5-£9.50 reductions. *May-Sept* £12; £6-£10 reductions. **Map** p56 A3 ❹

Dalí trademarks such as the *Mae West Lips* sofa and the *Spellbound* painting are major attractions in the main exhibition; less famous but at least as interesting are the series of Bible scenes by the Catholic-turned-atheist-turned-Catholic again. The gallery also shows work by new artists.

Design Museum

28 Shad Thames, Bermondsey, SE1 2YD (7403 6933/www.designmuseum. org). Tower Hill tube/London Bridge tube/rail. **Open** 10am-5.45pm daily. **Admission** £7; free-£4 reductions. **Map** p57 F2 ❺

Exhibitions in this white 1930s-style building focus on modern and contemporary design. The Tank is a little outdoor gallery of installations, while the smart Blueprint Café has a balcony overlooking the Thames. **Event highlights** Bruno Munari, Italian Futurist and book designer (13 Jan-6 May 2007).

Fashion & Textile Museum

83 Bermondsey Street, Bermondsey, SE1 3XF (7407 8664/www.ftm london.org). London Bridge tube/rail. **Open/admission** phone or check website for details. **Map** p57 F4 ❻

As flamboyant as its founder, fashion designer Zandra Rhodes, this pink and orange museum has 3,000 of her garments, along with her archive of paper designs, sketchbooks, silk screens and show videos. The exhibitions were in the process of being restructured as we went to press, with only pre-booked groups able to view the main collection, but full public access is expected to resume late in 2007.

The South Bank

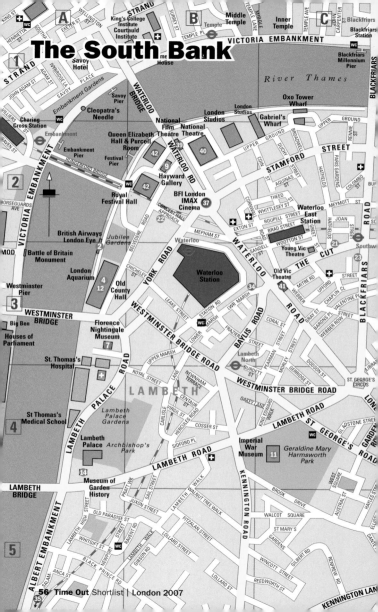

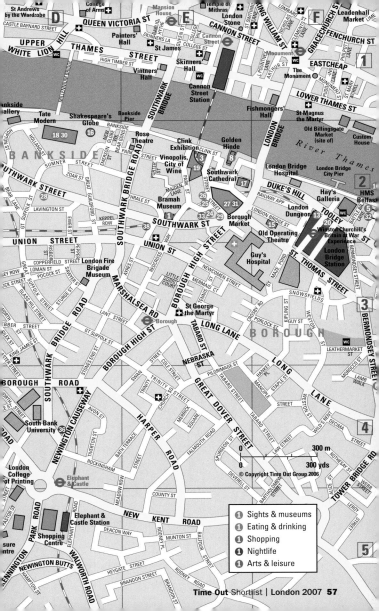

London Ducktours

Amazing Amphibious Adventure

visit LONDON
BRONZE WINNER
AWARDS 2005

A 75 minute adventure tour of the City of Westminster by road and river on board an amphibious 'Duck', including a live commentary.

London Ducktours offers more than just a sightseeing tour - its an exciting road and river adventure appealing to visitors of all ages taking in some of London's most famous landmarks.

Ask about our personalised tours for weddings, children's parties, hospitality, educational tours, special events etc!

ARRANGE YOUR OWN SPECIAL ADVENTURE!

In partnership with
visit LONDON
GOLD

www.londonducktours.co.uk 020 7928 3132

Florence Nightingale Museum

*St Thomas's Hospital, 2 Lambeth
Palace Road, Borough, SE1
7EW (7620 0374/www.florence-
nightingale.co.uk). Westminster
tube/Waterloo tube/rail.* **Open**
10am-5pm Mon-Fri; 10am-4.30pm
Sat, Sun (last entry 1hr before closing).
Admission £5.80; free-£4.80
reductions. **Map** p56 A3 **7**

The nursing skills and campaigning
zeal that made Florence Nightingale's
Crimean War work the stuff of legend
are honoured with a chronological tour
through her remarkable life.

Golden Hinde

*St Mary Overie Dock, Cathedral Street,
Bankside, SE1 9DE (0870 011 8700/
www.goldenhinde.co.uk). Monument
tube/London Bridge tube/rail.* **Open**
10am-5.30pm but times vary; phone to
check. **Admission** £3.50; free-£3
reductions. **Map** p57 E2 **8**

Weekends see this reconstruction of Sir
Francis Drake's little 16th-century flagship swarming with hordes of kids
dressed up as pirates for birthday
dos. When not taken over by cutlass-
wielding youths, the meticulously recreated ship is fascinating to explore.
Thoroughly seaworthy, it has reprised
Drake's circumnavigatory voyage itself.

Hayward Gallery

*Belvedere Road, South Bank, SE1
8XX (information 7921 0813/box
office 0870 169 1000/www.hayward.
org.uk). Embankment tube/Charing
Cross or Waterloo tube/rail.* **Open**
During exhibitions 10am-6pm Mon,
Thur, Sat, Sun; 10am-8pm Tue, Wed;
10am-9pm Fri. **Admission** £7.50;
free-£7 reductions. **Map** p56 B2 **9**

A roster of powerhouse events inhabit
London's major temporary exhibition
centre, a vast concrete block containing similarly vast white spaces (ideal
for intallation work). Recent visitors
have included a Dan Flavin restro-
spective and 'Undercover Surrealism'.
Event highlights 'Sixty Years of the
Arts Council Collection' (7 Sept-19 Nov):
not the most enticing of titles, yes, but

bear in mind that the collection holds
thousands of works by star British
artists from Henry Moore, Anthony Caro
and Bridget Riley to Gilbert & George,
Tracey Emin and Rachel Whiteread. In
late 2006 'Intimate Relations: the Art of
Sex' is pencilled in: it will explore repre-
sentations of copulation across the globe
and in all media down the ages.

HMS Belfast

*Morgan's Lane, Tooley Street,
Bankside, SE1 2JH (7940 6300/
www.iwm.org.uk). London Bridge
tube/rail.* **Open** *Mar-Oct* 10am-6pm
daily. *Nov-Feb* 10am-5pm daily.
Last entry 45mins before closing.
Admission £8.50; free-£5.25
reductions. **Map** p57 F2 **10**

This 11,500-ton battlecruiser, the last
surviving big-gun World War II ship
in Europe, is a floating branch of the
Imperial War Museum. It makes an
unlikely playground for children, who
tear easily around its cramped complex
of nine decks, boiler, engine rooms and
gun turrets. *Belfast* was built in 1938,
provided cover for convoys to Russia
and was instrumental in the Normandy
landings. She also supported UN forces
in Korea before being decommissioned
in 1965; a special exhibition looks at
that 'forgotten war'.

Imperial War Museum

*Lambeth Road, Lambeth, SE1 6HZ
(7416 5000/www.iwm.org.uk). Lambeth
North tube/Elephant & Castle tube/rail.*
Open 10am-6pm daily. **Admission**
free. **Map** p56 C4 **11**

The collection covers conflicts from
World War I to the present day.
Exhibits range from tanks, aircraft and
big guns to photographs, letters, film,
sound recordings and paintings.
Special areas include the smelly 'World
War I Trench Experience', the teeth-
chattering 'Blitz Experience' and
'Secret War', full of fascinating spying
artefacts worthy of Q. The cruel truths
are not far away, though, in the heart-
breaking 'Holocaust Exhibition' and
'Crimes Against Humanity'.
Event highlights 'D-Day' (to 10 Jan
2007). 'The Animals' War': the roles

HMS Belfast p59

played by birds and animals in 20th-century conflict (to Apr 2007). 'The Children's War': childhood in World War II (to 2008).

London Aquarium

County Hall, Riverside Building, Westminster Bridge Road, South Bank, SE1 7PB (7967 8000/tours 7967 8007/www.londonaquarium. co.uk). Westminster tube/Waterloo tube/rail. **Open** 10am-6pm daily (last entry 5pm). **Admission** *Summer & peak periods* £11.75; free-£9.50 reductions. *Off-peak periods* £10.75; free-£8.50 reductions. **Map** p56 A3 ⑫

The aquarium, one of Europe's largest, displays its inhabitants according to geographical origin, so there are tanks of bright fish from the coral reefs of the Indian Ocean, temperate freshwater fish from the rivers of Europe and North America, and crustaceans and rockpool plants from the shoreline. Rays glide swiftly around touch pools, surfacing frequently. There are also tanks devoted to jellyfish, octopuses, sharks and piranhas – and even one containing robotic fish.

London Dungeon

28-34 Tooley Street, Bankside, SE1 2SZ (7403 7221/www.thedungeons. com). London Bridge tube/rail. **Open** *Sept-June* 10.30am-5.30pm daily. *July, Aug* 9.30am-7.30pm daily; longer in school hols. **Admission** £15.95; £11-£12.50 reductions. **Map** p57 F2 ⑬

Join the queue for this disturbing world of torture, death and disease under the Victorian railway arches of London Bridge and you are led through a dry-ice fog past gravestones and hideously rotting corpses. White-faced visitors experience nasty symptoms from the Great Plague exhibition: an actor-led medley of corpses, boils, projectile vomiting, worm-filled skulls and scuttling rats. Other hysterical revisions of horrible London history include the Great Fire and Great Plague, Jack the Ripper Victoriana and the Judgement Day Barge, where visitors play the part of prisoners (death sentence guaranteed).

Museum of Garden History

Church of St Mary-at-Lambeth, Lambeth Palace Road, Lambeth, SE1 7LB (7401 8865/www.museumgarden history.org). Waterloo tube/rail. **Open** 10.30am-5pm daily. **Admission** free. *Suggested donation* £3; £2.50 reductions. **Map** p56 A4 ⑭

John Tradescant, intrepid plant hunter and gardener to Charles I, is buried here at the world's first museum of horticulture. In the garden, most of the plants are labelled with their country of origin and year of introduction to these islands. Inside are displays of ancient tools, exhibitions about horticulture through the ages, a collection of antique gnomes, a shop and a wholesome vegetarian café in the north transept. A little green-fingered marvel of a place.

Old Operating Theatre, Museum & Herb Garret

9A St Thomas's Street, South Bank, SE1 9RY (7188 2679/www.thegarret. org.uk). London Bridge tube/rail. **Open** 10.30am-5pm daily (last entry 4.45pm). Closed mid Dec-early Jan. **Admission** £4.95; free-£3.95 reductions. No credit cards. **Map** p57 F2 ⑮

The tower that houses this salutary revelation of antique surgical practice used to be part of the chapel of St Thomas's Hospital, founded on this site in the 12th century. The centrepiece is a Victorian operating theatre, with tiered viewing seats for students, but just as disturbing are the displays of operating equipment that look like torture implements and worrying objects in glass jars.

Shakespeare's Globe

21 New Globe Walk, Bankside, SE1 9DT (7902 1500/www.shakespeares-globe.org). Mansion House or Southwark tube/London Bridge tube/rail. **Open** *Box office* (theatre bookings) 10am-6pm Mon-Sat; 10am-5pm Sun. *Tours* 10am-5pm daily. From May-Sept, afternoon tours visit only the Rose Theatre, not the Globe. **Admission** *Tours* £9; £6.50-£7.50 reductions. **Map** p57 D2 ⑯

The original Globe theatre, where many of William Shakespeare's plays were first staged, burned down in 1613. Nearly 400 years later, it was rebuilt not far from its original site using construction methods and materials as close to the originals as possible. From May to September historically authentic (and frequently very good) performances are staged. You can tour the theatre year round, and there's a fine exhibition on the reconstruction.

Southwark Cathedral

London Bridge, Bankside, SE1 9DA (7367 6700/tours 7367 6734/ www.dswark.org/cathedral). London

Never stand still

Redevelopments are afoot at the South Bank.

To some, it's an unnavigable concrete monstrosity, and even those who appreciate the modernist brutality of the South Bank Centre agree that the arts complex would benefit from a few common-sense fixes. The metamorphosis, which got under way in 2003, enters its next major phase with the redevelopment of the National Film Theatre in September 2006, to coincide with the London Film Festival's 50th anniversary.

The new **British Film Institute Centre**, built in the old Museum of the Moving Image, will include a walk-in digital cinema, and a mediatheque that allows you to watch the BFI's extensive archive material. There will also be a gallery showing film-related art and a well-stocked film and DVD shop. The development is part of a larger, longer-term plan to create a National Film Centre by around 2012. One site being considered for this mammoth proposal is the King's Cross regeneration area.

Next up is the redevelopment of **Jubilee Gardens**, due to have completed in summer 2007; the **Royal Festival Hall** has been undergoing a gradual refurb; and the rest of the South Bank Centre will have a variety of cosmetic facelifts, including more trees, decorative paving, increased public seating and creative lighting. The idea is to open the centre up, creating a more user-friendly public space.

LONDON BY AREA

Bodo Sperlein p68

Bridge tube/rail. **Open** from 8.45am daily (closing times vary). *Services* 8am, 8.15am, 12.30pm, 12.45pm, 5.30pm Mon-Fri; 9am, 9.15am, 4pm Sat; 8.45am, 9am, 11am, 3pm, 6.30pm Sun. **Admission** *Audio tour* £3; £1.50-£2.50 reductions. **Map** p57 E2 ⑰

The oldest bits of this building, one of the few places south of the river that Dickens had a good word for, date back more than 800 years, but it's been a cathedral only since 1905. An interactive museum called the Long View of London, a refectory and a lovely garden are some of the millennial improvements that make the building look so shipshape these days. There are memorials to Shakespeare, John Harvard (benefactor of the US university), Sam Wanamaker (the force behind Shakespeare's Globe) and stained-glass windows with images of Chaucer, who set off on pilgrimage to Canterbury from a pub in Borough High Street.

Tate Modern

Bankside, SE1 9TG (7401 5120/ 7887 8888/www.tate.org.uk). Blackfriars tube/rail. **Open** 10am-6pm Mon-Thur, Sun; 10am-10pm Fri, Sat. Last entry 45mins before gallery closes. **Admission** free. *Temporary exhibitions* prices vary. **Map** p57 D2 ⑬

A powerhouse of modern art, Tate Modern is imposing even before you embark on a tour of the collection thanks to its industrial architecture: it was built as Bankside Power Station between 1947 and 1966, opening in its current incarnation in 2000. The original cavernous turbine hall is used to jaw-dropping effect as the home of large-scale installations; on 10 October 2006 a work by Carsten Höller will take over the space.

The collection is not an anticlimax. It draws from the Tate organisation's deep reservoir of modern art (1900 on, and international) and features 20th-century heavy-hitters including Matisse, Rothko, Giacometti and Pollock. In May 2006 the permanent galleries were completely rehung,

with the artworks grouped according to movement rather than theme. Amost half of the works are new to Tate Modern (*Whaam!* by Roy Lichtenstein, for example), and many newly acquired pieces will go on show, from artists including Francis Picabia, Anish Kapoor, Tacita Dean, the Guerrilla Girls, John Baldessari and Cildo Meireles.

The Tate-to-Tate boat service – decor courtesy of Damien Hirst – links Tate Modern with Tate Britain in Pimlico (p190), and runs every 40 minutes, stopping along the way at the London Eye. Tickets are available from desks at the Tates, on board the boat, online or by phone (7887 8888). Adult tickets are £4.30.

Event highlights An exhibition focusing on the early career of Wassily Kandinsky (to 1 Oct 2006). Mid 20th-century American abstract sculptor David Smith (1 Nov 2006-14 Jan 2007). Contemporary Swiss duo Peter Fischli and David Weiss (11 Oct 2006-14 Jan 2007). Gilbert and George (15 Feb-7 May). Dali & Film (1 June-9 Sept). Oiticica (7 June-23 Sept).

Vinopolis, City of Wine

1 Bank End, Bankside, SE1 9BU (0870 241 4040/www.vinopolis.co.uk). London Bridge tube/rail. **Open** noon-9pm Mon, Fri, Sat; noon-6pm Tue-Thur, Sun. Last entry 2hrs before closing. **Admission** £15; free-£12 reductions. **Map** p57 E2 ⑲

Participants in this wine visitor attraction are furnished with a wineglass and an audio guide, and given five opportunities to taste wine and champagne from different regions. Highlights include a virtual voyage around Chianti on a Vespa and a virtual flight to the wine-producing regions of Australia. A whisky-tasting area and a microbrewery were recently added. The wine shop has some interesting offers for dedicated tipplers; there's also a smart restaurant and a tourist information centre. You do need to be interested in wine to get the most out of Vinopolis, but not an expert.

Winston Churchill's Britain at War Experience

64-66 Tooley Street, Bankside, SE1 2TF (7403 3171/www.britainatwar. co.uk). London Bridge tube/rail. **Open** *Apr-Sept* 10am-6pm daily. *Oct-Mar* 10am-5pm daily. Last entry 1hr before closing. **Admission** £9.50; free-£5.75 reductions. **Map** p57 F2 ⍟

This old-fashioned exhibition recalls the privations endured by the British during World War II. Displays on rationing, food production and Land Girls are fascinating, and the set-piece walk-through bombsite (you enter just after a bomb has dropped on the street) quite disturbing. A funny old place, but it conjures up wartime austerity well.

Eating & drinking

Anchor & Hope

36 The Cut, Waterloo, SE1 8LP (7928 9898). Southwark tube/Waterloo tube/rail. **Open** 5-11pm Mon; 11am-11pm Tue-Sat. **££. Gastropub.** **Map** p56 C3 ⍟

The Anchor & Hope is walk-in only, and you'll rarely snag a table without a wait at peak hours. The reason? The interesting British food – garlic soup, for example, or crab on toast – is terrific, the ale well kept, and the surroundings and atmosphere highly congenial. If you can wait, 2.15pm is the best time to turn up for lunch.

Archduke

Concert Hall Approach, South Bank, SE1 8XU (7928 9370). Waterloo tube/rail. **Open** 8.30am-11pm Mon-Fri; 11am-11pm Sat. **Wine bar.** **Map** p56 B2 ⍟

South Bank culture vultures are attracted to this glass-fronted, split-level bar by decent modern European cooking and an affordable, varied wine list.

Baltic

74 Blackfriars Road, Waterloo, SE1 8HA (7928 1111/www.baltic restaurant.co.uk). Southwark tube. **Open** *Restaurant* noon-11pm Mon-Sat; noon-10.30pm Sun. **££. Eastern European.** **Map** p56 C3 ⍟

Baltic's spacious interior, complete with a 'wall of amber' bar, makes a terrific setting for its varied, modern menu and efficient waiting staff. The food is a rare combination for an eastern European restaurant: both adventurous and authentic.

Glas

3 Park Street, Borough, SE1 9AB (7357 6060/www.glasrestaurant.com). Borough tube/London Bridge tube/rail. **Open** noon-2.30pm, 6.30-10pm Mon-Sat. **££. Swedish.** **Map** p57 E2 ⍟

Glas is undeniably Swedish. The smörgåsbord-style menu offers enticing dishes of distinctly Scandinavian flavour but with a modern twist.

Konditor & Cook

10 Stoney Street, Borough, SE1 9AD (7407 5100/www.konditorand cook.com). London Bridge tube/rail. **Open** 7.30am-6pm Mon-Fri; 8.30am-5pm Sat. **£. Bakery.** **Map** p57 E2 ⍟

Famed for excellent cakes, this delightful mini chain is a one-stop spot for indulgence of both the sweet and savoury kind (pastas, soups, pizza), and great for takeaway lunch or a hamper. There's another branch at 22 Cornwall Road, behind the South Bank complex.

Market Porter

9 Stoney Street, Borough, SE1 9AA (7407 2495). London Bridge tube/rail. **Open** 6-8.30am, 11am-11pm Mon-Fri; noon-11pm Sat; noon-10.30pm Sun. **Pub.** **Map** p57 E2 ⍟

Wedged beneath the railway arches next to London's main foodie market, this atmospheric Borough pub has standing room only on most nights. If you're a fan of real ale, you'll understand why: there are up to eight different, strangely named brews on tap at any given time (Slater's Top Totty being a typically silly example).

Roast

NEW *Floral Hall, Stoney Street, Borough, SE1 1TL (7940 1300/ www.roast-restaurant.com). London Bridge tube/rail.* **Open** 7am-10am, noon-3pm, 5.30-11pm Mon-Fri; 7am-

LONDON BY AREA

Working-class heroes

Fish Club

It took a while for the British food renaissance, with its emphasis on first-quality ingredients, to have a trickle-down effect on our everyday nosh. But now food-lovers have been reclaiming the dishes that you once risked heart disease, dental caries or botulism to sample. Our favourite is the **Square Pie Company**, which has managed to make the traditional cockney dish of pie and mash not just palatable, but incredibly delicious, by using top-quality ingredients where once only the cheapest rubbish would do. Fish and chip shops have also had a fillip from the likes of **Fish Club**, which has turned the once-humble dish into a gourmet choice. Sausage and mash has also been made respectable – or nearly so, given that London's leading purveyor is called the **S&M**

Café (p171). Explain *that* when it appears on your credit card bill. There are even Cornish pasty franchises prominent at stations and on high streets.

Why did this happen? We think it can be traced back to **St John** restaurant (p88) opening its doors in Clerkenwell in 1994, with a shocking menu that reclaimed offal and other once-repugnant dishes by doing them really, really well. If you can persuade people to eat tripe and pig's spleen in a fancy restaurant, then reclaiming pies or sausages for the gourmets is child's play.

■ Square Pie Company (www.squarepie.com) has outlets in Spitalfields Market, Selfridges and Canary Wharf
■ Fish Club is at 189 St John's Hill, SW11 1TH (7978 7115), in south London

4pm, 6-11pm Sat; 9-11.30am, noon-4pm
Sun. **££££**. **British**. Map p57 E2 ㉖
The best of British in both – food and
architecture. Roast sits in a grand new
hall, imaginatively built into railway
arches over Borough Market and
fronted by Covent Garden's lovely old
market portico (reclaimed for a token
£1). The menu similarly features rein-
vigorated British classics, cooked
with verve and care using prime-qual-
ity, seasonal ingredients.

The Table
NEW *83 Southwark Street,
Borough, SE1 0HX (7401 2760
www.thetablecafe.com). London
Bridge tube/rail.* **Open** 8am-6pm
Mon-Thur; 8am-11pm Fri. **£**.
Bar/café. Map p57 D2 ㉗
Sparse and open with a refectory feel,
the Table functions equally well for
self-service breakfasts or lunch and as
a bar. Dishes range from pasta made
on the premises to beautiful lemon
tarts. The salad bar is pretty good too,
adding West Coast invention to Med-
style salads. When the Bankside 1-2-3
development opens across the street in
2007, it should become a fully fledged
evening restaurant.

Tapas Brindisa
*18-20 Southwark Street, Borough, SE1
1TJ (7357 8880/www.brindisa.com).
London Bridge tube/rail.* **Open** noon-
3pm Mon-Thur; 9-11am, noon-4pm,
5.30-11pm Fri, Sat. **££**. **Tapas**.
Map p57 E2 ㉘
This top-rate tapas bar perched on
the edge of Borough Market sets
the benchmark for others of its kind.
Showcasing produce on sale at
Brindisa's stall in the market and
its shop in Clerkenwell (32 Exmouth
Market, EC1), it conjures quintessentially Spanish fare with gusto and flair.

Tate Modern Café: Level 2
*2nd Floor, Tate Modern, Bankside,
SE1 9TG (7401 5014/www.tate.org.uk).
Southwark tube/London Bridge tube/
rail.* **Open** 10am-5.30pm Mon-Thur,
Sat, Sun; 10am-9.30pm Fri. **£**. **Café**.
Map p57 D2 ㉚

Market Porter p65

LONDON BY AREA

With three separate daytime menus (breakfast, lunch and tea) – as well as tapas when the museum is open late on Fridays and Saturdays – this café offers plenty of choice from its modern British menu (poached salmon, corn-fed chicken, fish and chips).

Shopping

There are some great design and crafts shops in the Oxo Tower between Blackfriars and Waterloo Bridge (we particularly like Bodo Sperlein in unit 1.05). Gabriel's Wharf, however, is missable.

Borough Market

8 Southwark Street, Borough, SE1 1TL (7407 1002/www.borough market. org.uk). London Bridge tube/rail. **Open** 10am-around 5pm Thur; noon-6pm Fri; 9am-4pm Sat. **Map** p57 E2 ③

There's been a market here for two millennia, and even the Victorians thought it was pretty swanky. Now it sells produce of such impeccable quality and sourcing that London's chefs love it – Jamie Oliver is a valued client. Even if you're not buying to cook, it's good fun: there are picnic ingredients and takeaway snacks aplenty, and the atmosphere under the London Bridge railway arches is lovely.

Design Museum Shop

Shad Thames, Bermondsey, SE1 2YD (7940 8753/www.designmuseum.org). Tower Hill tube/London Bridge tube/rail. **Open** 10am-5.45pm daily. **Map** p57 F2 ③

Small items prevail at this pleasing shop, such as the Vitra miniature chair range, vases from Rosenthal, Pigeon lights by Ed Carpenter and various beautiful design classics, current and future.

Paul Smith

NEW *13 Park Street, Borough, SE1 9AB (7403 1678).* **Open** 10am-6pm Mon-Sat. **Map** p57 E2 ③

The front of this shop, lit with bare bulbs and plastered with framed album covers, is an anarchic jumble of toys, kitsch novelties, art books and Rococo chocs. Urban-casual clothes for men, women and kids, including arty T-shirts and selections from the Jeans and Pink collections, are in the minimalist back room, but you'll have to cross the river to the Covent Garden store for the quirky-classic main lines.

Radio Days

87 Lower Marsh, Waterloo, SE1 7AB (7928 0800). Waterloo tube/rail. **Open** 10am-6pm Mon-Fri, Sat; 10am-7pm Fri. **Map** p56 B3 ③

This lovingly put-together vintage shop, selling clothes and collectibles from the 1920s to 1970s, is eminently browsable. Look out for glamourous cocktail accessories and ephemera like gift cosmetics.

Nightlife

Crash

Arch 66, Goding Street, Kennington, SE11 5AW (7793 9262/www.crash london.co.uk). Vauxhall tube/rail. **Open** Alternate Saturdays; call for details. **Admission** £12-£15. No credit cards. **Map** p56 A5 ③

Under the arches of this gay dance club are four bars, two dancefloors, chill-out areas… and lots of muscles.

Ministry of Sound

103 Gaunt Street, off Newington Causeway, Newington, SE1 6DP (0870 060 0010/www.ministryof sound.com). Elephant & Castle tube/rail. **Open** 10pm-3am Wed; 10.30pm-5am Fri; 11pm-7am Sat. **Admission** £5 Wed; £12 Fri; £15 Sat. **Map** p57 D4 ③

With millions of compilations to its name, the Ministry of Sound has to be the world's most recognised clubbing brand. As such, it's sometimes sneered at by cutting-edge clubbers, but it is one of the few UK clubs that can afford to put on the likes of NYC house legends Masters at Work all night long. The sound system is shockingly good.

Borough Market

Arts & leisure

BFI London IMAX Cinema

1 Charlie Chaplin Walk, South Bank, SE1 8XR (0870 787 2525/www.bfi. org.uk/imax). Waterloo tube/rail. **Map** p56 B2 ③⑦

The biggest screen in the country for 3-D delights.

Menier Chocolate Factory

51-53 Southwark Street, Bankside, SE1 1RU (7907 7060/www.menierchocolate factory.com). London Bridge tube/rail. **Map** p57 E2 ③⑧

This attractive fringe venue is housed, unsurprisingly, in a former chocolate factory. There's a pleasant bar and restaurant attached, serving reliable, sometimes excellent, mainstream fare.

National Film Theatre (NFT)

South Bank, SE1 8XT (information 7928 3535/bookings 7928 3232/ www.bfi.org.uk/nft). Embankment tube Waterloo tube/rail. **Map** p56 B2 ③⑨

London's best cinema, with an unrivalled programme of retrospective seasons and previews in three well-designed screens. For the new British Film Institute centre, see box p61.

National Theatre

South Bank, SE1 9PX (information 7452 3400/box office 7452 3000/www. nationaltheatre.org.uk). Embankment or Southwark tube/Waterloo tube/rail. **Map** p56 B2 ④⓪

The National Theatre continues to be fighting fit during the watch of Nicholas Hytner, its artistic director. It can still afford to cherry-pick new writers and sponsor innovative performing groups. During the summer the free outdoor performing arts stage is a great way to see all sorts of entertainment, from booty-shaking bhangra to fire-swallowing avant-garde dancers.

Event highlights *The Coram Boy*, an 18th-century children's adventure following the intertwined fates of two orphans, returns from 29 November 2006 to 20 January 2007.

Old Vic

Waterloo Road, Waterloo, SE1 8NB (0870 060 6628/www.oldvictheatre. com). Waterloo tube/rail. **Map** p56 C3 ④①

Kevin Spacey's reign at this two-century-old theatre has been less stellar than some expected. He has drawn criticism for playing safe, as well as allowing some under-par productions through, recently the Robert Altman-directed *Resurrection Blues*, the last play written by Arthur Miller.

Event highlights Spacey has cast himself in Eugene O'Neill's *A Moon for the Misbegotten*, booking from September 2006.

South Bank Centre

Belvedere Road, South Bank, SE1 8XX (0870 380 0400/www.rfh.org.uk). Embankment tube/Waterloo tube/rail. **Map** p56 B2 ④②

The South Bank Centre is the name given to the South Bank's three concert halls, which inhabit two buildings. The 3,000-seat Royal Festival Hall, closed for renovations until January 2007 (see box p61) hosts major orchestral concerts – house ensembles include the Philharmonia and the London Philharmonic orchestras – and large-scale rock and jazz shows. The smaller Queen Elizabeth Hall stages anything from classical dance to alternative folk; its tiny Purcell Room has chamber and contemporary music concerts. Both offer well-raked seating and good sound.

Unicorn Theatre

147 Tooley Street, Bankside, SE1 2HZ (08700 534 534/www.unicorntheatre. com). London Bridge tube/rail/Tower Hill tube. **Map** p57 F3 ④③

Unicorn Theatre, one of Britain's leading producers of professional theatre for children, moved into its new multi-million pound South Bank home at the end of 2005. It's a striking modern building containing two auditoriums: the Weston Theatre, with 340 seats, for larger-scale work and, for new work and education, a smaller, second space called the River Theatre. The foyer also houses a family-friendly café.

St Paul's Cathedral p76

The City

The City

The City of London today, the self-governing 'square mile' of all things financial, has pretty much exactly the same boundaries as the Romans gave it. This was the original Londinium, and as such it is full of history and heraldry, institutions and monuments. It also has, of course, the offices to house, tall buildings to glorify and expensive restaurants to feed the incumbent financial establishment. Its pleasures lie in wandering the maze of streets whose ancient geography and names not even the Great Fire of London could eradicate, getting glimpses of the past and people-watching the present. The City is most itself at either end of the business day, when hordes of commuters throng its tube stations, but it's also a pleasure to explore at weekends and in the evenings, when the streets can be eerily quiet. (Be warned that many businesses in the area don't open at weekends, though that's gradually starting to change.)

City Information Centre

St Paul's Churchyard, EC4M 8BX (7332 1456). St Paul's tube. **Open** *Apr-Sept* 9.30am-5pm daily. *Oct-Mar* 9.30am-5pm Mon-Fri; 9.30am-12.30pm Sat. **Map** p72 C4 ❶
Information and brochures on sights, events and walks in the Square Mile, including a map of City churches.

Sights & museums

Bank of England Museum

Entrance on Bartholomew Lane, EC2R 8AH (7601 5491/www.bank ofengland.co.uk/museum). Bank

The City

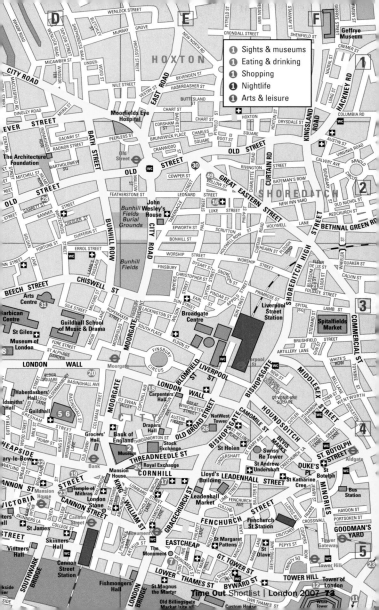

Baking hot

Some credit *Sex and the City* for the unstoppable rise of the fairy cake, but we see it as part of a wider trend: the reclassification of homespun crafts from mumsy to desirable (remember the improbable trendification of knitting?). Craft bakeries are something of a global trend, but Britain – with its sweet tooth, its bring-and-buy sale heritage and its particular gift for inspired eccentricity – has developed it into an endearing cottage (bedsit?) industry. At markets around London you'll find small stalls whose wares are limited to just a few beautifully made cakes or biscuits, baked at dawn by their enthusiastic purveyors and popped on purchase into hand-lettered paper bags. The Eccles cakes at Hackney's Broadway Market, for example, are something truly special.

Our favourite example of the genre is Choc Star, a one-woman operation based in a converted ice-cream van. Petra Barran makes chocolate concoctions guaranteed to hit your C-spot every time: Malteser muffins, millionaires' shortbread and a walnut and chocolate brownie that even an experienced journalist could only describe as 'yumptious'. Other treats include Mexican chocolate ice-cream and espresso-style Venezuelan choc shots. 'It's accessible chocolate, not snooty,' says Barran. 'Life can get a bit serious at times; I provide the escapism.'

The Choc Star van moves around, of course, but it can usually be found on Brick Lane on Sunday mornings, just north of Hanbury Street. It also makes appearances at other visitable spots, including East Greenwich Food Market and the Wallace Collection. Check the website for the latest.

■ www.chocstar.co.uk

tube/DLR. **Open** 10am-5pm Mon-Fri.
Admission free; £1 audio guide.
Map p73 E4 ❷

The bank's Stock Office has been restored to its original 1788 glory. You can see ancient coins and bills, original banknote artwork, minting machines and dioramas based on 18th-century political cartoons. Try lifting the real gold bar – it's worth about £98,000 at current rates and weighs more than two stone. The museum should be spick and span after redecoration in 2006.

College of Arms

130 Queen Victoria Street, EC4V 4BT (7248 2762/www.college-of-arms. gov.uk). St Paul's tube/Blackfriars tube/ rail. **Open** 10am-4pm Mon-Fri. *Tours* by arrangement. 6.30pm Mon-Fri. **Admission** free. *Tours* prices vary. **Map** p72 C5 ❸

The emblems of Britain's noble families are maintained by the heralds at the College of Arms. You can arrange tours to view the records or commission hand-drafted certificates of your family arms.

Dr Johnson's House

17 Gough Square, off Fleet Street, EC4A 3DE (7353 3745/www. drjohnsonshouse.org). Chancery Lane or Temple tube/Blackfriars tube/rail. **Open** *May-Sept* 11am-5.30pm Mon-Sat. *Oct-Apr* 11am-5pm Mon-Sat. *Tours* by arrangement; groups of 10 or more only. **Admission** £4.50; free-£3.50 reductions. *Tours* free. **Map** p72 B4 ❹

Hidden away in a grand court of Georgian townhouses is the home of Dr Samuel Johnson (1709-84), author of the first *Dictionary of the English Language*, published in 1755. The museum is lent tremendous atmosphere by its creaky floorboards and Queen Anne furniture; you can almost feel the old wit's presence.

Guildhall

Gresham Street, EC2P 2UJ (7606 3030/tours ext 1463/www.corpof london.gov.uk). St Paul's tube/Bank tube/DLR. **Open** *May-Sept* 9.30am-5pm daily. *Oct-Apr* 9.30am-5pm Mon-Sat. Last entry 4.30pm. Closes for functions, so phone ahead. *Tours* by arrangement; groups of 10 or more only. **Admission** free. **Map** p73 D3 ❺

The cathedral-like Great Hall in the centre of the Guildhall compound has been the home of the Corporation of London for more than 800 years and is encrusted with historical symbolism.

Guildhall Art Gallery

Guildhall Yard, off Gresham Street, EC2P 2EJ (7332 3700/ www.guildhall-art-gallery.org.uk). Mansion House or St Paul's tube/ Bank tube/DLR/Moorgate tube/rail. **Open** 10am-5pm Mon-Sat (last entry 4.30pm); noon-4pm Sun (last entry 3.30pm). **Admission** £2.50; free-£1 reductions. **Map** p73 D3 ❻

Many of the paintings displayed here are stuffy portraits of long-dead politicians, but there are a few surprises, including a delightful collection of pre-Raphaelite paintings including works by Rossetti and Millais. The centrepiece of the exhibition is the vast *Siege of Gibraltar* by John Copley; it's the largest painting in Britain. Elsewhere in the collection are grand paintings by Constable, Reynolds and others. Down in a sub-basement you can see the ruins of London's Roman amphitheatre, built in around AD 70.

The Monument

Monument Street, EC3R 8AH (7626 2717/www.towerbridge.org.uk). Monument tube. **Open** *Oct-Mar* 10am-5pm daily. *Apr-Sep* 9.30am-5.30pm daily. Last entry 1hr before closing. **Admission** £2; free-£1 reductions. No credit cards. **Map** p73 E5 7 ❼

This gigantic Doric column was raised by Sir Christopher Wren in 1677 as a monument to the Great Fire of London. Its 202ft (62m) height is the distance to the site of the bakery in Pudding Lane where the fire began. Inside, a 311-step staircase leads to a narrow gallery with giddying views.

Museum of London

150 London Wall, EC2Y 5HN (0870 444 3851/2/www.museumoflondon.

LONDON BY AREA

org.uk). St Paul's tube/Barbican tube/ rail. **Open** 10am-5.50pm Mon-Sat; noon-5.50pm Sun. Last entry 5.30pm. **Admission** free. *Exhibitions* £5; £3 reductions. **Map** p73 D3 ❽

This well-thought-out museum traces the history of the capital from the earliest settlers to the outbreak of World War I. Highlights include a model of the Great Fire, with a narrative from Pepys's diaries, an atmospheric walk-through Victorian street scene and an outrageous red and gold coach belonging to the Lord Mayor. The museum is in the process of a major upgrade, with Roman and medieval galleries added recently. The latter covers the period of the Black Death, interpreted in a multi-voiced audio chamber.

St Bartholomew-the-Great

West Smithfield, EC1A 7JQ (7606 5171/www.greatstbarts.com). Barbican tube or Farringdon tube/rail. **Open** 8.30am-5pm Tue-Fri (until 4pm Nov-Feb); 10.30am-1.30pm Sat; 8.30am-1pm, 2.30-8pm Sun. **Admission** free; £3 suggested donation. **Map** p72 C3 ❾

This is probably the City's finest medieval church, and it's very atmospheric. Parts of the building belong to a 12th-century hospital priory. The church was chopped about during Henry VIII's reign and the interior is now firmly Elizabethan. It was used as a location for *Shakespeare in Love*.

St Paul's Cathedral

Ludgate Hill, EC4M 8AD (7236 4128/ www.stpauls.co.uk). St Paul's tube. **Open** 8.30am-4pm Mon-Sat. *Galleries, crypt & ambulatory* 9.30am-4pm Mon-Sat. Hours may change & special events cause closures; check before visiting. **Admission** *Cathedral, crypt & galleries* £9; free-£8 reductions. *Tours* £3; £1-£2.50 reductions. No credit cards. **Map** p72 C3 ❿

London's most famous cathedral has been wrapped up in scaffolding for most of the last decade in preparation for its 300th anniversary in 2008. Now the bulk of the work is finished, and Sir Christopher Wren's masterpiece glows. The Portland stone has been returned to its original gleaming white, while the paintings held in the Whispering Gallery and the Byzantine-inspired mosaics below the dome are radiant.

Be sure to take the 530 steps up to the open-air Golden Gallery for inspiring views over London. En route, you'll pass the outdoor Stone Gallery and the Whispering Gallery inside the dome, designed to bounce even a whisper clearly to someone on the opposite side of the gallery. Look out for the 18th-century graffiti.

Before leaving St Paul's, head down to the maze-like crypt, which contains memorials and graves of many great Britons, including Wren himself. The bookshop in the crypt sells a commendably useful guidebook for £4.

Tower Bridge Exhibition

Tower Bridge, SE1 2UP (7403 3761/ www.towerbridge.org.uk). Tower Hill tube. **Open** *Apr-Sept* 10am-6.30pm daily. *Oct-Mar* 9.30am-6pm daily. Last entry 1hr before closing. **Admission** £5.50; free-£4.25 reductions. **Map** p73 F5 ⓫

In its day (it was finished in 1894) the bridge was a triumph of Victorian technology, and even though it's only opened a few times a week these days, it still performs its drawbridge trick impressively. Two towers and the west walkway have been converted into an exhibition on its history – interesting stuff, and the views from the top are stupendous.

Tower of London

Tower Hill, EC3N 4AB (0870 756 6060/www.hrp.org.uk). Tower Hill tube/ Fenchurch Street rail. **Open** *Mar-Oct* 10am-6pm Mon, Sun; 9am-6pm Tue-Sat (last entry 5pm). *Nov-Feb* 10am-5pm Mon, Sun; 9am-5pm Tue-Sat (last entry 4pm). **Admission** £15; free-£12 reductions. **Map** p73 F5 ⓬

One of the city's essential tourist attractions, the Tower of London was founded more than 900 years ago. It has served as a fortress, royal palace, prison and execution site for traitors to the state – two of Henry VIII's wives were beheaded here. Visitors mob the fortress daily, but there's so much to see that most people are happy to put up with the inconvenience. Getting into the Tower used to be a fairly convoluted process, but these days you just buy your ticket (self-guided or free Beefeater-led tour) at the separate ticket office and enter through the Middle Tower. Before you come in, check out the interesting audio-visual display in the modernist Welcome Centre.

The highlight is almost certainly the Crown Jewels, which you glide past on airport-style travelators; the other big drawcard is the armoury in the White Tower, with its execution axe and chopping block. Executions were carried out on the green in front of the Tower – a glass memorial by Brian Catling was unveiled there in autumn 2006. The Medieval Palace recently re-opened with new interactive displays.

Eating & drinking

City eating tends to be formal and expensive. In addition to the suggestions below, the Great Eastern Hotel (p180), the Royal Exchange (p80) and Leadenhall Market (p80) each contain several options, the latter more humble than the first two.

Bar & Grill
2-3 West Smithfield, EC1A 9JX (0870 442 2541/www.barandgrill.co.uk). Farringdon tube/rail. **Open** noon-midnight Mon-Thur; noon-1am Fri; 6pm-2am Sat. **££-££££**. **International**. Map p72 C3 ⑬
This striking newcomer is a meat-eater's delight. There's an exotic choice of steaks – including ostrich and Kobe – then choose your own rub and sauce. Pizzas, fish and burgers are also served.

Black Friar
174 Queen Victoria Street, EC4V 4EG (7236 5474). Blackfriars tube/rail. **Open** 11am-11pm Mon-Wed, Sat; 11am-11.30pm Thur, Fri; noon-10.30pm Sun. **Pub**. Map p72 C5 ⑭
This beautiful wedge-shaped landmark, isolated among traffic and office buildings, retains its original 1905 stained glass, wooden floors, elaborate carvings and mosaics. The selection of ales includes guest brews, and the bar food (nice pies) is excellent too.

De Gustibus
53-55 Carter Lane, EC4V 5AE (7236 0056/www.degustibus.co.uk). St Paul's tube/Blackfriars tube/rail. **Open** 7am-5pm Mon-Fri. **£**. **Bakery café**. Map p72 C4 ⑮
This award-winning baker supplies upmarket restaurants with a mouth-watering range of artisan breads, also used to make deep-filled sandwiches or accompany own-made soups. The place also boasts a great salad bar, and serves hearty full English breakfasts.

Eyre Brothers
70 Leonard Street, EC2A 4QX (7613 5346/www.eyrebrothers.co.uk). Old Street tube/rail. **Open** noon-3pm, 6.30-11pm Mon-Fri; 7-11pm Sat. **££**. **Mediterranean**. Map p73 E2 ⑯
Subtle retro style combined with the Eyre brothers' fondness for Spanish flavours and Portuguese regional cooking make this a top-notch and unapologetically hearty dining experience.

Jamaica Wine House
St Michael's Alley, EC3V 9DS (7929 6972/www.massivepub.com). Bank tube/Monument tube/DLR. **Open** 11am-11pm Mon-Fri. **Pub**. Map p73 E4 ⑰
The site of London's first coffee house, this pub was razed in the Great Fire. Rebuilt, it became a meeting place for slave traders and Jamaican plantation owners. These days its dark-wood interior is divided into intimate spaces lined with banquettes; there's a restaurant upstairs. Wines and draught ales are tailored to the suited custom.

K-10
20 Copthall Avenue, EC2R 7DN (7562 8510/www.k10.net). Moorgate tube/rail. **Open** 11.30am-3pm Mon-Fri. **£-££**. **Japanese**. Map p73 E4 ⑱
The tiny, ground-floor takeaway on Copthall Avenue gives no clue to the hi-tech kaiten-zushi bar that occupies the large basement. An astonishing

Cellar Gascon, at Club Gascon, p86

variety of dishes rolls past, including immaculate sashimi and sushi dishes both classic and gourmet. A cut above most other *kaiten* contenders.

Le Coq d'Argent

1 Poultry, EC2R 8EJ (7395 5000/ www.conran.com). Bank tube/DLR. **Open** *Bar & grill* 11.30am-3pm Mon-Fri. *Restaurant* 7.30-10am, 11.30am-3pm, 6-10pm Mon-Fri; 6.30-10pm Sat; noon-3pm Sun. **££. Bar & grill. ££. French**. **Map** p73 D4 ⑲
The regional French cooking is as much a magnet here as the luxuriant Mediterranean garden setting and spectacular roof-top location. Popular with business types during the day and well-heeled diners after office hours.

Noto

2-3 Bassishaw Highwalk, off London Wall, EC2V 5DS (7256 9433/www. noto.co.uk). Moorgate tube/rail. **Open** 11.30am-2.30pm, 6-9.30pm Mon-Fri. **££. Japanese**. **Map** p73 D4 ⑳
Noto has an outlet in Harrods but the flagship restaurant is tucked away in the charmless walkways of Moorgate. It's a bit like the Japanese equivalent of a chippy, with busy deep-fryers, plastic chairs and easy-wipe tables. It's all super-fast, cheap and cheerful; don't expect high-end perfection and you won't be disappointed.

1 Blossom Street

1 Blossom Street, E1 6BX (7247 6530/ www.1blossomstreet.com). Liverpool Street tube/rail. **Open** noon-3pm, 6-9pm Mon-Fri. **£££. Italian**. **Map** p73 F3 ㉑
A new chef has improved the food at this spacious basement bar and restaurant near Spitalfields. The modern Italian menu now tastes as good as it reads, bringing it into line with the high quality of the rest of the operation.

The Place Below

St Mary-le-Bow, Cheapside, EC2V 6AU (7329 0789/ www.theplace below.co.uk). St Paul's tube/Bank tube/DLR. **Open** 7.30-11am, 11.30am-3pm Mon-Fri. **£. Vegetarian**. **Map** p73 D4 ㉒

Located in the Norman crypt of St Mary-le-Bow church, this smart canteen, atmospheric with its high, domed ceiling, columns and alcoves, is an unlikely hit with the area's stockbrokers; in fine weather, it's possible to sit in the churchyard. Food quality varies but it's imaginative and often scores highly. Lovely breakfasts.

Rosemary Lane

61 Royal Mint Street, E1 8LG (7481 2602). Tower Hill tube/Fenchurch Street rail/Tower Gateway DLR. **Open** noon-2.30pm, 5.30-10pm Mon-Fri; 5.30-10pm Sat. **£££. French**. **Map** p73 F5 ㉓
Word of mouth has done a lot to help Rosemary Lane get around its duff location and somewhat dull frontage and it is no longer one of the best-kept secrets in the City. Its reputation has been built on exceptional food, a modern take on French cuisine. Tables in the tastefully converted pub are closely spaced, but even this hasn't dampened our enthusiasm.

Sauterelle

Royal Exchange, EC3V 3LR (7618 2483/www.conran.com). Bank tube/ DLR. **Open** noon-2.30pm, 6-10pm Mon-Fri. **£££. French**. **Map** p73 E4 ㉔
Terence Conran's latest French restaurant delivers classic French cooking with simplicity, style and precision. Perched on the beautiful Exchange's mezzanine, overlooking the hubbub, it manages to be detached without being rarefied. Indulgent, elegant, relaxed.

Sweetings

39 Queen Victoria Street, EC4N 4SA (7248 3062). Mansion House tube. **Open** 11.30am-3pm Mon-Fri. **£££. Fish**. **Map** p73 D5 ㉕
Comfortingly old school and therefore unsurprisingly popular with (mainly male) City workers, Sweetings's dishes are good – sometimes excellent – and unfussy fishy fare, accompanied by buttered sliced bread which you can wash down with tankards of British ale.

Vertigo 42

Tower 42, 25 Old Broad Street, EC2N 1HQ (7877 7842/www.vertigo42.co.uk). Bank tube/DLR/Liverpool Street tube/rail. **Open** noon-3pm, 5-11pm Mon-Fri (reservations essential). **Bar**. **Map** p73 E4 **②⑥**

Champers and charming staff aside, there's only one thing that really counts at Vertigo 42: the view. Situated on the 42nd floor of the tallest building in the City, the bar enjoys a truly stunning panorama. Dress nicely, and eat before you come, unless you want (and can afford) a supper of caviar and pricey desserts from the short menu.

Ye Olde Cheshire Cheese

145 Fleet Street, EC4A 2BU (7353 6170/www.yeoldecheshirecheese.com). Blackfriars tube/rail. **Open** 11am-11pm Mon-Sat; noon-2.30pm Sun. **Pub**. **Map** p72 B4 **②⑦**

This marvellous labyrinth of a pub (hidden behind a dark, unwelcoming entrance) has ten rooms of varying size and character, between them involving wooden panelling, roaring fires and low beams. Dickens, Dr Johnson and WB Yeats have all been regulars.

Shopping

You don't come to the City to shop. For a start, it closes at weekends. You can browse the chainstores along Bishopsgate Arcade and in Liverpool Street Station (middle market). Between Cornhill and Threadneedle Street, the handsome Royal Exchange shopping centre, previously a futures trading floor, is distinctly upmarket: think Richard James, Tiffany, Gucci, Montblanc, but also Jo Malone, Agent Provocateur and Lulu Guinness. Leadenhall Market, at the south end of Leadenhall Street, is a beautiful Victorian arcade with glass roof and cobbled floor. It's home to upmarket and food shops, as well as pubs and restaurants. Whitecross Street is an old market street on which trendy shops have

started springing up, and there are some good food shops around nearby Smithfield meat market (which has recently been given fully protected status).

Bread & Honey

205 Whitecross Street, EC1Y 8QP (7253 4455/www.breadnhoney.com). Barbican tube/Old Street tube/rail. **Open** 10am-6.30pm Mon-Wed, Fri; 10am-7pm Thur; 11am-5pm Sat. **Map** p73 D2 **②⑧**

An eclectic collection of funky, upscale streetwear mixing familiar labels like Stüssy with younger contenders such as MHI and Misericordia. There are also bags by Ollie & Nic, shoes from Swear, Block headwear and extras such as toys.

Flâneur Food Hall

41 Farringdon Road, EC1M 3JB (7404 4422). Farringdon tube/rail. **Open** 9am-10pm Mon-Sat; 9am-6pm Sun. **Map** p72 B3 **②⑨**

Tall shelves and a large service area dominate this toothsome deli, whose every inch is crammed with astonishing products ranging from everyday (piccalilli, fresh pasta) to exotic (fresh Japanese mushrooms, pistachio oil). A daily changing menu of great quality food is available to eat in or take away.

Nightlife

There's nothing going on in the central city, but you'll find some action where it abuts nightlife zones Shoreditch and Hoxton.

Aquarium

256-260 Old Street, EC1V 9DD (7251 6136/www.clubaquarium.co.uk). Old Street tube/rail. **Open** *Bar* noon-11pm Mon-Wed, Sun; 11am-midnight Thur, Fri; 1pm-midnight Sat. *Club* 10pm-3am Mon-Wed, Sun; 10pm-4am Thur-Sat. **Admission** £5-£20. No credit cards. **Map** p73 E2 **③⓪**

This is apparently the only club in the country with its own swimming pool and bubblelicious jacuzzi: lifeguards

Magic bus

Your ticket to ride on the near-extinct Routemaster

For over 50 years the conductor-operated Routemaster bus served London both as a uniquely practical means of travel and an international symbol of the capital. At the start of 2006 the red double-deckers headed a list of the nation's most popular icons, along with Stonehenge and the FA Cup. Enduringly popular for their open design, which allowed passengers to hop on or off whenever they liked, the model was finally withdrawn from service on 9 December 2005, despite prior assurance from Mayor Ken Livingstone that this would not happen (to wit: 'only a ghastly dehumanised moron would want to get rid of the Routemaster').

Slightly happier news for Routemaster lovers arrived when Transport for London announced that the bus would live on along two 'heritage' routes. Beautifully refurbished Routies now run through the Central London sections of routes 9 and 15.

The vehicles used first went into service between 1960 and 1964. They have been lovingly repainted in their original colour scheme, complete with a cream-coloured horizontal stripe, and fitted with new engines that meet European emission standards.

The buses run daily every 15 minutes from 9.30am to 6.30pm and supplement the normal bus services. Route 9 takes in the Royal Albert Hall (westbound service only), Aldwych, the Strand, Trafalgar Square and Piccadilly Circus; Route 15 runs from Trafalgar Square to Tower Hill and allows passengers to glimpse the Strand, Fleet Street and St Paul's Cathedral.

Routemaster fares match the rest of the bus network (£1.50, less with an Oyster card), and Travelcards are accepted. Note that conductors now only check tickets rather than selling them – you must buy one before you board.

■ www.tfl.gov.uk/buses

Princess p88

are on hand, as are fluffy towels. For more traditional frugging the 500-capacity space has two dancefloors and a great lounge bar.

Arts & leisure

A tradition of midday performing has grown up in a number of lovely City churches, with admission usually free or by donation. They include **St Bride's** (7427 0133, www.stbrides.com), **St Margaret Lothbury** (7606 8330, www.stml.org.uk) and **St Mary-le-Bow** (7248 5139, www.stmarylebow.co.uk).

Barbican Centre

Silk Street, EC2Y 8DS (7638 4141/ box office 7638 8891/www.barbican. org.uk). Barbican, Farringdon or Moorgate tube/rail. **Map** p73 D3 **31**
This visionary arts centre, reviled and adored in equal measure for its concrete-slab architecture and confusing layout, turns 25 in 2007 (see box p90). Wherever you stand on its aesthetics, there's little argument about the quality of the arts programme in its concert hall, two theatres, art gallery, three cinemas and occasionally even in its lovely conservatory.

Musically, it's home to the London Symphony Orchestra (LSO), widely regarded as the capital's best orchestra. After a £25-million renovation, the auditorium now enjoys better acoustics and attracts high-prestige ensembles; the modern music programming is finding ever larger audiences.

The main and Pit theatres offer an eclectic mix of touring regional and foreign theatre and dance companies during the year-round BITE season, and the well-specced cinemas offer the arthouse end of mainstream releases.
Event highlights *The Bull* by Fabulous Beast Dance Theatre (2wks mid Feb); Overhead (7 Mar-22 Apr), on composer Thomas Adès; New Crowned Hope (4 July 4-12 Aug, a multidisciplinary festival curated by maverick director Peter Sellars; Ozmosis, celebrating all things Australian (1 Oct-mid Nov 2007).

Holborn & Clerkenwell

Holborn and Clerkenwell developed as service centres for the City on one side and Westminster on the other: home to markets, the media and religious and legal institutions.

Clerkenwell, to the north-west of the City across from Smithfields meat market, has a particularly bloody history, taking in plague and burnings-at-the-stake. Today's clutch of clubs around Clerkenwell Road can be quite intense but they don't quite match that. Come here instead for the pleasures of a relatively residential inner-city area: great pubs, bars and restaurants on characterful streets.

To the south, **Holborn** (pronounced 'Hoe-bn') is an office district, home to the four medieval Inns of Court, whose august courtyards and wig and gown shops give them the air of an otherwordly company town.

Sights & museums

Hunterian Museum

35-43 Lincoln's Inn Fields, Holborn, WC2A 3PE (7869 6560/www.rcseng. ac.uk/museums). Holborn tube. **Open** 10am-5pm Tue-Sat. *Tours* 1pm Wed (book in advance). **Admission** free. *Tours* free. **Map** p72 A4 ㉜
Named after 18th-century surgeon and anatomist John Hunter, this is the museum of the Royal College of Surgeons. It contains a terrifying collection of historic surgical instruments alongside items from Hunter's collection of human and animal specimens. Everything is beautifully displayed and interpreted; the Hunterian was longlisted for the prestigous Gulbenkian prize in 2006.

Inns of Court

Opposite the Royal Courts of Justice, between Fleet Street and the Embankment, are **Middle Temple**

(7427 4800, www.middletemple.org. uk) and **Inner Temple** (7797 8183, www.innertemple.org.uk). The Inns aren't open to the public but you can look into the courtyards; the Inner Temple has several fine buildings and its lawns are a lovely spot for picnics. **Temple Church** (King's Bench Walk, 7353 8559), consecrated in 1185, is London's only round church. Part of Dan Brown's *The Da Vinci Code* is set here. **Lincoln's Inn** (7405 1393, www.lincolnsinn.org.uk) is a catalogue of architectural styles (its Old Hall is well over 500 years old) surrounding London's largest public square. The gardens of serene **Gray's Inn** (7458 7800, www.graysinn.org.uk) are open to the public on weekday mornings.

Museum & Library of the Order of St John

St John's Gate, St John's Lane, Clerkenwell, EC1M 4DA (7324 4000/ www.sja.org.uk/history). Farringdon tube/rail. **Open** 10am-5pm Mon-Fri; 10am-4pm Sat. *Tours* 11am, 2.30pm Tue, Fri, Sat. **Admission** free. *Tours* free. Suggested donation £5; £4 reductions. **Map** p72 C3 ㉝
This museum charts the evolution of the medieval Order of Hospitaller Knights into its modern incarnation as St John's ambulances. There are objects and artworks relating to this varied history, which visits Jerusalem, Malta and the Ottoman Empire.

Sir John Soane's Museum

13 Lincoln's Inn Fields, Holborn, WC2A 3BP (7405 2107/www. soane.org). Holborn tube. **Open** 10am-5pm Tue-Sat; 10am-5pm, 6-9pm 1st Tue of mth. *Tours* 2.30pm Sat. **Admission** free; donations appreciated. *Tours* £3; free reductions. **Map** p72 A4 ㉞
A leading architect in his day, Sir John Soane (1753-1837) was a passionate collector of decorative objects. His house, now a museum, is a pleasant chaos of sculptures, paintings, architectural models, antiquities, jewellery and other miscellanea in a cornucopia of domestic and artistic delights. In the run-up to

Christmas, there are atmospheric candle-lit evening openings. Be sure to ask to see the hidden Hogarths.

Somerset House

Strand, Holborn, WC2R 1LA (7845 4600/www.somerset-house.org.uk). Holborn or Temple tube (closed Sun). **Open** 10am-6pm daily (last entry 5.15pm); extended hours for courtyard & terrace. *Tours* phone for details. **Admission** *Courtyard & terrace* free. *Exhibitions* £5; £4 reductions. No credit cards. **Map** p72 A5 ③⑤

This quite lovely neo-classical mansion beside the Thames was built to house learned societies, and has also served as a tax office. These days it's home to three formidable art and museum collections, the beautiful fountain court (which hosts an outdoor ice rink in winter), a little café, a classy restaurant and a pleasant river terrace, with terrific views. Check *Time Out* for details of the outdoor film and music events held here in summer; the courtyard is a breathtaking setting.

Somerset House museums

Strand, Holborn, WC2R 0RN. Holborn or Temple tube (closed Sun). **Open** 10am-6pm daily (last entry 5.15pm). **Admission** *1 collection* £5; free-£4 reductions. *2 collections* £8; free-£7 reductions. *3 collections* (valid for 3 days) £12; free-£11 reductions. *Tours* phone for details. No credit cards. **Map** p72 A5 ③⑤

Courtauld Institute of Art Gallery

7848 2526/www.courtauld.ac.uk/gallery. The Courtauld has one of Britain's most important collections of paintings. It is excitingly diverse and eclectic, yet on a more manageable scale than, say, the National. Old Masters, Impressionists and post-Impressionists are here alongside a range of prints, drawings, pieces of sculpture and other works. Some of the most famous exhibits on display are Manet's *A Bar at the Folies Bergère*, Vincent Van Gogh's *Self-Portrait with Bandaged Ear* and *Two Dancers on the Stage* by Degas.

Gilbert Collection

7420 9400/www.gilbert-collection.org.uk. The late Sir Arthur Gilbert had a predilection for all that glisters, collecting silver, gold and all sorts of gemmed, gilt and shiny objects. In 1996 he donated his entire collection to the nation. Two floors are shamelessly bedecked with candelabras, mosaics, vases, urns, plates, mosaics, snuff boxes and more.

Hermitage Rooms

7845 4630/www.hermitagerooms.co.uk. These rooms host rotating exhibitions of items belonging to the Winter Palace in St Petersburg; they even recreate in miniature the decor of their Russian parent. New shows arrive twice a year and can include everything from paintings and drawings to decorative art and fine jewellery.

Eating & drinking

Ambassador

NEW *55 Exmouth Market, EC1R 4QL (7837 0009). Angel tube.* **Open** 9am-11pm Mon-Fri; 11am-11pm Sat; 11am-5pm Sun. **££-£££**. **Gastropub**. **Map** p72 B2 ③⑥

Fine gastropub food – simple at lunch and more ambitious in the evening – and a sleek formica-and-lino decor are appealing, but what stands out here is an excellent and approachable wine list, with choices by the glass.

Bountiful Cow

NEW *51 Eagle Street, Holborn, WC1R 4AP (7404 0200). Holborn tube.* **Open/food served** 11am-11pm Mon-Sat. **££**. **Diner.** **Map** p72 A3 ③⑦

Roxy Beaujolais's new baby is a sassy two-floor diner with a witty and well-sourced bovine theme – retro Vache Qui Rit and Bovril ads, cowboy posters and steaks aplenty (as well as non-meaty specials).

Clerkenwell House

23-27 Hatton Wall, Clerkenwell, EC1N 8JJ (7404 1113/www. clerkenwellhouse.com). Chancery Lane tube/Farringdon tube/rail. **Open** noon-11pm Mon-Wed;

Peasant p87

noon-midnight Thur-Sat; noon-10.30pm Sun. **Cocktail bar**.
Map p72 B3 ㉝

A serious contender for Match's crown as Clerkenwell's king of cocktails. Just reading the menu induces salivation, and ambrosial recipes such as Blueberry Amaretto Sour don't disappoint. The design mixes monochrome with shabby chic and psychedelia – surprisingly well.

Club Gascon

57 West Smithfield, Clerkenwell, EC1A 9DS (7796 0600). Barbican tube/ Farringdon tube/rail. **Open** noon-2pm, 7-10pm Mon-Thur; noon-2pm, 7-10.30pm Fri; 7-10.30pm Sat. **££££**. **French**. Map p72 C3 ㉟

Pascal Aussignac's accomplished eaterie is plush and clubby – fitting for a foie gras specialist. Assured staff serve imaginative concoctions in witty presentations. Dishes are served tapas-style and it's easy to spend more than you expected: consider going for the tasting menu. The basement wine bar, Cellar Gascon, has an excellent list. A good special-occasion restaurant.

Coach & Horses

26-28 Ray Street, Clerkenwell, EC1R 3DJ (7278 8990/www.thecoachand horses.com). Farringdon tube/rail. **Open** 11am-11pm Mon-Fri; 6-11pm Sat; noon-3pm Sun. **££**. **Gastropub**. Map p72 B2 ㊵

Expect delicious, unfussy British food at this updated (as opposed to refurbished) gastropub. The menu changes daily, ingredients are lovingly selected, and the interesting wine list shows that real effort has been made with the drinks too. In its quest for British authenticity, it impressed us by serving Christmas mince pies with actual meat in it; it also serves hitherto unfashionable offal dishes.

Dovetail

9 Jerusalem Passage, Clerkenwell, EC1V 4JP (7490 7321/www.belgian bars.com). Farringdon tube/rail. **Open** noon-11pm Mon-Sat. **Bar**. Map p72 C2 ㊶

The only beer served at Dovetail is Belgian – in 101 varieties. Taps supply Leffe Blonde and Brune, Jupiler and Maes Pils, and the drinks menu makes a good guidebook for the beer explorer. The Trappist brews fit in spirit with the stone-flagged floors and pew-style seating. Food is served.

Eagle

159 Farringdon Road, Clerkenwell, EC1R 3AL (7837 1353). Farringdon tube/rail. **Open** noon-11pm Mon-Sat; noon-5pm Sun. **££**. **Gastropub**. Map p72 B2 ㊷

With its dedication to offering decently priced seasonal food, this slightly raffish local, beloved of *Guardian* hacks, is not only London's very first gastropub, it continues to be one of the city's best. The flavours are big and brash, and the cooking mixes simple Mediterranean with hearty British. It can be hard to get a seat at peak times, but there are barstool perches, too.

Jerusalem Tavern

55 Britton Street, Clerkenwell, EC1M 5UQ (7490 4281). Farringdon tube/ rail. **Open** 11am-11pm Mon-Fri. **Pub**. Map p72 C3 ㊸

The small but perfectly formed Jerusalem isn't quite as old as its 1810 shopfront suggests, but we forgive it: as the only London pub associated with the St Peter's Brewery, it serves exemplary booze from the barrel. It's all pretty tight and cosy: the green-painted wood, chipped walls and candles work well with original tiles, and it's usually packed out.

Match EC1

45-47 Clerkenwell Road, Clerkenwell, EC1M 5RS (7250 4002/www. matchbar.com). Farringdon tube /rail. **Open** 11am-midnight Mon-Fri; 5pm-midnight Sat. **Cocktail bar**. Map p72 C2 ㊹

Match forms the old guard of bars in Clerkenwell, and much of its continued success is down to Dale DeGroff's definitive and frequently changing cocktail list. The space consists of a table-lined balcony overlooking a

Seven Stars p88

sunken standing and dancing space, which faces the excellently stocked and styled bar. Food includes sharing bowls for up to four people.

Matsuri

71 High Holborn, Holborn, WC1V 6EA (7430 1970. Chancery Lane or Holborn tube. **Open** noon-2.30pm, 6-10pm Mon-Sat. **£££-££££. Map** p72 A3 ⓖ
Decked out with sleek polished surfaces, white walls, wooden screens and lots of glass, Matsuri St James's style-conscious younger sister is a champion all-rounder. The cooking and ingredients are nothing short of superb. Expensive, but worth it.

Medcalf

40 Exmouth Market, Clerkenwell, EC1R 4QE (7833 3533/www.medcalf bar.co.uk). Angel tube/Farringdon tube/ rail. **Open** noon-11pm Mon-Thur, Sat; noon-12.30am Fri; noon-5pm Sun. **££.**
British. **Map** p72 B2 ⓖ
Set, mod-retro style, in a former butcher's shop, Medcalf is a fine purveyor of top-quality British food in portions

both snacky and substantial. A louche vibe allows it to slip effortlessly into drinking-den mode after the kitchen shuts at 10pm.

Moro

34-36 Exmouth Market, Clerkenwell, EC1R 4QE (7833 8336/www.moro. co.uk). Farringdon tube/rail. **Open** 12.30-10.30pm Mon-Sat. **£££.**
Spanish. **Map** p72 B2 ⓖ
This bustling mainstay continues to set the standard for Spanish and North African fare, nearly a decade after it opened. Either pop in for a snack (tapas are available all day, and tasting menus at Saturday lunchtime) or settle down for a full meal.

Peasant

240 St John Street, Clerkenwell, EC1V 4PH (7336 7726/www.thepeasant. co.uk). Angel tube/Farringdon tube/rail. **Open** noon-11pm daily. **££-£££.**
Gastropub. **Map** p72 C2 ⓖ
The Peasant's cosy downstairs, with its battered sofas and welcoming fireplace, is the perfect place to share

sumptuous bar snacks. Upstairs there's a posher dining space for sampling the diverse, top-notch menu.

Princess

76 Paul Street, Clerkenwell, EC2A 4NE (7729 9270). Old Street tube/rail. **Open** noon-11pm Mon-Fri; 5.30-11pm Sat; noon-5.30pm Sun. **££-£££**. **Map** p73 E2 ㊾

Comprising a downstairs boozing area and comfortable galleried upstairs restaurant with trademark swirly wallpaper, there's no doubt the Princess is a gastropub. But its Mediterranean-influenced food is gaining plaudits that set it alongside the best restaurants. With good service, some excellent international wines and a couple of real ales, this one's quality all round.

Seven Stars

53 Carey Street, Holborn, WC2A 2JB (7242 8521). Chancery Lane, Holborn or Temple tube. **Open** 11am-11pm Mon-Fri; noon-11pm Sat; noon-10.30pm Sun. **££**. **Gastropub**. **Map** p72 A4 ㊿

Roxy Beaujolais's fabulous little pub manages to squeeze the best ales, wines and food into an interior whose compactness is dictated by the constraints of its 1602 construction. Nobody seems to mind the crush, certainly not the jolly clientele from the Royal Courts of Justice across the road. The tasty, not-too-fussy food is served on checked tablecloths.

Smiths of Smithfield

67-77 Charterhouse Street, Clerkenwell, EC1M 6HJ (7251 7950/www.smithsofsmithfield.co.uk). Farringdon tube/rail. **Open** *Ground-floor bar/café* 7am-5pm Mon-Fri; 10am-5pm Sat; 9.30am-5pm Sun. *Brasserie* noon-3pm, 6-11pm Mon-Fri; 6-10.45pm Sat. *Top floor* noon-3pm, 6.30-10.45pm Mon-Fri; 6.30-10.45pm Sat; noon-3.45pm, 6.30-10.30pm Sun. **£** Bar. **££** Brasserie. **£££** Restaurant. **Modern European**. **Map** p72 C3 (51)

This warehouse-like eaterie, opposite the famous meat market, caters for every mood. The ground-floor bar serves brunch, snacks and after-work drinks, and there's a small but swish cocktail bar upstairs. For more substantial food head upstairs to the lively brasserie or all the way up to the fine-dining restaurant on the top floor.

St John

26 St John Street, Clerkenwell, EC1M 4AY (7251 0848/4998/www.stjohnrestaurant.com). Farringdon tube/rail. **Open** noon-3pm, 6-11pm Mon-Fri; 6-11pm Sat. **£££** **British**. **Map** p72 C3 (52)

Proprietor Fergus Henderson was a pioneer in the renaissance of British food, earning a reputation for winkling out forgotten British dishes (pork is pressed and paired with gizzards for a starter, mains might be chitterlings or crispy pig's tails) and creating riffs on well-worn classics (gooseberry fool with toasted brioche). The atmosphere, however, is all white-painted modern, and very congenial. Both here and at St John's sister site by Spitalfields market, ingredients are seasonal, and cakes and breads are sold to take away.

Three Kings of Clerkenwell

7 Clerkenwell Close, Clerkenwell, EC1R 0DY (7253 0483). Farringdon tube/ rail. **Open** noon-11pm Mon-Fri; 7-11pm Sat. **Food served** noon-3pm Mon-Fri. **Pub**. Map p72 B2 ❸

Idle, creative and shambling souls congregate here under the watchful eye of a (fake) rhino head that thrusts out over the open fire; also for mellow DJ events, and a downstairs crush or quiet upstairs chats, Prestige jukebox allowing.

Vinoteca

7 St John Street, Clerkenwell, EC1M 4AA (7253 8786/www.vinoteca.co.uk). Farringdon tube/rail. **Open** 11am-11pm Mon-Sat. **Wine bar**. Map p72 C3 ❺

Vinoteca is a real find, with lovely staff, a nice atmosphere and one of the best wine lists we've seen in a London bar – with flat-rate rather than percentage mark-ups making the expensive bottles more accessible. The bar food's good, too, in snack-Brit mode.

Shopping

There's not much shopping around here, but Clerkenwell's artisan heritage is still evident in its crafts network and the gem traders of Hatton Garden. Exmouth Market also has some great local shops.

Brindisa

32 Exmouth Market, Clerkenwell, EC1R 4QE (7713 1666/www.brindisa. com). Farringdon tube/rail. **Open** 10am-6pm Mon; 9.30am-6pm Tue-Sat. Map p72 B2 ❺

An importer of top-quality Spanish foods. Items are sourced from the best-known Spanish producers (including organic ones) and tastings are held.

Lesley Craze Gallery

33-35A Clerkenwell Green, Clerkenwell, EC1R 0DU (7608 0393/www.lesley crazegallery.co.uk). Farringdon tube/rail. **Open** 10am-5.30pm Tue-Sat. Map p72 B2 ❺

Smiths of Smithfield

Barbican turns 25

Hot on the heels of a £30 million renovation, the love-it-or-hate-it Barbican centre is gearing up to celebrate its 25th birthday in 2007. Some see the place as a concrete monster, others a stroke of architectural genius, but few will deny its historical significance: a ground-breaking modernist vision emerging from the debris of post-war London.

Since opening in 1982, the distinctive concrete structures of the arts centre – with their fat columns and labyrinthine underground layers – have housed a concert hall, two theatres, three cinema screens and two art galleries. The arts programmes, some of London's most far-reaching, have evolved to make the Barbican a key player on the scene, taking in major performers in classical, world and pop music; arthouse and first-run cinema; cutting-edge art; and the highly acclaimed BITE international theatre and dance programme.

To mark its quarter-century, the Barbican is planning an impressive programme of events, starting on the birthday weekend (3-4 March 2007). Highlights will include performances by the London Symphony Orchestra; the Berlin Philharmonic; pianist Evgeny Kissin; dance from all-singing, all-dancing French outfit Les Grooms; and an aptly labyrinthine, art installation in the Curve gallery by Danish artist Jeppe Hein.

■ www.barbican.org.uk

Diamonds aren't the focus here, but the jewellery is certainly cutting-edge. Over 100 international designers are showcased, working in precious metals and imaginative mixed media. Prices run from the affordable to the unthinkable.

London Silver Vaults

Chancery House, 53-64 Chancery Lane, Holborn, WC2A 1QT (7242 3844/ www.thesilvervaults.com). Chancery Lane tube. **Open** 9am-5.30pm Mon-Fri; 9am-1pm Sat. **Map** p72 A3 ⑤⑦
This underground vault was originally a safety deposit, where London toffs stored their valuables in guarded strongrooms. It's now home to around 30 silver dealers, selling everything from £20,000 centrepieces to £30 napkin rings. Fun to wander.

Nightlife

Fabric

77A Charterhouse Street, Clerkenwell, EC1M 3HN (7336 8898/www.fabric london.com). Farringdon tube/rail. **Open** 9.30pm-5am Fri; 10pm-7am Sat. **Admission** £12-£15. **Map** p72 C3 ⑤⑧
World renowned, thanks to adoring reviews from punters and DJs alike, Fabric is all about the music, usually of the leftfield, extremely underground sort. Its three rooms get pretty packed: the main one is home to the stomach-wobbling Bodysonic dancefloor; the second's a rave-like warehouse (complete with laser); and the smaller third room is where the cool stuff happens.

Turnmills

63B Clerkenwell Road, Clerkenwell, EC1M 5PT (7250 3409/www.turn mills.co.uk). Farringdon tube/rail. **Open** 8pm-1am Wed; 9pm-3am Thur; 10.30pm-7.30am Fri; 10pm-6am Sat; 6pm-2am Sun. **Admission** £12-£15. **Map** p72 B3 ⑤⑨
Turnmills' neo-classical, acid-warehouse nooks and crannies are a hedonist's playground. Hugely friendly (rather than achingly fashionable) and offering the full musical spectrum, it's one of the most popular venues in town.

Soho Theatre p129

The West End

Bloomsbury & Fitzrovia

Bloomsbury is characterised by sweeping Georgian terraces and gracious squares. This was where the nobility built their townhouses and founded their instititions: it's a centre of academia, endowed with hospitals and museums, the British Museum prime among them. And of course it has a famous literary heritage, counting not only Virginia Wolfe's literary set among its former inhabitants, but Dickens, Trollope, Poe and Yeats. These days its grandeur is a little faded, and no one would call it buzzy or fashionable, but it's a pleasure to wander.

Fitzrovia, to its west, has come from a more raffish past as a gathering point for radicals, revolutionaries, punks and bohemians to a rather smarter present. It still has plenty of the pubs in which the above used to famously consort, but it also has some of this side of the capital's hippest restaurants and hotels, and some inviting small shops, particularly around the very strollable Charlotte Street.

Sights & museums

British Library

96 Euston Road, Bloomsbury, NW1 2DB (7412 7332/www.bl.uk). Euston Square tube/Euston or King's Cross tube/rail. **Open** 9.30am-6pm Mon, Wed-Fri; 9.30am-8pm Tue; 9.30am-5pm Sat; 11am-5pm Sun. **Admission** free; donations appreciated. **Map** p93 D1 ①

This is one of the greatest libraries in the world, with 150 million items. Its 1997 home has also been called one of the ugliest buildings in the world, but the interior is spectacular – all white

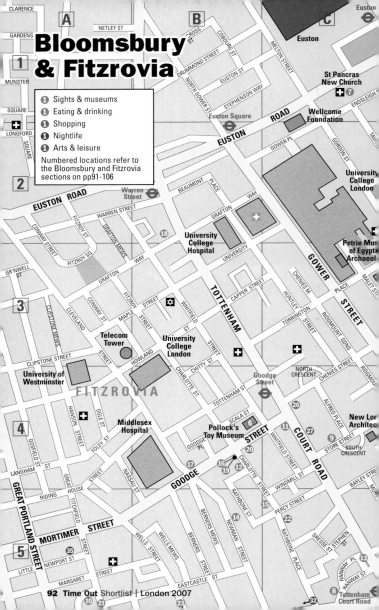

Bloomsbury
& Fitzrovia

❶ Sights & museums
❶ Eating & drinking
❶ Shopping
❶ Nightlife
❶ Arts & leisure

Numbered locations refer to
the Bloomsbury and Fitzrovia
sections on pp91-106

Euston

St Pancras
New Church

Wellcome
Foundation

University
College
London

University
College
Hospital

Petrie Mus
of Egyptian
Archaeol

Warren
Street

FITZROVIA

Telecom
Tower

University
College
London

University of
Westminster

Middlesex
Hospital

Pollock's
Toy Museum

New Lor
Architec

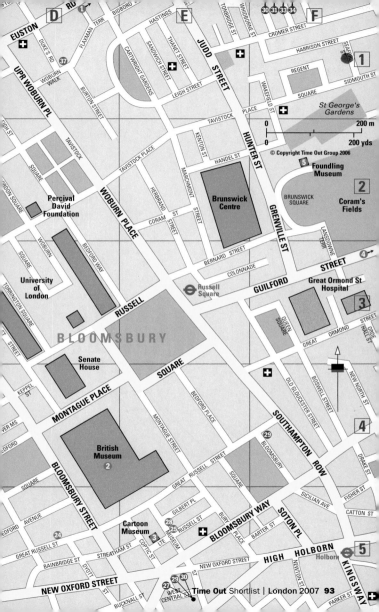

'THE FEEL-GOOD
FACTOR OF A GREEK
ISLAND HOLIDAY'
THE GUARDIAN

BENNY ANDERSSON & BJÖRN ULVAEUS'

MAMMA MIA!®

THE SMASH HIT MUSICAL BASED ON THE SONGS OF ABBA®

TICKETS RELEASED DAILY AT THE BOX OFFICE
0870 850 0393 | 0870 264 3333 | mamma-mia.com

PRINCE OF WALES THEATRE
COVENTRY STREET | LONDON | W1D 6AS

©LITTLESTAR

marble, glass and light. The main treasures are on display: the Magna Carta, the Lindisfarne Gospels and original manuscripts from Chaucer. There's fun stuff too, including Beatles lyric sheets and archive recordings of everyone from James Joyce to Bob Geldof.

British Museum

Great Russell Street, Bloomsbury, WC1B 3DG (7636 1555/recorded information 7323 8783/www.thebritishmuseum. ac.uk). Russell Square or Tottenham Court Road tube. **Open** *Galleries* 10am-5.30pm Mon-Wed, Sat, Sun; 10am-8.30pm Thur, Fri. *Great Court* 9am-6pm Mon-Wed, Sun; 9am-11pm Thur-Sat. **Admission** free; donations appreciated. *Temporary exhibitions* prices vary. *Highlights tours* £8; £5 reductions. *Eye opener tours* free. **Map** p92 D4 ❷

Officially London's most popular tourist attraction, the museum is a neo-classical marvel built in 1847 and updated in 2000 by Sir Norman Foster's glass-roofed Great Court, the largest covered space in Europe. This £100m landmark surrounds the domed Reading Room, where Marx, Lenin, Thackeray, Dickens, Hardy and Yeats once worked. Star exhibits include ancient Egyptian artefacts – the Rosetta Stone, statues of the pharaohs, and mummies – Greek antiquities, including the controversial marble friezes from the Parthenon, and massive fragments of ancient Middle Eastern buildings. The Celts gallery has the Lindow Man, killed in 300BC and preserved in peat. The Wellcome Gallery of Ethnography holds an Easter Island statue. The King's Library is the finest neo-classical space in London, and permanent home to 'Enlightenment: Discovering the World' in the 18th Century.

Event highlights 'French Drawings from the British Museum: Clouet to Seurat' (to 26 Nov 2006). 'From Life', work by Israeli artist Avigdor Arikha (to 6 Jan 2007). Coins, jewellery and art from a thousand years of Byzantine history (to 7 Jan 2007). 'Power and Taboo:

St Pancras New Church p97

Sacred Objects from the Pacific', exploring 18th and 19th century religious practice in Polynesia (to 7 Jan 2007).

Cartoon Museum

NEW *35 Little Russell Street, Bloomsbury, WC1A 2HH (7580 8155/www.cartoonmuseum.org). Holborn or Tottenham Court Road tube.* **Open** 10.30-5.30 Tue-Sat, noon-5.30 Sun. **Admission** £3; reductions free-£2. **Map** p93 E5 ❸

See box p96.

Charles Dickens Museum

48 Doughty Street, Bloomsbury, WC1N 2LX (7405 2127/www.dickens museum.com). Chancery Lane or Russell Square tube. **Open** 10am-5pm Mon-Sat; 11am-5pm Sun. *Tours* by arrangement. **Admission** £5; £3-£4 reductions. **Map** p93 F3 ❹

Dickens lived here between 1837 and 1840 while he wrote *Nicholas Nickleby* and *Oliver Twist.* Restored to its former condition, the house is packed with Dickens ephemera: letters, manuscripts and his writing desk.

A new draw

London's Cartoon Museum opens.

The global furore sparked by the publication of cartoons of the Prophet Mohammed in a Danish newspaper in 2006 highlighted the power and influence of the comic artform. The Cartoon Museum (p95), which opened in Bloomsbury in March 2006, reinforces the significance of cartoon art but also serves as a powerful reminder that cartooning is fun – you're actually encouraged to laugh out loud.

'Britain has a wonderful history of political satire,' enthuses Oliver Preston, the Cartoon Museum's chairman. 'This museum is about celebrating and promoting the very best in British cartoon art.' Opposite well-known World War II political cartoons by Low and Vicky hang gems by Thelwell – whose playful countryside images bring a smile to the face – and Giles, whose work reveals much about what people wore, thought and did in the mid 20th century.

On the ground floor of this transformed former dairy, the cartoons are displayed in chronological order, starting with the early 18th century, when high-society types back from the Grand Tour introduced the Italian practice of the *caricatura* to polite company. From Hogarth it moves through the much parodied *Plum Pudding* by James Gillray, plus works by John Bull and George Cruikshank (who was born around the corner from the museum) – British cartooning's 'golden age' (1770 to 1830). While 'Modern Times' may not be a label those under 50 would choose for the dates 1914 to 1961, in that section are interesting wartime cartoons and social commentary. The 'new satire' – works published from 1961 onwards – includes Ralph Steadman, Steve Bell, Dave Brown, Matt and others on topics from Brown and Blair to mad cow disease.

It's perhaps indicative of the gallery's bent that while downstairs the artists' names are immediately recognisable, upstairs – where comic strip art such as *2000AD*, the *Dandy*, the *Beano* and other favourites of our youth are displayed – is much more about the characters portrayed: from Rupert to Dan Dare and Judge Dredd. It is to be hoped that the Young Artists' Gallery will include underground work with a less 'authorised' feel that would appeal to younger audiences. The excellent shop is recommended, and there's a library where you can search, by appointment, a catalogue of some 3,000 books.

Foundling Museum

40 Brunswick Square, Bloomsbury, WC1N 1AZ (7841 3600/www. foundlingmuseum.org.uk). Russell Square tube. **Open** 10am-6pm Tue-Sat; noon-6pm Sun. **Admission** £5; free-£3 reductions. **Map** p93 F3 ⑤

The museum recalls the social history of the Foundling Hospital, set up in 1739 by shipwright and sailor Captain Thomas Coram, who was appalled by the number of abandoned children on London's streets. The museum recounts the social change in the period, with interactive exhibits and a case of mementos left by mothers for their babies. Sounds staid, but very involving for both children and adults. Coram's Fields nearby is a playground to which adults are only admitted if accompanied by a child.

Pollock's Toy Museum

1 Scala Street (entrance on Whitfield Street), Fitzrovia, W1T 2HL (7636 3452/www.pollockstoymuseum.com). Goodge Street tube. **Open** 10am-5pm Mon-Sat. **Admission** £3; free-£1.50 reductions. **Map** p92 B4 ⑥

Housed in a creaky Georgian townhouse, the old board games, clockwork trains and Robertson's gollies on display evoke enormous nostalgia in adults. Young children prefer the free puppet shows (usually on Saturdays).

St Pancras New Church

Euston Road (corner of Upper Woburn Place), Bloomsbury, NW1 2BA (7388 1461/www.stpancraschurch.org). Euston tube/rail. **Open** 12.45-2pm Wed; noon-2pm Thur; 9.15-11am, 3-5pm Sat; 7.45am-noon, 5.30-7.15pm Sun. Services 8am, 10am, 6pm Sun; 1.15pm Wed. **Admission** free. **Map** p92 C1 ⑦

Built in 1822, this church is a spectacular example of the Greek Revivalist style. Inspired by the Erechtheion on the Acropolis hill in Athens, its most notable feature is its Caryatid porches. The interior is more restrained but has beautiful stained-glass windows. Free lunchtime concerts are held on Thursdays at 1.15pm).

Fino p98

Eating & drinking

Bradley's Spanish Bar

42-44 Hanway Street, Fitzrovia, W1T 1UT (7636 0359). Tottenham Court Road tube. **Open** noon-11pm Mon-Sat; noon-10.30pm Sun. **Bar.** **Map** p92 C5 ⑧

Brazenly boho, yet still Iberian, Bradley's Spanish Bar carries on packing 'em into its two-floor retro casket of velour every night of the week – and spilling 'em out into the tiny street outside. No food, but good beers on tap, and beer is what people come for. The real deal: poseurs need not apply.

Busaba Eathai

22 Store Street, Fitzrovia, WC1E 7DS (7299 7900). Goodge Street or Tottenham Court Road tube. **Open** noon-11pm Mon-Thur; noon-11.30pm Fri, Sat; noon-10pm Sun. **££**. **Thai.** **Map** p92 C4 ⑨

Alan Yau has brought many good things to the London restaurant scene (and beyond), including slurp-and-go noodle chain Wagamama and high-end

LONDON BY AREA

Sardo p101

LONDON BY AREA

Hakkasan and Yauatcha. Busaba is a great way of sampling his style, teaming excellent Thai-inspired dishes with a classy version of communal-table design. This and the Marylebone and Soho locations are all conveniently close to visitor honeypots and the prices pleasing. No reservations.
Other locations: 8-13 Bird Street, Marylebone, W1U 1BU (7518 8080); 106-110 Wardour Street, Soho, W1F 0TR (7255 8686).

Carluccio's Caffè
8 Market Place, Fitzrovia, W1W 8AG (7636 2228/www.carluccios.com). Oxford Circus tube. **Open** 7.30am-11pm Mon-Fri; 10am-11pm Sat; 10am-10pm Sun. **££**. **Italian**. Map p92 A5 ⑩
With nearly 15 branches around London, Carluccio's may feel a bit chain-like, yet it continues to push the right buttons, blending classic and innovative regional Italian dishes with flair. Desserts are a high point, and include own-made ice-creams and sorbets. Staff are friendly and welcoming.

Crazy Bear
26-28 Whitfield Street, Fitzrovia, W1T 7DS (7631 0088/www.crazybeargroup. co.uk). Goodge Street or Tottenham Court Road tube. **Open** noon-11pm Mon-Fri; 6-11pm Sat. **Bar**. Map p92 C4 ⑪
Über-stylish yet supremely comfortable, the flagship of the namesake chain comprises a restaurant and opulent bar down an ornate staircase. Choose between a swivel cowhide bar stool, a red padded alcove or low leather armchair and pull up a menu – one for cigars, one for drinks (expertly and convivially mixed).

Fino
33 Charlotte Street, entrance on Rathbone Street, Fitzrovia, W1T 1RR (7813 8010/www.finorestaurant.com). Goodge Street or Tottenham Court Road tube. **Open** Restaurant noon-2.30pm, 6-10.30pm Mon-Fri; 12.30-2.30pm, 6-10.30pm Sat. **£££**.
Spanish. Map p92 B4 ⑫
Fino is invitingly bright despite its basement setting. Appearance is a priority that equally applies to its tantalisingly presented, uncontrived and directly flavoured tapas dishes (some also available at the bar, which is open throughout the afternoon). The desserts and wine list (including plenty of sherries) are further draws.

Hakkasan
8 Hanway Place, Fitzrovia, W1T 1HD (7907 1888). Tottenham Court Road tube. **Open** noon-2.45pm, 6-11.30pm Mon, Tue; noon-2.45pm, 6pm-12.30am Wed-Fri; noon-4.30pm, 6pm-12.30am Sat; noon-4.30pm Sun. **££££**.
Chinese. Map p92 C5 ⑬
There's no questioning the buzz about Alan Yau's flagship restaurant. Its slinky and stylish basement interior – black lattice screens and spotlit tables – is matched by its innovative Chinese cuisine. Lunchtime dim sum is excellent. The bar is effortlessly fashionable – and you'll need to dress nice.

Nordic
25 Newman Street, Fitzrovia, W1T 1PN (7631 3174/www.nordicbar.com).

Bowling bling

All-Star Lanes is the new alley cat.

Bowling in London used to mean a retail park in the suburbs: blaring arcade machines, sticky floors and fluorescent slush drinks that came from no earthly fruit. But a change is rollin' in. Perhaps due to the Stateside success of 'boutique' bowling alleys – more bar sport than sports bar – Londoners now have a stylish alternative to the retail parks: **All-Star Lanes** in Bloomsbury (p105).

Successful outfits like Elbow Room (for pool) and Bar Kick (for table football) have shown there's a market for bars trendifying gently accessible sports. Bowling has been waiting its turn. It's loud, destructive, but also sociable and agreeably cool, tapping a vein of zeitgeist running through cult films like *The Big Lebowski* and *Kingpin*.

You have to hand it to the chaps behind All-Star Lanes: this is a very well-realised endeavour. The four bowling lanes (plus two private lanes upstairs) here are only part of the set-up; the place also devotes commendable attention to food and drink, prepared with just enough swagger to legitimise the prices. Alongside the alleys run diner-style booths at which to enjoy a trailer-chow menu and the spectacle of players bowling gutterballs. In the modish, red-leather bar beyond, cocktails (as good here as at style bars that take themselves twice as seriously) are served in undulating circular booths. On the menu as a 'Caucasian' is the White Russian cocktail that made its inevitable and ubiquitous post-Lebowski appearance.

It's unlikely that bowling will ever be an Olympic discipline (especially when the tally of the sport's best practitioners can be matched by Matey Eightpints on a lucky streak). But as a drink-side pursuit, it is exactly what London needs – something fresh, flippant and not too straight-faced.

Not quite so trendy but cheaper, nearby Bloombsury Bowling Lanes (Tavistock Hotel, Bedford Way, WC1H 9EU, 7691 2610, www.bloomsburybowling.com) opened in 2005.

Thrillin' chillin'

The Big Chill festival folk take on London.

Larkin and Lawrence

At the risk of attracting some seriously nasty jinxes, it would seem that child-friendly festival organisers turned nightlife barons Big Chill can do no wrong. Since starting at Islington's Union Chapel 13 years ago, and hosting a small festival in Wales the year after, they have steadily grown to become something that can in all fairness tack the word 'phenomenon' after their name. Their festival in Eastnor, Herefordshire, now attracts 35,000 smiling folk each August and sells out faster every year, not to mention their other events around the globe, and there's a successful record label too.

In late 2005, the Big Chill Bar, off Brick Lane, took a grey steel bunker of a room and turned it into a super-friendly, constantly busy, vibrant DJ bar. No mean feat in the infamously competitive East End.

June 2006 and a new venue opened its doors between Islington and King's Cross: Big Chill House. Four independently themed floors and a suntrap of a south-facing terrace with its own cocktail bar, pretty much bringing all of the festival features under one roof. Despite the success of the bar, surely this was a very big step?

'I didn't want a project this big,' admits Katrina Larkin, co-founder of the Big Chill. 'But I put one foot inside the door and thought, "This is it". 'Pete [Lawrence] and I have always wanted to create multi-use spaces for people. There's dancing, film, chill-out, art. You can go for a working lunch, spend the afternoon drinking cocktails on the terrace or do a yoga class. That's what it's been about from day one for us in the House and the festival: something for everyone. I've always said that festivals get the people they deserve. We get fantastic people who make the festival fantastic.'

■ www.bigchill.net
■ Big Chill House, 257-259 Pentonville Road, N1 9NL
■ Big Chill Festival 2007 3-5 Aug
■ Big Chill Bar p180

Tottenham Court Road tube. **Open** noon-11pm Mon-Fri; 6-11pm Sat. **Bar**. **Map** p92 B5 ⓮

A long basement accessed at one end from Newman Street and from Newman Passage at the other, this Scandinavian-themed bar is kitsch when it wants to be (Ingrid Bergman with reindeer antlers, Max von Sydow triptych), but professional when it comes to cocktails, smörgåsbords and the drinks list. Be warned: it's standing (and shouting) room only on a Friday night, when post-work parties descend.

Rasa Samudra

5 Charlotte Street, Fitzrovia, W1T 1RE (7637 0222/www.rasa restaurants.com). Goodge Street tube. **Open** noon-3pm, 6-10.45pm Mon-Sat; 6-10.45pm Sun. **££-£££**. **Indian**. **Map** p92 B5 ⓯

Rasa's cochineal-pink frontage might suggest a sweet shop more than a Keralite seafood restaurant, but everything else about the place is true to tradition, particularly the exquisite flavours. And inside, it's much less candy-cute: we like the first floor for its lighter, more spacious feel.

Roka

37 Charlotte Street, Fitzrovia, W1T 1RR (7580 6464/www.rokarestaurant. com). Goodge Street or Tottenham Court Road tube. **Open** noon-midnight daily. **£££**. **Japanese**. **Map** p92 B4 ⓰

Conceived as a 'restaurant without walls', the gorgeously designed Roka (younger sister to Zuma in Knightsbridge) prides itself on appearances – and the food here is as beautifully turned out as the decor. A trip to the Shochu Lounge (p103), the lovely basement bar, is also recommended if you're not feeling too casual.

Salt Yard

54 Goodge Street, Fitzrovia, W1T 4NA (7637 0657/www.saltyard.co.uk). Goodge Street tube. **Open** noon-11pm Mon-Fri; 5-11pm Sat. **££**. **Spanish**. **Map** p92 B4 ⓱

Stylishly pared down and dotted with elegant design features, the compact Salt Yard is unusually restrained for a tapas bar/restaurant. But this is no ordinary tapas bar: it delivers dishes with a twist – adding Italian touches to the usual Spanish fare. Excellent for vegetarians too.

Sardo

45 Grafton Way, Fitzrovia, W1T 5DQ (7387 2521/www.sardo-restaurant.com). Warren Street tube. **Open** noon-3pm, 6-11pm Mon-Fri; 6-11pm Sat. **£££**. **Sardinian**. **Map** p92 B2 ⓭

This welcoming and unpretentious trattoria has acquired a reputation for

Salt Yard

LONDON BY AREA

being the place food critics go to spend their own money. Its speciality is seafood, but Sardo excels in applying a modern, imaginative twist to a variety of Italian dishes. It's good value too.

Shochu Lounge

Basement, Roka, 37 Charlotte Street, Fitzrovia, W1T 1RR (7580 9666/ www.rokarestaurant.com). Goodge Street or Tottenham Court Road tube. **Open** 5pm-midnight daily. **Bar.** **Map** p92 B4 ⑲

The alluring basement bar has a louche yet sociable mood conferred by low lighting, a low ceiling, and a pioneering focus on Japan's vodka-like spirit shochu, served neat or in cocktails. The crowd and the aspirations are fashionable, which is perhaps why the staff sometimes forget to be friendly.

Shopping

Bang Bang

21 Goodge Street, Fitzrovia, W1T 2PJ (7631 4191). Goodge Street tube. **Open** 10am-6.30pm Mon-Fri; 11am-6pm Sat. **Map** p92 B4 ⑳

This shop is full of eccentric, original and stylish clothes: a psychedelic-print dress from the '60s, a silk kimono or a crushed-velvet bed jacket, say, and many items are under a tenner. Accessories are a highlight, with quirky bags and a fantastic selection of big, bold earrings. Fancy selling your own cast-offs? You'll get 30% of the potential price tag in cash, or 50% in merchandise.

Borders Books & Music

203 Oxford Street, Fitzrovia, W1D 2LE (7292 1600/www.borders. co.uk). Oxford Circus tube. **Open** 8am-11pm Mon-Sat; noon-6pm Sat. **Map** p93 A5 ㉑

This US import offers an extensive selection of general interest and specialist titles spread over five floors, plus a decent CD/video/DVD section and a commendable stationery and magazine area at ground level – your best bet for US imports. There's also a coffee shop with plenty of seating.

Contemporary Applied Arts

2 Percy Street, Fitzrovia, W1T 1DD (7436 2344/www.caa.org.uk). Goodge Street or Tottenham Court Road tube. **Open** 10am-6pm Tue, Wed; 10am-8pm Thur; 10am-6pm Fri, Sat; 11am-5pm Sun. **Map** p92 C5 ㉒

Undoubtedly the best central London location to see leading contemporary craft. The award-winning gallery holds regular exhibitions on the upper level, showing top names such as ceramicist Rupert Spira. Museum and gallery curators buy and commission through CAA, and the gallery also arranges commissions of everything from furniture to jewellery for individuals.

HMV

150 Oxford Street, Fitzrovia, W1D 1DJ (7631 3423/www.hmv.co.uk). Oxford Circus tube. **Open** 9am-8.30pm Mon-Wed, Fri, Sat; 9am-9pm Thur; 9am-8.30pm Sat; noon-6pm Sun. **Map** p92 B5 ㉓

The first and last stop for the record-buying novice in London. With seasonal sales, cut-price box sets and hundreds of rarities and imports, there's little chance you'll leave this behemoth of a store empty-handed. The vast basement houses broad classical and jazz sections, and staff are always on hand to advise.

L Cornelissen & Son

105 Great Russell Street, Bloomsbury, WC1B 3RY (7636 1045/www. cornelissen.com). Holborn or Tottenham Court Road tube. **Open** 9.30am-5.30pm Mon-Fri; 9.30am-5pm Sat. **Map** p93 D5 ㉔

A delightfully old-fashioned shop, seemingly straight out of a period drama, L Cornelissen celebrated 150 years of trading in 2005. Striking displays of paints and brushes fill the walls, and dark wood shelves store everything from art books to cleaning soap for brushes. You'll also find Mussini resin oils, Horadam watercolours, calligraphy equipment, pastels, gouache, feather quills in glass jars and lovely papers.

Ulysses

London Review of Books

14 Bury Place, Bloomsbury, WC1A 2JL (7269 9030/www.lrb.co.uk/lrbshop). Tottenham Court Road tube. **Open** 10am-6.30pm Mon-Sat; noon-6pm Sat. **Map** p93 E5 **25**

This modern, well-run shop, owned by the eponymous literary-political journal, is all polished wood, quiet conversations and passionate staff. The range of books is extraordinary, from Alan Bennett's latest offerings and the most recent academic, political and biographical tomes, plus a good choice of the best poetry, cookery and gardening titles. Regular readings and talks.

Paperchase

213-215 Tottenham Court Road, Bloomsbury, W1T 7PS (7467 6200/ www.paperchase.co.uk). Goodge Street tube. **Open** 9.30am-7pm Mon-Wed, Fri, Sat; 9.30am-8pm Thur; noon-6pm Sat. **Map** p92 C4 **26**

The flagship of this stationery superstore is a dream world for office addicts, with its eclectic mix of useful, tasteful and fun items. The ground floor features cards, gift wrap, pens, invitations and coloured notepaper. More upmarket goods are displayed on the first floor, while the second floor is devoted to artists' materials. Great for cheap gift items, especially at Christmas, when it's also the place to come for fantastical decorations – and signature seasonal carrier bags.

Purves & Purves

220-224 Tottenham Court Road, Fitzrovia, W1T 7PZ (7580 8223/ www.purves.co.uk). Goodge Street tube. **Open** 10am-6pm Mon-Wed, Fri; 10am-7.30pm Thur; 9.30am-6pm Sat; 11.30am-5.30pm Sun. **Map** p92 C4 **27**

Affordable and high-end furniture is sold here, along with a great range of lighting, kitchenware, rugs and accessories. Top European brands like Alessi, Driade, Kartell, Magis and MDF Italia grace the large showroom spread across two floors. We heard as we went to press that Purves & Purves is planning to move; keep an eye on the website for details.

Ulysses

40 Museum Street, Bloomsbury, WC1A 1LU (7831 1600). Holborn tube. **Open** 10.30am-6pm Mon-Sat. **Map** p93 E5 ㉓

One of the premier bookshops for affordable modern first editions. The space has a smart but homely feel with plenty of scope for browsing.

Nightlife

All-Star Lanes

NEW *Victoria House, Bloomsbury Place, Bloomsbury, WC1B 4DA (7025 2676, www.allstarlanes.co.uk). Holborn tube.* **Open** 5-11.30pm Mon-Wed; 5pm-midnight Thur; noon-2am Fri, Sat; noon-11pm Sun. **Map** p92 F4 ㉙

See box p99.

Canvas

King's Cross Goods Yard, off York Way, King's Cross, N1 0UZ (7833 8301/www.canvaslondon.net). King's Cross tube/rail. **Open** 8pm-midnight Thur; 8pm-2am Fri; 10pm-5am Sat. **Map** p93 D1 ㉚

Part of a cluster of venues in the area that's put King's Cross firmly on the clubbing map, Canvas is a massive warehouse space that takes in three dancefloors, two bars, and a fun new Ibizan-flavoured terrace. On Thursdays and Fridays it becomes the stonkingly successful Roller Disco.

The Cross

The Arches, 27-31 King's Cross Goods Yard, off York Way, King's Cross, N1 0UZ (7837 0828/www.the-cross.co.uk). King's Cross tube/rail. **Open** 11pm-6am Fri; 10pm-6am Sat; 10pm-5am Sun. Bar closes 2am. **Map** p93 D1 ㉛

A cavernous but comfortable brick and arches space for house lovers. Its nights aim for the middle of the road and create huge queues: Renaissance, XPress2's Muzik Xpress and the Italo-house Vertigo are all regulars here. The crowd is good-looking, friendly and unafraid to wear sunglasses.

100 Club

100 Oxford Street, Fitzrovia, W1D 1LL (7636 0933/www.the100club.co.uk).
Oxford Circus or Tottenham Court Road tube. **Map** p92 C5 ㉜

The 100 Club has in its lifetime been a crucial swing, jazz and punk venue. These days, the eccentrically designed, red-walled room hosts a mix of indie wannabes and jazz/swing acts. Extra points for real ale at the bar, plus iconic posters and photos.

The Key

King's Cross Freight Depot, King's Cross, N1 0UZ (7837 1027/www.thekeylondon.com). King's Cross tube/rail. **Open** 11pm-5am Fri; 10pm-6am Sat. **Map** p93 D1 ㉝

This trendy, tiny club has the best dancefloor in London – all glass and flashing lights. Leave any notions of strutting your John Travolta moves at the door, though: it's strictly hedonistic house, deep tech, electro-a-go-go and party hip hop.

Scala

275 Pentonville Road, King's Cross, N1 9NL (7833 2022/box office 0870 060 0100/www.scala-london.co.uk). King's Cross tube/rail. **Map** p93 F1 ㉞

This dual-purpose venue manages to tick the right music boxes both as a varied club and a live venue. A balcony and mezzanine-type levels provide great views of the stage, which has been graced by acts such as the Scissor Sisters and Franz Ferdinand. Weekends are given over to club nights: all-inclusive gay regular Popstarz is on Fridays. It all added up to a nomination for a *Time Out* Live Award in 2006.

Social

5 Little Portland Street, Fitzrovia, W1W 7JD (7636 4992/www.thesocial.com). Oxford Circus tube. **Open** noon-midnight; Mon-Fri; 1pm-midnight Sat. **Map** p92 A5 ㉟

An easily missed opaque front hides this diner and DJ bar of supreme quality. Drinks include draught San Miguel and Guinness, bottled A Le Coq and Tsing Tao beer, Breton and Kopparberg ciders, plus 20 decent cocktails at a giveaway £5.40 each.

Social p105

Arts & leisure

Dominion Theatre

Dominion Theatre, Tottenham Court Road, Fitzrovia, W1P 0AG (ticketmaster 0870 53444/www.london dominion.co.uk). Tottenham Court Road tube. **Map** p93 D5 **③⑥**

At press time the Queen musical *We Will Rock You!* was firmly in residence having extended its run due to popular demand. Production subject to change.

The Place

17 Duke's Road, Bloomsbury, WC1H 9PY (7387 0031/www.theplace.org.uk). Euston tube/rail. **Map** p93 D1 **③⑦**

This internationally recognised dance school and venue has a 300-seat theatre presenting innovative contemporary dance from around the globe.

Covent Garden

Covent Garden is looked on as a little touristy by locals, particularly its piazza. But as the world's tourist honeypots go, it deserves the crowds it attracts. The piazza, home to a market of some kind since the 17th century, is a handsome galleried space with lots of outdoor restaurant seating, decent shops in a gifty/fashion/chainy way and no traffic allowed to venture on to its cobblestones. The majority of the street entertainment (quality-vetted but, yes, living statues make it through) takes place under the portico of St Paul's (the Actors' Church). Covent Garden is home to several theatres and a couple of opera houses, along with the restaurants to feed their audiences. Its northern side has a pleasant human scale: people actually live here, and not just the well-off.

Sights & museums

Benjamin Franklin House

NEW *36 Craven Street, Covent Garden, WC2N 5NF (7930 6601/www. benjaminfranklinhouse.org). Charing Cross tube/rail.* **Open** pre-book tour by phone or online. **Admission** £8. **Map** p109 E4 **①**

See box opposite.

London's Transport Museum

39 Wellington Street, WC2E 7BB (020 7379 6344/www.ltmuseum.co.uk). Covent Garden tube. **Open/admission** check before visiting. **Map** p109 F2 **②**

When the renovated museum reopens in July 2007, the old Covent Garden flower market building will house lovingly preserved buses from the horse age to the present day, plus trains, taxis, trams and trolleybuses. It's also a collector's paradise of uniforms, posters, models, timetables – even tickets. And there's a beguiling shop.

Theatre Museum

Tavistock Street (entrance on Russell Street), WC2E 7PA (7943 4700/ www.theatremuseum.org). Covent Garden tube. **Open** 10am-6pm Tue-Sun. Last entry 5.30pm. **Admission** free. **Map** p109 F2 **③**

The permanent galleries commemorate the stars of a bygone age – David

Benjamin Franklin House

A former residence of the Founding Father and pioneering scientist opens to the public.

Who came up with the idea of lightning conductors, bifocal spectacles and fire insurance? Who identified the Gulf Stream and designed the armonica, an instrument based on glass vessels filled with different volumes of water, for which Mozart, Bach and Beethoven all composed? Who coined the following aphorisms: 'Eat to live, not live to eat'; 'Early to bed and early to rise, makes a man healthy, wealthy and wise'; 'Fish and visitors stink after three days'? The answer to all these questions is Benjamin Franklin, to whom is also attributed the saying 'Beer is living proof that God loves us and wants us to be happy', although our money would have been on Homer Simpson there.

Restoration of the house in Craven Street (opposite) where Franklin – scientist, diplomat, philosopher, inventor and Founding Father of the United States – lived for nearly 16 years between 1757 and 1775 has recently been completed: in January 2006, on the 300th anniversary of Franklin's birth, it was officially opened to the public. It's now home to a centre for academic research concerning Franklin and a science workshop where school parties can replicate some of his famous experiments. The house is not a museum in the conventional sense, but it can be explored on well-run tours pre-booked by phone or online.

An actress in character as the daughter of Franklin's landlady Margaret Stevenson conducts small groups around the house, a Grade I-listed building, beautifully restored but largely unfurnished. Projections and recorded sound conjure up Franklin's London years, recount his many achievements and flesh out his personal life. It's a short, intense experience: the tours last around 45 minutes and cover a lot of ground. You'll come away with a strong sense of the man and the times in which he lived.

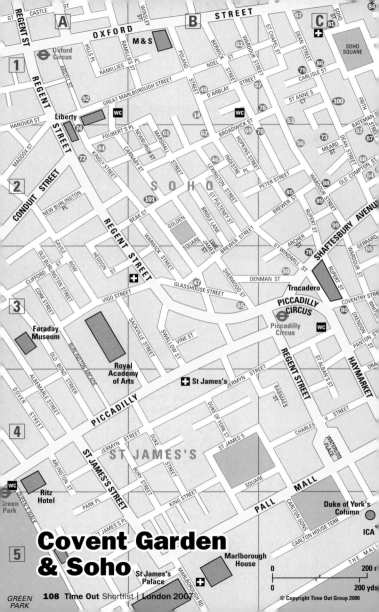

Covent Garden & Soho

© Copyright Time Out Group 2006

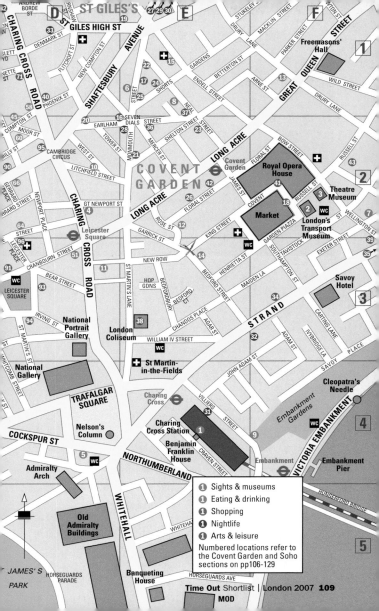

Sights & museums
Eating & drinking
Shopping
Nightlife
Arts & leisure

Numbered locations refer to the Covent Garden and Soho sections on pp106-129

Abeno Too

Garrick, Edmund Kean, Eliza Vestris – as well as the plays that made them famous. There are daily make-up classes and costume workshops, while larger exhibitions include an interactive biography of the Redgrave family. A good museum for children too, with activities such as dressing-up boxes and art projects, plus daily workshops.

Eating & drinking

Abeno Too

17-18 Great Newport Street, WC2H 7JE (7379 1160). Leicester Square tube. **Open** noon-11pm Mon-Sat; noon-10.30pm Sun. **£. Japanese.** **Map** p109 D2 ❹

Its discreet exterior makes it easy to miss, but this modest place is packed with hungry local office workers and Japanese regulars. The furnishings are simple, the staff are polite and efficient, and the food is heartily delicious.

Albannach

NEW *66 Trafalgar Square, WC2N 5DS (7930 0066/www.albannach.co.uk). Charing Cross tube/rail.* **Open** noon-1am Mon-Wed; noon-3am Thur-Sat. **Bar. Map** p109 D4 ❺

With an unrivalled location overlooking Nelson's Column, striking design, postmodern Scottish theme and fare and Caledonian-inspired cocktails, this lavish venue also has a decent snack menu and an encyclopedic whisky list, including a £12,000 bottle of 1937 Glenfiddich. There's even an illuminated stag in the basement bar.

Canela

NEW *33 Earlham Street, WC2H 9LS (7240 6926/www.canelacafe.com). Covent Garden tube.* **Open** 9.30am-10pm Mon-Sat; 10am-8pm Sun. **£. Café. Map** p109 E1 ❻

This friendly Portuguese and Brazilian café, in a corner of Thomas Neals Centre, has a converted warehouse feel. On the menu are delicious Portuguese snacksmain courses such as chorizo tart and vegetable lasagne, and gluten-and wheat-free cakes. Pavement tables.

Christopher's

18 Wellington Street, WC2E 7DD (7240 4222/www.christophersgrill.com). Covent Garden tube. **Open** noon-3pm, 5-11pm Mon-Fri; 11.30am-3pm, 5-11pm Sat; 11.30am-3pm Sun. **£££. North American. Map** p109 F2 ❼

LONDON BY AREA

This casual-elegant eaterie's dining room is spacious, with huge windows, a creamy colour scheme and polite, friendly staff. In recent years the modern American menu has veered from banal to elaborate; at the moment it's the best it's been in a long while, with a fine refurbished Martini bar.

Food for Thought

31 Neal Street, WC2H 9PR (7836 9072). Covent Garden tube. **Open** 9.30-11.30am, noon-5pm, 5-8.30pm Mon-Sat; noon-5pm Sun. **£.** No credit cards. **Vegetarian.** Map p109 E1 ⑧

The dining room is in a tiny basement, the queues are always huge, and the food isn't wildly adventurous – so why has this place remained so popular for so long? Because the prices are low, portions enormous and service friendly. Also good for take-outs.

Gordon's

47 Villiers Street, WC2N 6NE (7930 1408/www.gordonswinebar. com). Embankment tube/Charing Cross tube/rail. **Open** 11am-11pm Mon-Sat; noon-10pm Sun. **Wine bar.** Map p109 F4 ⑨

Unchanged since the era of *Brief Encounter*, this crumbling, candlelit wine bar was practically invented for affairs. Madeira is served from the wood in dock glasses, Graham's LBV comes by the schooner, beaker or bottle, and doorsteps of cheddar form the backbone of the ploughman's lunch.

The Ivy

1 West Street, WC2H 9NQ (7836 4751/www.caprice-holdings.co.uk). Leicester Square tube. **Open** noon-3pm, 5.30pm-midnight Mon-Sat; noon-3.30pm, 5.30pm-midnight Sun. **£££. Modern European.** Map p109 D2 ⑩

It's still possible to go to the Ivy and feel pretty damn good about the world. Station yourself at a table by the bar near the entrance if you want to observe the flow of celebs. The food's just what it should be – mainly homey British classics done well. Booking is essential but if you don't mind an off-peak time, not always ridiculously far ahead.

J Sheekey

28-32 St Martin's Court, WC2N 4AL (7240 2565/www.caprice-holdings.co.uk). Leicester Square tube. **Open** noon-3pm, 5.30pm-midnight Mon-Sat; noon-3.30pm, 6pm-midnight Sun. **£££. Fish.** Map p109 D3 ⑪

Sister establishment to the Ivy, Sheekey's is worth a splurge. From the restrained elegance of the decor to the perfectly executed cooking (including the famous fish pie), it's hard to fault.

Lamb & Flag

33 Rose Street, WC2E 9EB (7497 9504). Covent Garden tube. **Open** 11am-11pm Mon-Sat; noon-10.30pm Sun. **Pub.** Map p109 E2 ⑫

By far the best pub in the Covent Garden area – so you'll be hard pushed to get anywhere near its 350-year-old (or more) interior at busy times. It's got a picture-perfect location, at the head of a narrow cobbled lane, with an ancient tunnelled passageway squeezing down one side. Great staff, great ales and proper pub grub.

Lowlander

36 Drury Lane, WC2B 5RR (7379 7446/www.lowlander.com). Covent Garden or Holborn tube. **Open** noon-11pm Mon-Sat; noon-10.30pm Sun. **Bar.** Map p109 F1 ⑬

The bar at this great Dutch and Belgian beer café is a vision of gleaming chrome beer taps (pilsners, blondes, wheat, red, dark, fruit – tasting selections available), backed by 40 bottles. Close rows of communal tables are attended by waiting staff in white starched pinnies. Food includes snacks (charcuterie or cheese platters, moules frites) and good value two- and three-course prix fixes.

Paul

29 Bedford Street, WC2E 9ED (7836 3304/www.paul.fr). Covent Garden tube. **Open** 7.30am-9pm Mon-Fri; 9am-9pm Sat, Sun. **£. Café.** Map p109 E3 ⑭

With its elegant cake counter, dark wood panelling and black-and-white prints on the walls, Paul is the embodiment of an old-fashioned Parisian tea

LONDON BY AREA

room. Our gold star goes to the buttery croissants and crusty walnut bread, though the salads, omelettes and sarnies are contenders too.

Rock & Sole Plaice
47 Endell Street, WC2H 9AJ (7836 3785). Covent Garden tube. **Open** 11.30am-11pm Mon-Sat; noon-10pm Sun. **£. Fish & chips. Map** p109 E1  ⑮
London's oldest surviving fish and chip shop has been playing a few fish fingers since 1871 and it continues to thrive. As long as you avoid Sundays and bank holidays, the fish will be fresh, well prepared and succulent.

Shopping

Covent Garden satisfies shopping needs from not-too-tacky tourist browsing in and around the piazza via individualist Neal Street and its environs to the boutique sector near the tube station. Don't miss sweetly hippy Neal's Yard; Thomas Neal Centre is a more mainstream mall but pleasurable nonetheless.

Adidas Originals Store
9 Earlham Street, WC2H 9LL (7379 4042/www.adidas.co.uk). Covent Garden tube. **Open** 10.30am-7pm Mon-Sat; noon-6pm Sun. **Map** p109 E2 ⑯
The Adidas Originals Store aims to capitalise on the enormous retrospective value of the Adidas brand. Here you'll find remakes of classic footwear, T-shirts, zip-ups and accessories. The 1980s are as productive an influence as ever, inspiring branded hip hop jackets and zip-ups in retro colourways.

Coco de Mer
23 Monmouth Street, WC2H 9DD (7836 8882/www.coco-de-mer.co.uk). Covent Garden tube. **Open** 11am-7pm Mon-Wed, Fri, Sat; 11am-8pm Thur; noon-6pm Sun. **Map** p109 E1 ⑰
Coco de Mer does sex in a risqué, vaguely Victorian and rather intellectual way, with erotic literature among the ticklers, spankers and other assorted boudoir tools. The lingerie collection is small but well edited, with the sort of flirty items that manage to leave something to the imagination without sacrificing any eroticism.

Covent Garden Market
Apple Market *The Piazza, WC2E 8RF (0870 780 5001/www.covent gardenmarket.co.uk). Covent Garden or Embankment tube/Charing Cross tube/rail.* **Open** *Arts & crafts* 10.30am-6.30pm Tue-Sun. *Antiques & collectibles* 10.30am-6.30pm Mon.
Jubilee Market *1 Tavistock Court, The Piazza, WC2E 8BD (www.jmh. company.org.uk). Covent Garden or Embankment tube/Charing Cross tube/rail.* **Open** *Antiques* 5am-4pm Mon. *General goods* 10am-5pm Tue-Fri. *Arts & crafts* 10am-5pm Sat, Sun. **Map** p109 F2 ⑱
These few rows of Victorian-style wooden stalls inside Covent Garden's old market building sell mainly cottage-industry handicrafts: hand-knitted jumpers, paper lampshades, chunky jewellery, hand-printed baby clothes, fork sculptures and the like. Stalls change regularly. Jubilee Market has a wider range of gear, selling leather goods (bags, belts, wallets), velvet scarves, silver and gold jewellery, photography (and découpage), wooden

Adidas Originals Store

toys and Japanese papercraft. On Mondays antiques stalls sell porcelain, silverware, objets d'art and jewellery.

Forbidden Planet Megastore

179 Shaftesbury Avenue, WC2H 8JR (7420 3666/www.forbiddenplanet. com). Tottenham Court Road tube. **Open** 10am-7pm Mon-Wed, Fri, Sat; 10am-8pm Thur; noon-6pm Sun. **Map** p109 E1 ⑲

Heaven for *Star Wars*, Tolkien and Buffy fans, FP is the HMV of the sci-fi, fantasy and cult entertainment world. The colossal selection of books in the megastore's basement covers the spectrum from science fiction and ufology to crime, graphic novels and political and anarchist titles.

Fopp

1 Earlham Street, WC2H 9LL (7379 0883/www.fopp.co.uk). Covent Garden or Tottenham Court Road tube. **Open** 10am-10pm Mon-Sat; 11am-6pm Sun. **Map** p109 D2 ⑳

Boasting a delightfully minimalist aesthetic and low prices, this burgeoning national CD chain is especially brilliant for those looking to replenish their prog back catalogues on the cheap. Also good for picking up cult fiction and art-house DVDs.

Koh Samui

65-67 Monmouth Street, WC2H 9DG (7240 4280/www.kohsamui.co.uk). Covent Garden tube. **Open** 10am-6.30pm Mon, Sat; 10.30am-6.30pm Tue, Wed, Fri; 10.30am-7pm Thur. **Map** p109 E2 ㉑

One of the capital's premier cutting-edge clothes emporiums. The collection is as strong as ever, with Chloé, Marc Jacobs, Balenciaga and Missoni much in evidence, plus a smattering of rising stars like Victim and Misconception.

Monmouth Coffee House

27 Monmouth Street, WC2H 9EV (7379 3516/www.monmouthcoffee. co.uk). Covent Garden tube. **Open** 8am-6.30pm Mon-Sat. **Map** p109 E1 ㉒

Connoisseurs will appreciate the small but discerning selection of predominantly South American and African coffees on display at this atmospheric bean merchant. There's a small café area at the back, so you can sample the brews before you buy, and well-chosen coffee-nalia for sale.

LONDON BY AREA

Natural Shoe Store

*21 Neal Street, WC2H 9PU
(7836 5254/www.thenaturalshoe
store.com). Covent Garden tube.*
Open 10am-6pm Mon, Tue;
10am-7pm Wed, Fri; 10am-8pm
Thur; 10am-6.30pm Sat; noon-5.30pm
Sun. **Map** p109 E2 ㉓
The small parent shop of the slick
Birkenstock store down the road was
the first to introduce the cult German
sandal brand to the UK. It's dedicated
to selling comfortable shoes from
brands such as Trippen, Think! and
Arche (£30-£130) in a low-key, earthy
atmosphere.

Neal's Yard Dairy

*17 Shorts Gardens, WC2H 9UP (7240
5700). Covent Garden tube.* **Open**
11am-6.30pm Mon-Thur; 10am-6.30pm
Fri, Sat. **Map** 109 E1 ㉔
Dozens of restaurants and delis in
London serve Neal's Yard cheeses,
which are, quite simply, shorthand for
quality. They're sourced from artisan
producers in Britain and Ireland, and
matured in the company's own cellars.
Breads and relishes are also on sale.

Orla Kiely

NEW *31 Monmouth Street, WC2H
9DD (7240 022/www.orlakiely.
com). Covent Garden tube.* **Open**
10.30am-7pm Mon-Sat; noon-5pm Sun.
Map p109 E1 ㉕
A new flagship brings the designer's
full collection of clothing and accessories under one roof. Delectable bags
come in a wide range of materials, from
her famous graphic prints to richly
hued leather and ponyskin. Plus
scarves, hats, wellies, luggage, cush-
ions and blankets.

Tintin Shop

*34 Floral Street, WC2E 9DJ (7836
1131/www.thetintinshop.uk.com).
Covent Garden tube.* **Open** 10am-
5.30pm Mon-Sat. **Map** p109 E2 ㉖
This shop does what is says on the
Tintin: here you'll find a comprehensive range of books, toys, DVDs, T-
shirts and so forth starring the quiffed
Belgian boy reporter.

Nightlife

AKA

*18 West Central Street (7836 0110/
www.akalondon.com). Holborn or
Tottenham Court Road tube.* **Open**
10pm-5am Tue; 6pm-3am Thur; 6pm-
4am Fri; 7pm-5am Sat; 10pm-4am Sun.
Map p109 E1 ㉗
Set in a former Victorian sorting office,
this chic two-storey warehouse space,
one of London's finest club-bars, has
quality stamped all over it. The DJ
agenda, like the minimal but comfy
decor, is done with taste, and the cus-
tomer's enjoyment in mind. A good
drinks list and highly edible snacks
add to the classy mix.

The Box

*32-34 Monmouth Street, WC2H 9HA
(7240 5828/www.boxbar.com).
Leicester Square tube.* Open 11am-
11pm Mon-Sat; noon-10.30pm Sun.
Map p109 E1 ㉘
Smart, bright by day and easy-going,
the Box is a welcoming gay bar-café in
which straights can also feel at home.
Table service enhances a West Coast
feel and the drinks selection is more
sophisticated than most. By night, it
naturally gets cruisier.

Discotec

*The End, 18 West Central Street,
WC1A 1JJ (7419 9199/www.discotec-
club.com). Holborn or Tottenham Court
Road tube.* **Open** 10pm-4am Thur.
Credit at bar only. Map p109 E1 ㉙
Equipped with air-conditioning, a
couple of dancefloors and great sounds,
this is one of London's most eclectic
gay nights.

The End

*18 West Central Street, WC1A 1JJ
(7419 9199/www.the-end.co.uk).
Holborn or Tottenham Court Road
tube.* **Open** 10pm-3am Mon, Wed;
10pm-4am Thur; 10pm-5am Fri; 11pm-
7am Sat. **Map** p109 E1 ㉚
Winner of Time Out's 2006 Live
Award for best venue, the End may be
in the West End, but it remains at the
forefront of all things leftfield in the
world of electronica. The heady main

room boasts an island DJ booth that a few jocks loathe but most love. Monday night's Trash is a meeting of indie and dance, with frequent ahead-of-the-curve live acts. The Trash dress code – thrift shop meets haute couture – is as cutting-edge as the music.

Heaven

Under the Arches, Villiers Street, WC2N 6NG (7930 2020/www.heaven-london.com). Embankment tube/ Charing Cross tube/rail. **Open** 10.30pm-3am Mon, Wed; 10.30pm-6am Fri; 10pm-6am Sat. **Credit at bar only.** **Map** p109 E4 ③①

London's most famous gay club. The best nights are Popcorn (Mondays) and Fruit Machine (Wednesdays) but it really comes alive on Saturdays, thanks to a new influx of DJs who've helped bring the muscle boys back from the Vauxhall gay village.

Retro Bar

2 George Court, off Strand, WC2N 6HH (7321 2811). Charing Cross tube/ rail. **Open** noon-11pm Mon-Fri; 5-11pm Sat; 5-10.30pm Sun. **Map** p109 F3 ③②

True to its name, this mixed gay indie/retro bar plays '70s, '80s, goth and alternative sounds, and has a friendly atmosphere.

12 Bar Club

22-23 Denmark Place, WC2H 8NL (office 7240 2120/box office 240 2622/www.12barclub.com). Tottenham Court Road tube. **Open** Café 9am-9pm daily. Gigs 7.30pm; nights vary. **Map** p109 D1 ③③

This tiny hole-in-the-wall venue books a real grab-bag of stuff, though its size (the stage is barely big enough for three people) dictates a predominance of singer-songwriters. Wonderfully charcterful and intimate.

Arts & leisure

Adelphi Theatre

Strand, WC2E 7NA (Ticketmaster 08704 030303/www.ticketmaster. co.uk). Charing Cross tube/rail. **Map** p109 F3 ③④

NEW A new production of *Evita* took over from *Chicago* here in June 2006. Production subject to change.

Aldwych Theatre

Aldwych, WC2B 4DF (0870 400 0805). Charing Cross tube/rail/Embankment tube. **Map** p109 F3 ③⑤

NEW *Dirty Dancing* shimmies in to town in November 2006, written by Eleanor Bergstein, who also wrote the film's screenplay. Production subject to change.

Cambridge Theatre

Earlham Street, WC2H 9HU (0870 890 1102. Covent Garden tube. **Map** p109 E2 ③⑥

Chicago continues to Razzle Dazzle. Production subject to change.

Donmar Warehouse

41 Earlham Street, WC2H 9LX (0870 060 6624/www.donmarwarehouse. com). Covent Garden or Leicester Square tube. **Map** p109 E1 ③⑦

Less warehouse, more intimate chamber, the Donmar is a favourite crossover spot for actors more often seen on screen. The quality and creativity of its productions explains the lure.

London Coliseum

The Coliseum, St Martin's Lane, WC2N 4BR (box office 7632 8300/fax 7379 1264/www.eno.org). Leicester Square tube/Charing Cross tube/rail. **Map** p109 E3 ③⑧

Built in 1904 by renowned architect Frank Matcham, the London Coliseum is home to the English National Opera (ENO). This magnificent building has recently undergone a mammoth £80m restoration: from its patterned marble floor to the ornate and colourful foyer, the auditorium has been redecorated in accordance with the original style, and there's a glass-walled public bar with dramatic views of Trafalgar Square. The company has been beleaguered in recent years, so predictions of artistic merit are hard to make.

Event highlights The 2006-7 season mixes classics (*La Traviata, The Gondoliers, The Marriage of Figaro*)

Royal Opera House

with the more adventurous (*Gaddafi*, a collaboration with Asian Dub Foundation, from 7 Sept 2006; Phillip Glass's Ghandi-themed *Satyagraha*, from 5 April 2007; Britten's *Death in Venice*, from 24 May; and *Kismet*, from 27 June)

Lyceum Theatre

Wellington Street, WC2E 7DA (7420 8112/box office 0870 243 9000/www. disney.co.uk). Charing Cross tube/rail. **Map** p109 F3 ㊵
Lair of *The Lion King*, the widely acclaimed Disney extravaganza about an orphaned lion cub struggling to find his place on the savannah. Production subject to change.

Phoenix Theatre

Charing Cross Road, WC2H 8OJ (0870 060 6629). Tottenham Court Road tube. **Map** p109 D1 ㊿
Home of *Blood Brothers*, a grand, melodrama infused with sentiment and great songs. Production subject to change.

Royal Opera House

Bow Street, WC2E 9DD (box office 7304 4000/www.royaloperahouse. org.uk). Covent Garden tube. **Map** p109 F2 ㊶
'Covent Garden' is one of the great opera houses of the world, and the millennial conversion of Floral Hall, the old flower warehouse, into a restaurant and bars is one of London's wonders. It's home to the Royal Opera and Royal Ballet companies; facilities and programming are tip-top all round. Top-end tickets are famously expensive, but the mid-range is not unaffordable (clear-view tickets start at £15). A backstage tour is available most days.
Event highlights The 2006/7 opera season concentrates on works in French, with new productions of *Carmen*, *Pelléas et Mélisande* and *L'Heure espagnol*. Recent hit productions of *The Tempest* and *Lady Macbeth of Mtsensk* are also being revived. The Royal Ballet, which also performs here, continues to put on classic tutu faves such as *Coppélia*, *The Sleeping Beauty*, *The Nutcracker* and *Swan Lake*, leavened with new ballet work.

The Sanctuary

12 Floral Street, WC2E 9DH (0870 063 0300/www.thesanctuary.com). Covent Garden tube. **Map** p109 E2 ㊷
London's best day spa offers a welter of enjoyable face and body treatments from dry floats to hot stone therapy via various massages and facials. But it's the chillout areas, including a koi carp lounge, two whirlpools and a hammam, that make it special. Unpretentious and

therefore a reasonable £65 Monday to Thursday, £75 Friday to Sunday (plus treatments), women only.

Theatre Royal Drury Lane

Catherine Street, WC2B 5JF (0870 890 1109). Covent Garden tube.
Map p109 F2 ㊽

The Producers is Mel Brooks's hilarious story of two producers whose insurance fraud is bungled when their deliberately awful show, *Springtime for Hitler*, becomes a hit. The show closes in early 2007; *The Lord of the Rings* takes over on 9 May.

Soho

We don't list a single 'sight' in Soho – because there aren't any. It's not that kind of place, and never has been. It swiftly fell from its early status as hunting playground to the aristocracy when refugees made homeless by the Great Fire of London moved in, soon followed by the first of several waves of immigrants. The incomers gave Soho the anarchic, non-conformist and sometimes dangerous character that it hasn't quite lost today. Its streets are home to after-work partiers, media companies, theatre workers, hookers, market traders, tourists and queers, plus the odd hip venture hoping to aquire its louche charm by association. It has few chains, character in spades – and it almost never closes.

Good places to start exploring Soho's skinny streets are Old Compton Street, its main artery, and Soho Square, almost impassable for sunbathing bodies in summer. Berwick Street's market is also Soho in spades. Leicester Square is really only of any use for its giant picture palaces, but don't miss Chinatown to its north and east (the arches are on Gerrard Street): not the world's biggest, but the real thing.

Eating & drinking

Ain't Nothin' But? The Blues Bar

20 Kingly Street, W1B 5PZ (7287 0514/www.aintnothinbut.co.uk). Oxford Circus or Piccadilly Circus tube. **Open** 6pm-1am Mon-Wed; 6pm-2am Thur; noon-3am Fri, Sat; 7.30pm-midnight Sun. **Bar**. **Map** p108 A2 ㊹

This rather splendid music enthusiasts' bar and modest live venue recently celebrated '10 Rockin' Years', and well it might. Twelve-bar sheet music, photos and concert bills constitute the main bar's decor; a wall of fame covers the tiny staircase and cellar. Bands play each night.

Amato

14 Old Compton Street, W1D 4TH (7734 5733/www.amato.co.uk). Leicester Square or Tottenham Court Road tube. **Open** 8am-10pm Mon-Sat; 10am-8pm Sun. **£**. **Café**. **Map** p109 D2 ㊺

Amato's Art Deco posters and dark wood furnishings are an impressive backdrop to its lush pastry and cake display, heaving with calorific treats. There's also a good choice of pasta dishes, soups and salads.

Andrew Edmunds

46 Lexington Street (7437 5708). Oxford Circus or Piccadilly Circus tube. **Open** 12.30-3pm, 6-10.45pm Mon-Fri; 1-3pm, 6-10.45pm Sat; 1-3.30pm, 6-10.30pm Sun. **££**. **Modern European**. **Map** p108 B2 ㊻

This whole operation – from the unaffected decor to the straightforward menu to the casual bonhomie of the staff – runs with effortless ease. The short menu offers high-quality seasonal ingredients, cooked simply and with aplomb, and prices are exceedingly fair. Come in a suit or in torn jeans; either way, you'll feel equally special.

Astor Bar & Grill

NEW *20 Glasshouse Street, W1B 5DJ (7734 4888). Piccadilly Circus tube.* **Open** 5pm-3am Mon-Sat (meals served 6-11pm). **£££**. **Modern European**. **Map** p108 B3 ㊼

This gorgeous venue, a listed Art Deco basement with glamour in its every curve, has recently changed ownership and lost a little cachet. Prices are high, but the steaks – from a luxury-oriented grill menu – are excellent. The late-licence bar remains a big draw.

Bar Italia

22 Frith Street, W1V 5PS (7437 4520/www.baritaliasoho.co.uk). Leicester Square, Piccadilly Circus or Tottenham Court Road tube. **Open** 24hrs Mon-Sat; 7am-4am Sun. **£**. **Café**. Map p108 C2 ❹
Now into its sixth decade, this Soho landmark coasts on much as it always has, with red leatherette stools, Formica surfaces and the famous Rocky Marciano poster. Like the coffee, the food isn't too bad, but this place is really all about the atmosphere.

Bodean's

10 Poland Street, W1F 8PZ (7287 7575/www.bodeansbbq.com). Oxford Circus or Piccadilly Circus tube. **Open** noon-3pm, 6-11pm Mon-Fri; noon-11pm Sat; noon-10.30pm Sun. **£**. **BBQ**. Map p108 B1 ❹
The atmosphere at this good-hearted US-style BBQ joint is laid-back and friendly. Downstairs is classy, with leather banquettes and wood-panelled walls; upstairs is a big, communal cafeteria. Service is professional and the meat is sublimely cooked (head straight for the ribs).

Chowki

2-3 Denman Street, W1D 7HA (7439 1330/www.chowki.com). Piccadilly Circus tube. **Open** noon-11.30pm Mon-Sat; noon-10.30pm Sun. **£**. **Indian**. Map p108 C3 ❺
Don't be put off by Chowki's gloomy appearance; an abundance of dark wood, rows of red leatherette stools and industrial piping do it few favours. No matter: customers, mainly small office groups, tourists and nostalgic Asians, come here for affordable, authentically prepared meals from various Indian regions, overseen by attentive staff.

Cork & Bottle

44-46 Cranbourn Street, WC2H 7AN (7734 7807/www.donhewitson. com). Leicester Square tube. **Open** 11am-11.30pm Mon-Sat; noon-11pm Sun. **Wine bar**. Map p109 D3 ❺
Now in its 35th year, Don Hewitson's homely cellar is a celebration of what good wine is all about (even if it is jammed between a sex shop and a cheap pizza place). Average prices are £20 and each bottle is given a personal thumbnail sketch. The bar food too is exemplary. Timeless.

Dog & Duck

18 Bateman Street, W1D 3AJ (7494 0697). Tottenham Court Road tube. **Open** noon-11pm Mon-Sat; noon-10.30pm Sun. **Pub**. Map p108 C2 ❺
Soho has always been a hunting ground, but back in the day it was actual hounds and hares – hence this pub, built in 1734. Downstairs, in the tiny bar area and cosy back room, ale rules, even in steak pie.

Floridita

100 Wardour Street, W1F 0TN (7314 4000/www.floriditalondon.com). Leicester Square, Piccadilly Circus or Tottenham Court Road tube. **Open** 5.30pm-2am Mon-Wed; 5.30pm-3am Thur-Sat. **Bar**. Map p108 C1 ❺
Terence Conran teamed up with Cuba's renowned (if tourist-pitched) Floridita bar to open this outpost. Glitzy couples gaze at the film-set scene of hot waitresses swaying past with exotic drinks, to the rhythms of the house band. It's all a little forced, but the quality of the cocktails can't be gainsaid.

French House

49 Dean Street, W1D 5BG (7437 2799). Leicester Square or Piccadilly Circus tube. **Open** noon-11pm Mon-Sat; noon-10.30pm Sun. **Pub**. Map p108 C2 ❺
These days this stalwart Soho local is a bit arty, with John Claridge's black and white shots of Tommy Cooper et al on the walls, but it was built on legends larger than these (it was a London base for De Gaulle and his Resistance cohorts). A boho vibe lingers.

Chinatown p117

Brilliant Korean

London's latest breakthrough Asian cuisine.

Until recently Korean restaurants were staid places catering mainly to first-generation immigrants and business travellers. If other Londoners visited, they were intrigued by the flavours but daunted by the unfamiliar and complex menus and the size of the bill. But over the last few years, a rash of cheap and informal Korean eating houses have opened around Soho, run by a younger generation and populated by a lively mix of custom. In the noodle- or sushi-bar mode, they're ideal for a quick and tasty fill-up at the start of an evening out.

The cooking at **Nara** is exemplary, with dishes radiating freshness and packed with flavour: the most interesting are on the specials menu, the cheapest comprise the set lunch. **Woo Jung** is the best of three Korean restaurants on St Giles High Street. It's a small and unassuming eaterie that's usually packed and noisy, with a long menu whose main courses are notably good value.

Most recently, a couple of places have opened with the intention of taking the cuisine a little more upmarket and bringing in some style. First was **Wizzy** (616 Fulham Road, 7736 9171), out in South-west London. Chef Hwi Shim (aka Wizzy) successfully interprets traditional dishes in a contemporary fashion. **Asadal**, in Holborn, is a new branch of the best restaurant in New Malden, home to London's main Korean community. Its decor is chic and its service gracious but it's the complex, unusual and ambititous cooking that set it apart.

Korean food is distinctly different from that of its neighbours, Japan and China. Chilli appears in most dishes; other common flavours include sesame oil, soy sauce, fermented bean paste and sugar. Pickles are a national obsession, particularly kimchee (cabbage). Barbecue dishes and hotpots are commonplace, and many dishes are prepared at the table.

■ Asadal, 227 High Holborn, Holborn, WC1V 7DA (020 7430 9006).

■ Nara, 9 D'Arblay Street, Soho (7287 2224).

■ Wizzy, 616 Fulham Road, Parsons Green, SW6 5PR (7736 9171).

■ Woo Jung, 59 St Giles High Street, WC2H 8LH (7836 3103)

Glass

NEW *9 Glasshouse Street, Piccadilly Circus, W1R 5RL (7439 7770/www. paperclublondon.com). Piccadilly Circus tube.* **Open** 5-11pm Tue-Thur; 5pm-1am Fri, Sat. **Cocktail bar.** **Map** 108 B3 ⑤⑤

Glass is part of Paper, a press-themed restaurant and nightclub. Its stunning decor features glossy black and white walls and pillars, black glass chandeliers, padded white alcoves, and a long bar. A sophisticated cocktail list incorporates Martinis, rocks, highballs, Champagne cocktails and shooters.

Hummus Bros

NEW *88 Wardour Street, W1F 0TJ (7734 1311). Tottenham Court Road tube.* **Open** 11am-11pm Mon-Fri; noon-11pm Sat. **£.** **Middle Eastern.** **Map** p108 C2 ⑤⑥

Choose from a brief but perfectly executed menu of Levantine dishes at this stylishly designed fast-food place. Recommended.

Imli

NEW *167-169 Wardour Street, W1F 8WR (7287 4243). Leicester Square or Piccadilly Circus tube.* **Open** 11am-11pm daily. **££.** **Indian.** **Map** p108 C1 ⑤⑦

Asian street food is cropping up on lots of London menus right now. At Imli it's offered in a range of traditional and contemporary guises including chaats and bhajis. The canteen-like chocolate and orange decor is fairly basic but the food is carefully prepared with a fresh, light touch, and the service is friendly.

LAB

12 Old Compton Street, W1D 4TQ (7437 7820/www.lab-townhouse.com). Leicester Square or Tottenham Court Road tube. **Open** 4pm-midnight Mon-Sat; 4-10.30pm Sun. **Cocktail bar.** **Map** 109 D2 ⑤⑧

The London Academy of Bartending has always been at the forefront of the capital's cocktail scene. Set over two floors decorated with a tinge of retro, Lab operates on a huge range of original cocktails, its list recently reinvented. All are £7 or as near as dammit. Bar snacks are Thai. Outstanding.

Lindsay House

21 Romilly Street, W1V 5AF (7439 0450/www.lindsayhouse.co.uk). Leicester Square tube. **Open** noon-2.30pm Mon-Fri; 6-11pm Mon-Sat. **£££.** **British.** **Map** p108 C2 ⑤⑨

The dining area of Soho's most elegant townhouse restaurant is a pleasant mix of modern minimalism and discreet period detail. Richard Corrigan's spectacular cooking is robust and colourful, drawing on a larder of top-notch European ingredients. A great wine list and charming staff add to the appeal.

Maison Bertaux

28 Greek Street, W1V 5LL (7437 6007). Leicester Square, Piccadilly Circus or Tottenham Court Road tube. **Open** 8.30am-11pm daily. **£.** **Café.** **Map** p109 D2 ⑥⓪

A true Soho landmark, Maison Bertaux has wobbly tables, mismatched chairs and quirky artefacts, making it more like a theatre set than a French café. Ask for a menu and you'll draw a blank: the specials are whatever's come out of the oven. Service is charming.

Masala Zone

9 Marshall Street, W1F 7ER (7287 9966/www.realindianfood.com). Oxford Circus tube. **Open** noon-3pm, 5.30-11pm Mon-Fri; 12.30-11pm Sat; 12.30-3.30pm, 6-10.30pm Sun. **£.** **Pan-Indian.** **Map** p108 B2 ⑥①

A stamping ground for young office types on a limited budget, this is a café that does chic on the cheap. The affable staff deliver meals in a jiffy. Starters tend to be more memorable than mains, but the prices are hard to beat.

Milk & Honey

61 Poland Street, W1F 7NU (7292 9949/0700 065 5469/www.mlkhny. com). Oxford Circus tube. **Open** Non-members 6-11pm Mon-Fri; 7-11pm Sat. **Bar.** **Map** p108 B2 ⑥②

Milk & Honey oozes exclusivity, with the unmarked door and ring-for-entry arrangement. The interior is a jazz-age

Floridita p118

affair of dimly lit booths, low pressed-tin ceiling and a businesslike corner bar area lit like a Hopper painting. Cocktails and the few bar snacks are very fine indeed. Anyone can visit, but you must ring ahead and book.

Mr Jerk

189 Wardour Street, W1F 8ZD (7287 2878/www.mrjerk.co.uk). Tottenham Court Road tube. **Open** 9am-11pm Mon-Sat; 10am-8pm Sun. **£**.
Caribbean. **Map** p109 B1 ⑥

This cheap and cheery caff does a brisk day-long trade in filling, tasty meals dished up by friendly staff. Think patties, jerk chicken, rice and peas, and roti, and make sure you don't leave without sampling the Guinness punch.

Mr Kong

21 Lisle Street, WC2H 7BA (7437 7341/9679). Leicester Square or Piccadilly Circus tube. **Open** noon-2.45am Mon-Sat; noon-1.45am Sun.
££. **Chinese**. **Map** p109 D2 ⑥

Kong's menu has several enticing, unusual dishes, and this is surely the draw for the many Chinese who eat here. The list of 'special vegetarian dishes' lives up to the billing, especially the mock abalone. The food and the service are generally both up to scratch, although it's a bit cramped.

New Mayflower

68-70 Shaftesbury Avenue, W1B 6LY (7734 9207). Leicester Square or Piccadilly Circus tube. **Open** 5pm-4am daily. **££**. **Chinese**. **Map** p108 C3 ⑥

This is a genuine Cantonese restaurant of the first order. Service is willing, spirited and efficient, and the customers, almost all of them Chinese, are much too busy enjoying the delicious food to worry about the rather cramped surroundings in the restaurant basement.

New World

1 Gerrard Place, W1D 5PA (7734 0396). Leicester Square or Piccadilly Circus tube. **££**. **Chinese**.
Map p109 D2 ⑥

The dim sum trolley system at this multi-floored behemoth takes the guesswork out of ordering. The lengthy full menu is also worth a look.

LONDON BY AREA

Either way, for a uniquely Chinese dining experience, you should lunch here at least once.

Opium

1A Dean Street, W1D 3RB (7287 9608/www.opium-bar-restaurant.com). Tottenham Court Road tube. **Open** 6pm-3am Mon-Fri; 7.30pm-3am Sat. **Bar**. Map p108 C1 ⑥

This sumptuous French-Vietnamese bar-restaurant offers a luxurious sunken interior with delicately carved alcoves and imaginative, original cocktails of fine quality and oriental influence. Bar food is of the highest quality and cocktails are sheer artistry.

Pâtisserie Valerie

44 Old Compton Street, W1D 4TY (7437 3466/www.patisserie-valerie.co.uk). Leicester Square, Piccadilly Circus or Tottenham Court Road tube. **Open** 7.30am-8.30pm Mon, Tue; 7.30am-9pm Wed-Fri; 8am-9pm Sat; 9.30am-7pm Sun. **£**. **Café**. Map p108 C2 ⑥

Step back in time to the 1950s: Formica tables, an old-fashioned pastry counter and, more to the point, a selection of classic pâtisserie. Grab a window table upstairs, a cheerier, lighter and airier space than the hemmed-in café downstairs.

Yauatcha

15 Broadwick Street, W1F 0DE (7494 8888). Oxford Circus tube. **Open** noon-11pm Mon-Fri; 11am-11pm Sat; 11am-10pm Sun. **£££**. **Chinese**. Map p108 B2 ⑥

This Michelin-starred restaurant occupies two floors of Sir Richard Rogers's Ingeni building. Dim sum is the highlight of the menu – and, unusually, it is served all day – but service can verge on amateur. The tea menu is wonderful, and so are the cakes from the pâtisserie counter.

Shopping

Carnaby Street hasn't completely lost its boho charm; behind it, Kingly Court is a haven of independent boutiques in a three-storey Victorian building with courtyard.

Berwick Street Market

Berwick Street & Rupert Street, W1. Piccadilly Circus or Tottenham Court Road tube. **Open** 9am-6pm Mon-Sat. Map p108 C2 ⑦

A traditional fruit and veg market in the seedy heart of Soho, Berwick Street also has stalls selling flowers, nuts, fs, sweets, knickers and curiosities. The fresh produce is delicious, and the character strong. Like the rest of Soho, the market takes a while to get going.

Foyles

113-119 Charing Cross Road, WC2H 0EB (7437 5660/www.foyles.co.uk). Tottenham Court Road tube. **Open** 9.30am-9pm Mon-Sat; noon-6pm Sun. Map p109 D1 ⑦

This famous independent store has wonderful stocks of books popular and obscure. Its café area offers organic food and music events organised by Ray's Jazz (incorporated into the store as part of a recent refurbishment, along with Silver Moon women's bookshop). Author book signings and talks take place throughout the year. There's also a good audio choice.

Hamleys

188-196 Regent Street, W1B 5BT (0870 333 2455/www.hamleys. com). Oxford Circus tube. **Open** 10am-8pm Mon-Sat; noon-6pm Sun. Map p108 A2 ⑦

The largest toyshop in the world is a loud, frenetic, exciting experience. The ground floor has the latest toys and high-tech gadgets and games. The first floor does science, the second preschool, the third girlie heaven and the fourth remote-controlled vehicles. On the fifth floor is Lego World, which has its own café.

John Pearse

6 Meard Street, W1F 0EG (7434 0738/www.johnpearse.co.uk). Piccadilly Circus tube. **Open** 10am-7pm Mon-Fri; noon-7pm Sat. Map p108 C2 ⑦

Rays Jazz at Foyles, p123

Hailed by many as the godfather of new British tailoring, JP combines a playful eccentricity (ready-to-wear is displayed in Gothic wardrobes) with rock-solid tailoring credentials.

Liberty

210-220 Regent Street, W1B 5AH (7734 1234/www.liberty.co.uk). Oxford Circus tube. **Open** *10am-7pm Mon-Wed, Fri, Sat; 10am-8pm Thur; noon-6pm Sun.* **Map** *p108 A2* **74**

Liberty's famous prints are coveted the world over, but there are many other riches behind its façade. Menswear, women's shoes and lingerie are in the Regent House on Regent Street, as is the cosmetics department. For body and bath products, as well as the celebrated scarf hall, hop over to the 1920s Tudor House on Great Marlborough Street. The fourth floor houses furniture.

Milroy's of Soho

3 Greek Street, W1V 6NX (7437 9311/www.milroys.co.uk). Tottenham Court Road tube. **Open** *10am-8pm Mon-Fri; 10am-7pm Sat.* **Map** *p108 C1* **75**

London's most famous whisky specialist, founded in 1964, stocks a fine range of over 700 malts and whiskies from around the world, including a selection of rare bottles. Also on offer is a full range of wines. Regular tutored tastings are held in the cellar.

Space NK

8 Broadwick Street, W1F 8HW (7287 2667/www.spacenk.com). Piccadilly Circus or Tottenham Court Road tube. **Open** *10am-7pm Mon-Wed, Fri, Sat; 10am-8pm Thur.* **Map** *p108 C1* **76**

This beauty multiple broke the mould with its constantly rotating roster of cult lines under the one roof, not all off-the-scale expensive. Treatment room.

Nightlife

Astoria

157 Charing Cross Road, WC2H 0EL (information 8963 0940/box office 08701 500044/www.meanfiddler. com). Tottenham Court Road tube. **Map** *p109 D1* **77**

Although a major fixture for alt.rockers old and new, this 2,000-capacity sweat box represents some of the more frustrating aspects of live music in London. Its future is uncertain: we heard recently it may be sold to a developer.

Bar Rumba

36 Shaftesbury Avenue, W1D 7EP (7287 6933/www.barrumba.co.uk). Piccadilly Circus tube. **Open** 9pm-3.30am Mon; 6pm-3am Tue; 9pm-3am Wed; 6pm-3.30am Thur, Fri; 9pm-4am Sat; 8pm-2am Sun. **Map** p108 C3 ⓴
This basement club is home to some of the most respected leftfield nights in town. Drum 'n' bass fans worship at Movement's altar every Thursday and reggaeton fans cram in for Tuesday's essential Barrio Latino.

Candy Bar

4 Carlisle Street, W1D 3BJ (7494 4041/www.thecandybar.co.uk). Tottenham Court Road tube. **Open** 5-11.30pm Mon-Thur; 5pm-2am Fri, Sat; 5-10.30pm Sun. **Map** p108 C1 ⓴
London's best-known lesbian bar attracts a mixed clientele, from students to lipstick lesbians. Drinks aren't cheap, but there's a late licence at weekends, and erotic dancers in the basement bar.

Comedy Store

1A Oxendon Street, SW1Y 4EE (Ticketmaster 0870 060 2340/ www.thecomedystore.biz). Leicester Square or Piccadilly Circus tube. **Map** p108 C3 ⓴
The legendary Comedy Store is still the place every comic wants to play, with the best bills on the circuit. Go on Tuesdays for the topical Cutting Edge shows, or on Wednesdays for the skilled improv outfit the Comedy Store Players.

The Edge

11 Soho Square, W1D 3QE (7439 1313/www.edge.uk.com). Tottenham Court Road tube. **Open** noon-1am Mon-Sat; noon-11.30pm Sun. **Map** p108 C1 ⓴
Once at the cutting edge of the gay scene, this busy polysexual bar set out over several floors has just had a refurb. DJs play most nights, plus there's a piano bar.

The Tour's in town

In July 2007 the Tour de France visits London for the first time in its history – and not just for a quick 'bonjour' but for the start of the race. Expect three days of cheerful Francophile mayhem, sporting excitement and traffic chaos in the capital.

An opening ceremony will be held on 6 July in Trafalgar Square (under the watchful eye of Napoleon's vanquisher, Lord Nelson, atop his column); the prologue, a short warm-up race to allocate the yellow jersey, goes out on Saturday 7. It starts on Whitehall, passes Buckingham Palace, crosses Green Park and makes a loop in Hyde Park before returning through Green Park and finishing on the Mall. On Sunday 8 July, Stage One of the race proper leaves for Canterbury from the Mall, passing more spectacular backdrops – the Houses of Parliament, the British Airways London Eye, St Paul's Cathedral – before heading off for Kent.

Physically punishing, tactically devious and frequently touched by scandal, the Tour is one of the world's greatest sporting events. It's also one of the most fun to watch. If the Tour's last visit to England, in 1997, is anything to go by, locals will throw themselves into the experience, chalking messages of support on the road, shouting encouragement and waving banners as each wave passes, from outriders to peleton to press. If you're in town, TV is not an option.

G.A.Y.

Astoria, 157 Charing Cross Road, WC2H 0EN (7434 9592/www.g-a-y. co.uk). Tottenham Court Road tube. **Open** 11pm-4am Mon, Thur, Fri; 10.30pm-4.30am Sat. No credit cards. **Map** p109 D1 ❷

London's largest gay venue isn't its swankiest, but hordes of disco-bunnies still congregate to dance to poppy tunes and sing along to Saturday PAs.

Ghetto

5-6 Falconberg Court (behind the Astoria), W1D 3AB (7287 3726/ www.ghettolondon.co.uk). Tottenham Court Road tube. **Open** 10.30pm-3am Mon-Thur; 10.30pm-4am Fri; 10.30pm-5am Sat; 10.30am-3pm Sun. No credit cards. **Map** p108 C1 ❸

Done out in raving red, this fabulously sweaty gay venue is home to some of London's hippest electro synth fests. Wednesday's Nag Nag Nag is one for electro-loving fashion kids; Friday's The Cock is the night that prompted gay bible *Attitude* to dub Ghetto 'a welcome break from your typical homo hangout'.

Metro

19-23 Oxford Street, W1D 2DN (7437 0964/www.blowupmetro.com). Tottenham Court Road tube. No credit cards. **Map** p108 C1 ❹

Mushy sound and haphazard layout, but this basement dive earned a reputation as the place to play during the garage-rock boom a few years back. It's not quite what it was, but it can still get enjoyably messy.

Madame Jo Jo's

8 Brewer Street, W1F 0SE (7734 3040/www.madamejojos.com). Leicester Square or Piccadilly Circus tube. **Open** 8pm-3am Tue; 10pm-3am Wed, Fri; 9pm-3am Thur; 7pm-3am Sat; 10pm-2am Sun. **Map** p108 C2 ❺

A great venue, enhanced by a touch of Soho cabaret sleaze – you'd be forgiven for mistaking the nature of the operation after seeing the name. The big draw remains Keb Darge's Deep Funk on Fridays, where blindingly cool people dance to obscure 1960s and '70s cuts.

Bar Rumba p125

Pizza Express Jazz Club

*10 Dean Street, W1D 3RW
(restaurant 7437 9595/Jazz Club
7439 8722/www.pizzaexpress.co.uk).
Tottenham Court Road tube.* **Open**
Restaurant 11.30am-midnight daily.
Jazz Club 7.45pm-midnight daily. Gigs
9pm daily. **Map** p108 C1 ⑤
The food takes second billing in the
basement of this eaterie: this place is
all about largely contemporary mainstream jazz. Despite the pizza, it's a
proper venue: there's no talking
through the sets.

Ronnie Scott's

*47 Frith Street, W1D 4HT (7439
0747/www.ronniescotts.co.uk). Leicester
Square or Tottenham Court Road tube.*
Map p108 C2 ⑥
Scott died in 1996, but his club, founded in 1959, remained an atmospheric
Soho fixture until it closed recently for
renovations. It should have reopened
by the time this book comes out; the
food should improve, but only time will
tell whether the vibe will stay the same.

Shadow Lounge

*5 Brewer Street, W1F 0RF (7287
7988/www.theshadowlounge.co.uk).
Piccadilly Circus tube.* **Open** 10pm-3am
Mon, Wed; 9pm-3am Tue, Thur-Sat.
Map p108 C2 ⑧
Recently refurbished, the original
lounge bar and gay members' club is
still popular with celebrities and gay
wannabes alike. Funky, comfy decor,
professional cocktail waiters, friendly
door staff and air-conditioning come as
standard.

The Yard

*57 Rupert Street, W1V 7BJ (7437
2652/www.yardbar.co.uk). Piccadilly
Circus tube.* **Open** Summer noon-11pm
Mon-Sat; noon-10.30pm Sun. Winter 2-
11pm Mon-Sat; 2-10.30pm Sun. **Map**
p108 C2 ⑧
Understandably popular in the summer, this gay men's bar has a coveted
courtyard. An upstairs loft bar keeps
the smarter, after-work crowd interested during the colder months.

Arts & leisure

Curzon Soho

*99 Shaftesbury Avenue, W1D 5DY
(information 7292 1686/bookings 7734
2255/www.curzoncinemas.com).
Leicester Square or Tottenham Court
Road tube.* **Map** p93 D2 ⑳
Superb programming at these comfortable three screens sets shorts, rarities and seasons alongside new fare
from around the world. Great bar, too.

Empire

*4-6 Leicester Square, WC2H 7NA
(0871 224 4007/www.uci.co.uk).
Leicester Square or Piccadilly Circus
tube.* **Map** p93 D3 ⑨
Lowest-common-denominator   programming at this first-run cinema, but
the immense and comfortable main
auditorium makes it worthwhile.

London Palladium

*Argyll Street, W1F 7TF (0870 890
1108/www.franksinatra.com). Oxford
Circus tube.* **Map** p92 A1 ⑨

LONDON BY AREA

Madame Jo Jo's p126

NEW As we went to press, *Sinatra at the London Palladium* was booking into October 2006. For those of you who've spotted the obvious flaw, Sinatra appears courtesy of a giant screen. Production subject to change.

Odeon Leicester Square

Leicester Square, WC2H 7LQ (0871 224 4007/www.odeon.co.uk). Leicester Square tube. **Map** p93 D3 ⓽⓷
Lots of premières – including London Film Festival gala events – at this big art deco house with its much-admired original 1937 organ.

Odeon West End

40 Leicester Square, WC2H 7LP (0871 224 4007/www.odeon.co.uk). Leicester Square tube. **Map** p93 D3 ⓽⓸
Two big screens at this crowd-pleaser.

Palace Theatre

Shaftesbury Avenue, W1A 4AF (0870 895 5579/www.dewynters. com/spamalot). Leicester Square or Tottenham Court Road tube. **Map** p93 D2 ⓽⓹

NEW With Eric Idle writing the book and co-scoring, *Spamalot*, the stage version of Monty Python's Holy Grail story, from 2 October 2006, should do well. Production subject to change.

Prince Charles

7 Leicester Place, WC2H 7BY (7494 3654/www.princecharlescinema.com). Leicester Square tube. **Map** p93 D3 ⓽⓺
This cherished cinema is the best value in town for releases ending their first run elsewhere. Tickets start at £1.50 for weekday matinees and ascend to the heady heights of £4 for evening screenings. It has interesting season-lets and singalongs, too.

Prince Edward Theatre

Old Compton Street, W1D 4HS (0870 850 9191/www.marypoppinsthe musical.co.uk). Leicester Square tube. **Map** p93 D2 ⓽⓻
Chipper chimney sweeps and spoon-fuls of magic in this enchanting take on *Mary Poppins*, directed by Sir Richard Eyre. Production subject to change.

Prince of Wales Theatre

31 Coventry Street, W1D 6AS (0870 850 0393/www.mamma-mia.com). Leicester Square tube. **Map** p93 C3 ⓘ
Home of *Mamma Mia!*, the feel-good musical links Abba's hits into a continuous but spurious story. Endlessly popular. Production subject to change.

Queen's Theatre

Shaftesbury Avenue, W1D 8AS (7494 5040/www.lesmis.com). Leicester Square or Piccadilly Circus tube. **Map** p92 C2 ⓘ
The RSC's definitive version of *Les Misérables* continues to idealise the struggles of the poor in Victor Hugo's revolutionary Paris. Production subject to change.

Soho Theatre

21 Dean Street, W1D 3NE (7478 0100/box office 0870 429 6883/www.sohotheatre.com). Tottenham Court Road tube. **Map** p92 C1 ⓘ
Its blue neon lights, front-of-house café and late-night performances have a Soho vibe echoed in the production style. Sets are usually frills-free: the priority is to provide a space for new writers. Good for stand-up and cabaret.

Triyoga

NEW *2nd Floor, 2-4 Kingly Court, W1B 5PW (7483 3344). Oxford Circus or Piccadilly Circus tube.* **Map** p92 B2 ⓘ
Triyoga became the celebrity yoga brand *du jour* after the success of its Primrose Hill branch, but is entirely admirable on its own merits, in its pursuit of 'authenticity, accessibilty and affordablility'. Not to say style. Fifty classes a week are held here.

Marylebone

Marylebone sits to the north of Oxford Street at its western side (with Mayfair to its south). The mood changes swiftly. Instead of the pavement jostle and undistinguished chainstore consumerism of central London's main shopping street, there are quiet squares and a pretty high street that looks as if it belongs in an affluent provincial town. In the past decade, the area has been branded 'Marylebone Village' and become increasingly fashionable and desirable, but still relaxed.

Sights & museums

London Zoo

Regent's Park, NW1 4RY (7722 3333/www.zsl.org/london-zoo). Baker Street or Camden Town tube then 274, C2 bus. **Open** Late Oct-mid Mar 10am-4pm daily. Mid Mar-late Oct 10am-5.30pm daily. **Admission** £14; free-£12 reductions. **Map** p131 B1 ⓘ
Opened in 1828, this was the world's first scientific zoo. Times have changed, though, and the elephants are gone – they've been given room to roam at sister site Whipsnade Wild Animal Park – and the penguins have been moved from Lubetkin's famous modernist pool to a more suitable space. 'Meet the Monkeys' gives personal encounters with squirrel monkeys in 1,500sq m of recreated Bolivian rainforest, and the African Bird Safari is a new walk-through habitat. Check the daily programme of events to get a good view at feeding times.
Event highlights At Easter 2007 'Gorilla Kingdom' will open at the centre of the zoo: a forest walk to see gorillas and other animals that share their world. The Clore Small Mammals Building will re-open at the same time, featuring a new South American rainforest display.

Madame Tussauds

Marylebone Road, NW1 5LR (0870 400 3000/www.madame-tussauds.com). Baker Street tube. **Open** 9am-6pm daily (last entry 5pm); times vary during holiday periods. **Admission** 9.30am-3pm £24.99; £15.99-£20.99 reductions. 3-5pm £15.99; £9-£12.99 reductions. **Map** p131 A1 ⓘ
Tussauds compensates for its inherently static silicone attractions with a flurry of attendant activity. As you enter you're dazzled by fake paparazzi flashbulbs; starry-eyed kids can take

part in a 'Divas' routine; and 'Robbie Williams' has a hidden sensor activated by kisses to produce a 'twinkle' in his eye. Figures are constantly being added to keep up with new stars, movies and TV shows – now resident are *Little Britain*'s Andy and Lou – but public figures past and present remain. The London Planetarium has now closed, displaced by yet more celebrity exhibits.

Regent's Park

Map p131 B1 ❸

With a landscape including formal flower beds and extensive playing fields, Regent's Park (open 5am-dusk daily) is one of London's most treasured green spaces. As well as the famous zoo, it has a boating lake (home to wildfowl), tennis courts, cafés and a lovely open-air theatre. To the west of the park is the London Central Mosque.

Wallace Collection

Hertford House, Manchester Square, W1U 3BN (7935 0687/www.wallace collection.org). Bond Street tube. **Open** 10am-5pm daily. **Admission** free. **Map** p131 A2 ❹
Presiding over leafy Manchester Square, this handsome and newly spruced-up 18th-century house contains a lavish, premier-league collection of furniture, old master paintings, armour and objets d'art. There are also regular temporary exhibitions. Café Bagatelle ranks among the best London museum eateries.

Eating & drinking

Café Bagatelle

Wallace Collection, Manchester Square, W1U 3BN (7563 9505). Bond Street tube. **Open** 10am-4.30pm daily. **££**. **International**. **Map** p131 A2 ❺
Located in a spacious, glass-roofed courtyard at the Wallace Collection (above), Café Bagatelle is one of London's most charming museum restaurants. The menu is short but ambitious, taking in Asian influences alongside more standard Modern European fare. Utterly delightful.

FishWorks

89 Marylebone High Street, W1U 4QW (7935 9796/www.fishworks.co.uk). Baker Street, Bond Street or Regent's Park tube. **Open** noon-2.30pm, 6-10.30pm Tue-Fri; noon-10.30pm Sat, Sun. **£££**. **Fish**. **Map** p131 A1 ❻
The formula is simple: a fishmonger at the front, and a light, bright eating area behind. Muse over the long menu or pick your own fish from the counter. The emphasis is on super-fresh ingredients, with no fuss, a formula that is doing very well for FishWorks, which is expanding into a mini chain. Locals appreciate the cooking classes here.

Garden Café

Inner Circle, Regent's Park, NW1 4NU (7935 5729/www.thegardencafe.co.uk). Baker Street or Regents Park tube. **Open** 10am-dusk daily. **Modern European**. Licensed. **Map** p131 B1 ❼
The spacious interior of this café has recently been given a smart retro-chic look; the tasteful Modern European menu celebrates great British produce with understatement and style. There's a take-away counter for picnickers, and outdoor tables in a pretty garden.

Golden Hind

73 Marylebone Lane, W1U 2PN (7486 3644). Bond Street tube. **Open** noon-3pm, 6-10pm Mon-Fri; 6-10pm Sat. **££**. **Fish & chips**. **Map** p131 A2 ❽
This beautifully preserved art deco chippy offers unusual items such as deep-fried mussels in batter alongside perceptibly fresh fish, golden-brown chips and perfect mushy peas.

La Fromagerie

2-4 Moxon Street, W1U 4EW (7935 0341/www.lafromagerie.co.uk). Baker Street or Bond Street tube. **Open** 10.30am-7.30pm Mon; 8am-7.30pm Tue-Fri; 9am-7pm Sat; 10am-6pm Sun. **££**. **Deli**. **Map** p131 A1 ❾
This cheese shop and deli has done well from its rustic-styled café, which heaves at lunchtime. And rightly so. Cooking is of a consistently high standard: earthy soups, exquisite cheese platters and salad dishes.

Marylebone & Mayfair

300 m

300 yds

© Copyright Time Out Group 2006

Original Tagines

*7A Dorset Street, W1H 3SE
(7935 1545/www.originaltagines.
com). Baker Street tube.* **Open** noon-
3pm, 6-11pm daily. ££. **Moroccan**.
Map p131 A1 ⑫

A great little neighbourhood restaurant, Original Tagines is blessedly free
of ethnic knick-knacks. The standard
double act of couscous and tagines
(several varieties of each) is lent support by an atypically good selection of
starters, although portions aren't huge.

Providores & Tapa Room

*109 Marylebone High Street, W1U 4RX
(7935 6175/www.theprovidores.co.uk).
Baker Street or Bond Street tube.* **Open**
Providores noon-2.45pm, 6-10.45pm
Mon-Sat; noon-2.45pm, 6-10pm Sun.
Tapa Room 9-11.30am, noon-10.30pm
Mon-Fri; 10am-3pm, 4-10.30pm Sat;
10am-3pm, 4-10pm Sun. £££.
International. **Map** p131 A2 ⑬

The buzzy street-level Tapa Room is
frequently packed with crowds attracted by the exquisite global tapas and
breakfasts. Upstairs, the restaurant
itself is white, small and refined, and
uses a rarefied fusion of mainly Asian
and Middle Eastern ingredients to produce unusual but very good dishes.

Prince Regent

*71 Marylebone High Street, W1U 5JN
(7467 3811) Baker Street or Regent's
Park tube.* **Open** noon-11pm Mon-Sat;
noon-10.30pm Sun. ££. **Gastropub**.
Map p131 A1 ⑭

The food here is a little too ordinary to
earn the place a bona fide gastro stamp,
but everything else makes the grade:
dark wood, lots of comfortable seating
(especially upstairs), warm lighting,
extensive wine list hand-chalked on a
big blackboard, and a very impressive
selection of wheat beers.

Shopping

Trawl Paddington Street and
Marylebone High Street for 21st-
century village pleasures for the
well-heeled. St Christopher's Place,
just north of Oxford Street, is a
well-designed shopping centre.

Le Pain Quotidien

Le Pain Quotidien

NEW *72-75 Marylebone High Street,
W1U 5JW (7486 6154/www.pain
quotidien.com). Bond Street tube.* **Open**
7am-7pm Mon-Fri; 8am-6pm Sat, Sun.
£. **Café**. **Map** p131 A2 ⑩

The Belgian bakery/café chain opened
this first UK branch in 2005. It twangs
all those country-kitchen heartstrings:
a central communal table, tasteful but
homely presentation, huge windows
and mother-couldn't-beat-'em baked
goods and snacks.

Locanda Locatelli

*8 Seymour Street, W1H 7JZ (7935
9088/www.locandalocatelli.com). Marble
Arch tube.* **Open** noon-3pm, 7-11pm
Mon-Thur; noon-3pm, 7-11.30pm Fri;
noon-3.30pm, 7-11.30pm Sat; noon-
3.30pm, 6.45-10pm Sun. ££££.
Modern Italian. **Map** p131 A2 ⑪

A meal at Locanda Locatelli seems
indulgent, from the prices to the exclusive nightclub feel within. Many dishes
put a contemporary spin on the Italian
classics, and the ravioli served here are
among the very best in the country.

Alfie's Antique Market

*13-25 Church Street, NW8 8DT
(7723 6066/www.alfiesantiques.com).
Edgware Road tube/Marylebone
tube/rail.* **Open** 10am-6pm Tue-Sat.
Map p131 A1 ⑮

The bigger spaces at Alfie's tend to
belong to 20th-century decorative arts,
antiques and vintage clothing. Vincenzo
Caffarella has some stunning lighting;
Ian Broughton has '30s to '50s kitsch.
You can also find advertising posters,
telephones, china and jewellery. The top
floor is the best. Don't miss The Girl
Can't Help It, fantastical American
pieces sourced by owner Sparkle Moore.

Daunt Books

*83-84 Marylebone High Street,
W1U 4QW (7224 2295/www.daunt
books.co.uk). Baker Street tube.* **Open**
9am-7.30pm Mon-Sat; 11am-6pm Sun.
Map p131 A1 ⑯

Marvel at the Edwardian interior of
this great independent bookshop, with
its oak galleries and central skylight
running the length of the shop.

Fresh

*92 Marylebone High Street, W1U 4RD
(7486 4100/www.fresh.com). Baker
Street tube.* **Open** 10am-7pm Mon-
Wed, Fri, Sat; 10am-8pm Thur; noon-
5pm Sun. **Map** p131 A1 ⑰

These high-end American body- and
haircare products aren't just lovely to
look at, but with ingredients such as
soy, rice and sugar, they smell good
enough to eat too. Book yourself in for
a mini treatment at the shop and you
can redeem the cost against products.

John Lewis

*278-306 Oxford Street, W1A 1EX
(7629 7711/www.johnlewis.co.uk).
Bond Street or Oxford Circus tube.*
Open 9.30am-7pm Mon-Wed, Fri,
Sat; 9.30am-8pm Thur; noon-6pm Sun.
Map p131 B2 ⑱

John Lewis represents the best of
British consumer values with its 'never
knowingly undersold' prices. Nothing's
super-stylish, but it's not embarrass-
ingly outdated either, and the staff
know what they're talking about.

Kabiri

*37 Marylebone High Street, W1U 4QE
(7224 1808/www.kabiri.co.uk).* **Open**
10am-6.30pm Mon-Sat; noon-5pm Sun.
Map p131 A1 ⑲

This small shop showcases an incred-
ible variety of contemporary jewellery
by over 50 designers, many of them
locally based. Established names are
juxtaposed with talent fresh out of
art college.

Margaret Howell

*34 Wigmore Street, W1U 2RS (7009
9009/www.margarethowell.co.uk).
Bond Street tube.* **Open** 10am-6pm
Mon-Wed, Fri, Sat; 10am-7pm Thur.
Map p131 B2 ⑳

Margaret Howell's label has become
highly desirable as her crisp English
aesthetic has reached the height of cool.
This shop houses the full collection,
including homewares, and also acts as
an occasional exhibition space for 20th-
century art and design.

Mint

*70 Wigmore Street, W1U 2SF
(7224 4406). Bond Street tube.*
Open 10.30am-6.30pm Mon-Wed,
Fri, Sat; 10.30am-7.30pm Thur.
Map p131 A2 ㉑

An inspiring collection of globally
sourced one-off or production pieces.
The ever-changing array of furniture,
lighting, ceramics, glass, tableware
and textiles, by both big-boy designers
and new talent, is housed in a cosy
space over two floors. Great for
unusual gifts around the £5 mark.

Paul Bakery & Tearoom

*115 Marylebone High Street, W1U
4SB (7224 5615/www.paul.fr). Baker
Street or Bond Street tube.* **Open**
7.30am-8pm Mon-Fri; 8am-8pm Sat,
Sun. **Map** p131 A2 ㉒

This family-run bakery expanded all
over France and now to London. In
fact, it's quite a chain now, but the
famously good breads are still made
using exacting traditional methods.
Around 140 varieties are offered,
including chapata, polka, benoîtons
and bio bread, plus pastries.

Selfridges

400 Oxford Street, W1A 1AB (0870 837 7377/www.selfridges.com). Bond Street or Marble Arch tube. **Open** 10am-8pm Mon-Fri; 9.30am-8pm Sat; noon-6pm Sun. **Map** p131 A3 ㉓

This handsome department store maintains its august reputation while keeping a very contemporary finger on the pulse. It offers stylish luxury for every room in the house, and most particularly the wardrobe. Cafés, restaurants and a Moët champagne bar offer plenty of refuelling options.

Skandium

86 Marylebone High Street, W1U 4QS (7935 2077/www.skandium.com). Baker Street or Bond Street tube. **Open** 10am-6.30pm Mon-Wed, 10am-7pm Thur; Fri, Sat; 11am-5pm Sun. **Map** 131 A1 ㉔

This bustling store houses a large selection of interiors products from Scandinavian designers and manufacturers. Classic and contemporary furniture is accompanied by lighting, rugs, and brands including iittala's lovely whimsical accessories.

Topshop

36-38 Great Castle Street, Oxford Circus, W1W 8LG (7636 7700/www.topshop.co.uk). Oxford Circus tube. **Open** 9am-8pm Mon-Wed, Fri, Sat; 9am-9pm Thur; noon-6pm Sun. **Map** p131 C2 ㉕

The high-street darling of the fashion pack is known for keeping a sharp eye on the catwalk and echoing its trends. It continues to feature ranges by recent graduates alongside established names in its Boutique on Level 1.

Tracey Neuls

NEW *29 Marylebone Lane, W1U 2NQ (7935 0039/www.tn29.com). Bond Street tube.* **Open** 11am-6.30pm Mon-Wed, Fri; 11am-8.30pm Thur; noon-5pm Sat. **Map** p131 A2 ㉖

Tracey Neuls is giving footwear clichés a kick in the kitten heels. After scooping a string of awards at Cordwainers college, the Canadian designer set up her TN_29 label and this, her first

stand-alone shop. Her fascination with detail and playful curiosity are reflected in her eye-catching designs, which cost from around £120 to £300.

Whistles

12 St Christopher's Place, W1U 1NQ (7487 4484/www.whistles.co.uk). Bond Street tube. **Open** 10am-6pm Mon-Wed, Fri, Sat; 10am-7pm Thur; noon-5pm Sun. **Map** p131 A2 ㉗

'Eclectic' best sums up the style of this well-loved label, which manages to interpret catwalk trends without losing its distinctive identity.

Arts & leisure

Open Air Theatre

Regent's Park, NW1 4NR (7935 5756/box office 0870 060 1811/www.openairtheatre.org). Baker Street tube. Repertory season June-Sept; phone for details. **Map** p131 B1 ㉘

The lovely verdant setting of this al fresco theatre lends itself perfectly to summery Shakespeare romps and music performances. Book well ahead and take an extra layer for chills in act three. You can buy good-value, tasty grub on-site, or bring a picnic.

Wigmore Hall

36 Wigmore Street, W1U 2BP (7935 2141/www.wigmore-hall.org.uk). Bond Street tube. **Map** p131 B2 ㉙

With its perfect acoustics, discreet art nouveau decor and excellent basement restaurant, this is one of the world's top concert venues for chamber music and song. The Monday lunchtime BBC concerts are excellent value.

Mayfair

Not for nothing is Mayfair the most expensive property on the Monopoly board. It was conceived as an elegant residential suburb arranged around squares with service mews tucked behind them – and other than the fact that the city has advanced beyond it, that's how it remains. International toffs are still in residence, as are the rarefied shops, restaurants and galleries they frequent. In the commercial areas, you can feel out of place without a platinum credit card (but if you have one, there's no better place to push your limit). The quieter streets are fascinating to wander for their architecture, atmosphere and traditional pubs, and the voyeuristic pleasures of spying on how the other half live. Which, this being England, isn't showily – though even tiny mews homes originally built as stables would cost you several racehorses these days.

The streets are so quiet at night that only the security cameras will see you pass. Nightlife, such as it is, takes place in swanky bars and restaurants, many of them in hotels.

Sights & museums

Handel House Museum

25 Brook Street (entrance at rear in Ranger's Lodge, Lancashire Court), W1K 4HB (information 7495 1685/www.handelhouse.org). Bond Street tube. **Open** 10am-6pm Tue, Wed, Fri, Sat; 10am-8pm Thur; noon-6pm Sun. **Admission** £5; free-£4.50 reductions. **Map** p131 B3 ③⓿

George Frederick Handel moved to Britain from his native Germany aged 25 and settled in this house 12 years later, remaining here until his death in 1759. The house has been beautifully restored with original and recreated furnishings, paintings and a welter of the composer's scores (in the same room as photos of Jimi Hendrix, who lived here rather more recently).

Hyde Park & Kensington Gardens

7298 2100, www.royalparks.gov.uk. **Map** p131 A5 ③①

At 1.5 miles long and about a mile wide, Hyde Park is the largest of London's Royal Parks. It has a stately feel, though there's plenty of picnicking and general outdoor activity. It

became a hotspot for mass demonstrations in the 19th century and remains so today – a march against war in Iraq in 2003 was the largest in its history, and the Live8 concert of July 2005 was attended by thousands who had sent a text to Sir Bob Geldof. The legalisation of public assembly in the park led to the establishment of Speakers' Corner in 1872, where ranters sane and bonkers have the floor. Other points of interest include a bronze statue of Peter Pan, sculpted by Sir George Frampton in 1912 to honour Peter's creator, JM Barrie, and the Serpentine, London's oldest boating lake and home to ducks, coots, swans and tufty-headed grebes. You can rent rowing boats and pedalos from March to October.

To the west is Kensington Gardens, home of the Diana, Princess of Wales Memorial Playground and the less successful Princess Diana Memorial Fountain, more aesthetic than practical.

Kensington Palace

Kensington Gardens, W8 4PX (7937 9561/booking line 0870 751 5180/ www.hrp.org.uk). Bayswater, High Street Kensington or Queensway tube. **Open** *Mar-Oct* 10am-6pm daily. *Nov-Feb* 10am-5pm daily. Last entry 1hr before closing. **Admission** £11; free-£8.30 reductions. **Map** p131 A3 ③②

Sir Christopher Wren rushed to extend this Jacobean mansion to palatial proportions for the new King William III when he was imported from Holland in 1689; the king thought that the countryside location would be good for his asthma. The sections of the palace that the public are allowed to see give the impression of intimacy.

The Royal Ceremonial Dress Collection is a fascinating display, with lavish ensembles worn for state occasions and a permanent collection of 14 dresses worn by Diana, Princess of Wales, the palace's most famous resident. Make time for tea in Queen Anne's Orangery and admire – through the hedge – the piece of horticultural perfection that is the Sunken Garden.

St Pancras reborn

The capital's most exciting architectural and transport development nears completion.

It's easy to forget that the British invented the railway, so accustomed are we to being the runt of the European networks. But with architectural treasure St Pancras station getting the mother of all makeovers in time to accommodate the new, higher-speed Eurostar route in autumn 2007, we might be entering a second golden age of rail.

The huge £500 million project will turn the neglected station into one of Europe's major transport hubs, with a projected 40 million passengers each year. The roster of transport links is nothing if not impressive: regular, high-speed routes to France and Belgium; the intersection of six London underground lines; and high-speed links to Kent (via Stratford in a spry seven minutes). Slick connections are, however, only half of the story. The developers envisage St Pancras International as a destination in its own right, a meeting place, somewhere to linger in original, high-end shops, bars and restaurants – dare we say London's answer to New York's Grand Central Station? It will have the longest champagne bar in Europe, a micro-brewery, major art displays and even – we are told – a farmers' market.

Victorian St Pancras station was originally conceived and funded by Midland Railway in the late 19th century. The immense dimensions of William Barlow's beautifully vaulted train shed made it the world's largest enclosed space by its completion in 1868. The station is fronted by George Gilbert Scott's impressive St Pancras Chambers, a riot of Victorian Gothic soon to become a hotel and apartments.

Those who fear this sort of rapid commercial development will be reassured to hear that English Heritage has been keeping a eagle eye on the transformation. The fabulous roof, bombed in World War II, will have its glass put back in, and its iron work will be returned to its original shade of blue – to match the sky.

■ Eurostar (www.eurostar.com)
■ London & Continental Railways (www.lcrhq.co.uk)

Event highlights An exhibition of photos of Diana by Mario Testino (to spring 2007) also features dresses that were auctioned off for charity shortly after the famous photo shoot for *Vanity Fair* in 1997.

Royal Academy of Arts

Burlington House, Piccadilly, W1J 0BD (7300 8000/www.royalacademy.org.uk). Green Park or Piccadilly Circus tube. **Open** 10am-6pm Mon-Thur, Sat, Sun; 10am-10pm Fri. **Admission** varies. **Map** p131 C4 ③③

Britain's first art school was founded in 1768 and moved to the extravagantly Palladian Burlington House a century later. It's best known these days for its galleries, which stage crowd-pulling exhibitions. Those in the John Madejski Fine Rooms are drawn from the RA's holdings – ranging from Constable to Hockney – and are free, providing a good excuse to peek at the ornate interiors. The biggest event is the Summer Exhibition, which for more than two centuries has drawn from works entered by the public.
Event highlights Rodin sculptures (23 Sept 2006-1 Jan 2007). Chola Bronzes (11 Nov 2006-25 Feb 2007).

Serpentine Gallery

Kensington Gardens (near Albert Memorial), W2 3XA (7402 6075/ www.serpentinegallery.org). Lancaster Gate or South Kensington tube. **Open** 10am-6pm daily. **Admission** free; donations appreciated. **Map** p131 A5 ③④

This light and airy gallery has a rolling exhibition programme of contemporary art is an attractive place for a spontaneous visit while walking in the park.
Event highlights Works from Damien Hirst's collection of other people's art is on from November to January 2007.

St James's Church Piccadilly

197 Piccadilly, W1J 9LL (7734 4511/www.st-james-piccadilly.org). Piccadilly Circus tube. **Open** 8am-7pm daily. *Evening events* times vary. **Admission** free. **Map** p131 C4 ③⑤

This Wren church is a simple, calming building: delicate limewood garlanding by Grinling Gibbons is one of the few frills. It stages regular concerts and hosts markets in its churchyard: antiques Tuesday, arts and crafts Wednesday to Saturday.

Wellington Arch

Hyde Park Corner, W1J 7JZ (7930 2726/www.english-heritage.org.uk). Hyde Park Corner tube. **Open** *Apr-Oct* 10am-5pm Wed-Sun. *Nov-Mar* 10am-4pm Wed-Sun. **Admission** £3; free-£2.30 reductions. **Map** p131 A5 ③⑥

Built in the late 1820s to mark Britain's triumph over France, the arch has three floors of historical displays. From the balcony, there are views of the Houses of Parliament and Buckingham Palace, though trees intervene in summer.

Eating & drinking

China Tang

NEW *Dorchester Hotel, Park Lane, W1A 2HJ (7629 9988/www. dorchesterhotel.com). Green Park or Hyde Park Corner tube.* **Open** 11am-1am Mon-Sat; 11am-midnight Sun. **Bar**. **Map** p131 A4 ③⑦

The bar adjacent to the sumptuous Cantonese restaurant in the basement of the Dorchester is heaving with the rich and the famous. Decked out in chocolate and cream, the smart room looks like an old-fashioned cruise liner. There's great range of champagnes, and the wines include a spice-friendly selection from Alsace and Bordeaux.

Chisou

4 Princes Street, W1B 2LE (7629 3931). Oxford Circus tube. **Open** noon-2.30pm, 6-10.15pm Mon-Sat. **£££**. **Japanese**. **Map** p131 B3 ③⑧

London now has a large number of inexpensive, good-value Japanese restaurants. Chisou isn't one of them. This is a place where the quality of ingredients – from sushi and sashimi to select sakés and fundamentals like dashi – matters. They say you get what you pay for, and Chisou proves the point impeccably.

Chisou p137

Donovan Bar

NEW *Brown's Hotel, Albemarle Street, W1S 4BP (7493 6020). Green Park tube.* **Open** 11am-1am Mon-Sat; 11am-10.30pm Sun. **Bar.** Map p131 B4 ➌➒

After a reported £20 million refurbishment, the legendary Brown's Hotel reopened in 2006. Named after the celebrated British photographer Terence Donovan, its swanky bar incorporates a Bill Amberg-designed leather bar, a stained-glass window and walls hung with Donovan's photographs. Drop by to sip a glass of champagne, or settle down with a well-made classic or contemporary cocktail.

Dorchester Grill Room

Dorchester, 53 Park Lane, W1A 2HJ (7317 6336/www. dorchesterhotel.com). Hyde Park Corner tube. **Open** 7-11am, 12.30-2.30pm, 6-11pm Mon-Sat; 7.30-11am, 12.30-2.30pm, 7-10.30pm Sun. **££££.** **British/French.** Map p131 A4 ➍➋

This renowned hotel eaterie has just undergone a revamp, with a spruced-up interior by Thierry Despont, but it retains its usual high standards. Service is impeccable without being snooty, and the cuisine a sybaritic mix of British steaks and roasts, and classic French-style cooking.

Gordon Ramsay at Claridge's

Claridge's Hotel, 55 Brook Street, W1A 2JQ (7499 0099/www.gordon ramsay.com). Bond Street tube. **Open** noon-2.45pm, 5.45-11pm Mon-Fri; noon-3pm, 5.45-11pm Sat; noon-3pm, 6-11pm Sun. **££££.** **Haute cuisine.** Map p131 B3 ➍➊

Slick presentation adds yet another layer of glamour to the vintage sparkle of this beautifully restored art deco hotel. It's nigh on impossible to get a table, but worth persevering. We've had one curiously lacklustre meal here, but generally Ramsay's hand remains sure. Set lunch is the best value.

Maze

Marriott Grosvenor Square, 10-13 Grosvenor Square, W1K 6JP (7107 0000/www.gordonramsay. com). Bond Street tube. **Open** noon-3pm, 6-11pm daily. **£££.** **Modern European.** Map p131 A3 ➍➋

Ignore the fact it's in a hotel: Gordon Ramsay's protégé Jason Atherton is the reason people visit Maze. Judging from the dining room's laughter and chatter – oh, and the taste – his tapas-sized dishes are going down a storm (there's a more conventional menu too). The bar is worth a visit in its own right, too, sharing the restaurant's sleek decor.

Nobu

Metropolitan Hotel, 19 Old Park Lane, W1K 1LB (7447 4747/www.nobu restaurants.com). Hyde Park Corner tube. **Open** noon-2.15pm, 6-10.15pm Mon-Thur; noon-2.15pm, 6-11pm Fri; 12.30-3pm, 6-11pm Sat; 12.30-3pm, 6-9.30pm Sun. **££££. Japanese.** Map p131 A5 ⓭

It's still the most famous Japanese restaurant in town, yet Nobu is no longer the most fashionable or even the most expensive (judicious selection of dishes can yield a filling meal at under £90 for two). The trim, efficient staff seem less bossy now, but are quick to clear plates – no lingering over the views, folks.

Noura Central

122 Jermyn Street, SW1Y 4UJ (7839 2020/www.noura.co.uk). Piccadilly Circus tube. **Open** noon-midnight Mon-Thur, Sun; noon-1am Fri, Sat. **£££. Middle Eastern.** Map p131 C4 ⓮

This branch of the Parisian chain is a glam, air-conditioned sanctuary, offering numerous tasty Levantine mezes and main courses for both vegetarians and omnivores. To make the most of it, pick several dishes, dive in and share.

Postcard Teas

NEW *9 Dering Street, W1S 1AG (020 7629 3654/www.postcardteas.com). Bond Street or Oxford Circus tube.* **Open** 10.30am-6.30pm Tue-Sat. **£. Tearoom.** Map p131 B3 ⓯

This tea sanctuary is the pet project of Timothy d'Offay, son of art gallery proprietor Anthony d'Offay and tea conoisseur. It sells a score of brews, for a mere £1.50 per pot, which is cheap for varieties of this excellence: black, green and oolongs (semi 'fermented' teas) of many different styles. Well-matched nibbles too, such as chocolate cake and dates.

Red Lion

1 Waverton Street, W1J 5QN (7499 1307). Green Park tube. **Open** 11.30am-11pm Mon-Fri; 6-11pm Sat; 6-10.30pm Sun. **Pub.** Map p131 A4 ⓰

This carefully kept Mayfair secret is out, though its miniature tables, toby jugs and intimate, front-room atmosphere still keep it feeling like a local. The landlord is as hospitable as ever, pulling pints of Greene King IPA, Bombardier and Young's ales with a cheeky wink. Honest, unpretentious pub fare doesn't come much better.

Rhodes W1

The Cumberland, Great Cumberland Place, W1A 4RF (7479 3838). Marble Arch tube. **Open** 11am-11pm Mon-Sat; 11am-10.30pm Sun. **£££. British.** Map p131 A3 ⓱

Gary Rhodes' signature Modern British approach is writ large at this huge hotel restaurant. Oxtail is a favourite ingredient of the celebrity chef, but there are plenty of other British classics to salivate over.

Salt Whisky Bar

82 Seymour Street, W2 2JB (7402 1155/www.saltbar.com). Marble Arch tube. **Open** noon-1am Mon-Sat; noon-midnight Sun. **Bar.** Map p131 A3 ⓲

Salt is dedicated to the pleasures of whisky. The dark, ultra-modern bar has ample floor space and perches for a quick stopover, and comfy sofas upon which to set the world to rights. More than 200 whiskies are on offer – Scotch, American, Irish and Japanese – and some well-made cocktails, plus other drinks if you must.

Sketch

9 Conduit Street, W1S 2XZ (0870 777 4488/www.sketch.uk.com). Oxford Circus tube. **Open** Glade noon-3pm Mon-Sat. Gallery 7-10.30pm Mon-Sat. Lecture Room noon-2.30pm, 7-10.30pm Tue-Fri; 7-10.30pm Sat. **££-££££. Intenational.** Map p131 C3 ⓳

These trendy Mayfair premises are home to several dining options. On the lower level are the cheaper – relatively – Gallery (Modern Euro food; largely style over substance) and a new addition, Glade (French-inspired dishes that sound pretentious on paper but work well). The first-floor Lecture Room has dramatic food at dramatic prices.

Sketch p139

Tamarind

20 Queen Street, W1J 5PR (7629 3561/www.tamarindrestaurant.com). Green Park tube. **Open** noon-3pm Mon-Fri; 6-11.30pm Mon-Sat; noon-2.30pm, 6-10.30pm Sun. **££. Indian. Map** p131 B4 🟢

This classy, sumptuous, subterranean restaurant specialises in Mogul tandoori cuisine from the north-west of India. The cooking tends to the cautious rather than flamboyant, leaving the theatrics to kebab chefs in the open-view kitchen.

The Wolseley

160 Piccadilly, W1J 9EB (7499 6996/ www.thewolseley.com). Green Park tube. **Open** 7am-midnight Mon-Fri; 9am-midnight Sat; 9am-11pm Sun. **££-£££. European. Map** p131 C4 🟢

This handsome building was built in 1921 as a car showroom, and its huge windows and high vaulted ceilings doubtless fitted the role. But its current incarnation as a European-style grand café is surely the one it was born for. With quality French and European fare, a stunner of an afternoon tea and a permanent buzz, it's easy to see why it's always full to the rafters.

Shopping

Angela Hale

5 Royal Arcade, 28 Old Bond Street, W1S 4SE (7495 1920/www. angela-hale.co.uk). Green Park tube. **Open** 10am-6pm Mon-Sat. **Map** p131 B4 🟢

This little boutique, which showcases the romantic, whimsical aesthetics of Angela Hale's jewellery designs, will make any girl swoon. Hale's handmade creations are based on hypo-allergenic bronze and set with beautiful Swarovski crystals. All manner of accessories are also available to jazz up a feminine outfit.

b Store

6 Conduit Street, W1S 2XE (7734 6846/www.buddhahood.co.uk). Oxford Circus tube. **Open** 10.30am-6.30pm Mon-Sat. **Map** p131 C3 🟢

A little bit of Hoxton edginess in venerable Mayfair. The diverse stock includes Pelican Avenue (beautifully colourful stylised bibs for women), Peter Jensen sweatshirts and accessories like brooches starting from as little as £15. b Store is the exclusive stockist of several brands, including Judy Blame accessories and T-shirts; also check out its fab own-brand Buddhahood footwear.

Browns

23-27 South Molton Street, W1K 5RD (7514 0000/www.brownsfashion.com). Bond Street tube. **Open** 10am-6.30pm Mon-Wed, Fri, Sat; 10am-7pm Thur. **Map** p131 B3 🟢

Around 100 top designers jostle for attention in Joan Burstein's five interconnecting shops: Marc Jacobs, Chloé and Sophia Kokosalaki, plus an entire floor of Jil Sander. Those without a sugar daddy can peruse the almost-affordable diffusion and emergent-designer ranges at the adjacent Browns Focus, or Browns Labels for Less (No.50).

Burberry

21-23 New Bond Street, W1S 2RE (7839 5222/www.burberry.com). Bond Street tube. **Open** 10am-7pm Mon-Sat; noon-6pm Sun. **Map** p131 B3 🟢

Christopher Bailey, the hugely talented British designer, is bringing style and glamour into Burberry's Prorsum collection with sharp tailoring and cool British sensibilities. Tip: if you want Burberry threads on the cheap, check out the factory shop in Hackney (29-53 Chatham Place, E9 6 LY, 8328 4287).

Connolly

41 Conduit Street, W1S 2YQ (7235 3883). Bond Street tube. **Open** 10am-6pm Mon-Wed, Fri, Sat; 10am-7pm Thur. **Map** p131 B3 🟢

This seriously luxury label built its reputation by producing upholstery for the likes of Rolls-Royce and Maserati. You'll find driving shoes and jackets (£1,000) and a portable espresso set that plugs into the lighter socket. Luggage evokes a 1960s sports car.

Reiss

LONDON BY AREA

Dover Street Market

17-18 Dover Street, W1S 4LT (7518 0680). Green Park tube. **Open** 11am-6pm Mon-Wed, Fri, Sat; 11am-7pm Thur. **Map** p131 C4 ❺

Comme des Garçons designer Rei Kawakubo's mould-breaking six-storey space combines the edgy energy of London's indoor markets – concrete floors, tills housed in corrugated-iron shacks – with exclusive labels. Her deconstructed tailoring is sold alongside collections by Alaïa, Lanvin and others, plus such conversation pieces as taxidermy and vintage pornography.

Fortnum & Mason

181 Piccadilly, W1A 1ER (7734 8040/ www.fortnumandmason.co.uk). Green Park tube. **Open** 10am-6.30pm Mon-Sat. *Restaurant & food hall only* noon-6pm Sun. **Map** p131 B4 ❺

Fortnum's famed food hall can get as packed as a tin of Portuguese Sardines Picante (£2.25). In preparation for its tercentenary in 2007, London's oldest department store is expanding the section into the basement and introducing a traiteur and wine bar. The upper floors, also getting a spruce-up, are essentially a very large, classy gift shop.

Georgina Goodman

12-14 Shepherd Street, W1J 7JF (7499 8599/www.georginagoodman. com). Green Park tube. **Open** 10am-6pm Mon-Sat. **Map** p131 B4 ❺

Footwear is displayed like artwork in this light-filled gallery/shop, and the workshop downstairs is a hive of creativity. Each of Goodman's bespoke, sculptural shoes is made from a single piece of untreated leather (from £650 for women; from £900 for men). The ready-to-wear women's range brings her individualistic approach to the masses.

Grays Antique Market & Grays in the Mews

58 Davies Street, W1K 5LP, & 1-7 Davies Mews, W1K 5AB (7629 7034/ www.graysantiques.com). Bond Street tube. **Open** 10am-6pm Mon-Fri. **Map** p131 ❻

Grays is just moments away from the chain-store Anywheresville of Oxford Street, yet decades apart. A liveried doorman greets you as you enter from South Molton Street. Inside are small shops selling jewellery; further back there are silver, glass and other antiques sellers. The more varied dealers in the Mews building make hunting for affordable gifts rewarding.

Miller Harris

21 Bruton Street, W1J 6QD (7629 7750/www.millerharris.com). Bond Street or Green Park tube. **Open** 10am-6pm Mon-Sat. **Map** p131 B4 ③①
Perfumer Lyn Harris has built a reputation as one of the industry's most highly regarded 'noses'. Bespoke fragrances are concocted at the original shop at 14 Needham Road, W11, but in this sleek flagship, you'll find her range of off-the-peg perfumes and body products, packed with rich natural oils.

Mulberry

41-42 New Bond Street, W1S 2RY (7491 3900/www.mulberry.com). Bond Street tube. **Open** 10am-6pm Mon-Wed, Fri, Sat; 10am-7pm Thur. **Map** p131 B3 ③②
Mulberry won the British Fashion Council's Accessory Designer of the Year award in 2004. Bags have been at the forefront, with the delightful Phoebe and Tyler joining the cult Bayswater and Roxanne. The men's accessory collection includes the new bestselling Woody bag. Clothes are interesting too.

Reiss

51 South Molton Street, W1K 5SD (7491 2208/www.reiss.co.uk). Oxford Circus tube. **Open** 10am-7pm Mon-Wed, Fri, Sat; 10am-8pm Thur; noon-6pm Sun. **Map** p131 B3 ③③
The clothes at Reiss's womenswear offshoot have a designer feel: skirts with unusual stitching or abstract patterns in the weave, cotton tops in contemporary blouson shapes, modern tailoring and understated draped, ruched or wrapped dresses. While they're not cheap, they certainly look more expensive than they are.

Rigby & Peller

22A Conduit Street, W1S 2XT (7491 2200/www.rigbyandpeller.com). Bond Street tube **Open** 9.30am-6pm Mon-Wed, Fri, Sat; 9.30am-7pm Thur. **Map** p131 C3 ③④
The emphasis at the Queen's corsetiere is on getting the fit right: once expert staff have measured you, they'll bring you selections of underwear to try from banks of drawers at the back. Rigby & Peller's own lacy, feminine designs are supplemented by high-quality brands. It's best to make an appointment.

Rupert Sanderson

33 Bruton Place, W1J 6NP (0870 750 9181/www.rupertsanderson.co.uk). Bond Street or Green Park tube. **Open** 10am-6pm Mon-Fri; 11am-6pm Sat. **Map** p131 B3 ③⑤
Feted by the fashion press, Sanderson prefers to focus on craftsmanship rather than passing trends. Yet his shoes somehow capture the current zeitgeist in a quintessentially English way. Shoes from £300.

Sac Frères

NEW *7 Grafton Street, W1S 4EJ (7495 9040/www.sacfreres.com). Green Park tube.* **Open** 10am-6pm Mon-Fri; 11am-5pm Sat. **Map** p131 B4 ③⑥
Iconic British style is in the bag. Sac Frères turns all sorts of unlikely materials into handbags and carry-alls: tanned soccer-ball cowhide, cricket-pad canvas, crimson cavalry twill, even the same burgundy, buttoned leather used on the seats in the House of Lords – all displayed alongside the objects that inspired them.

Smythson

40 New Bond Street, W1S 2DE (7629 8558/www.smythson.com). Bond Street tube. **Open** 9.30am-6pm Mon-Wed, Fri; 10am-6pm Thur, Sat. **Map** p131 B3 ③⑦
An elegant and classic selection of fine English stationery and gifts for those who see the luxuries of creamy paper, bespoke gold stamping and hand-engraving as de rigueur. Other classy (and pricey) items in the range include diaries, photo albums and wallets.

LONDON BY AREA

Westminster Abbey p152

Westminster to Kensington

LONDON BY AREA

Westminster & St James's

Westminster is for many the heart of London – if not England. It has been the seat of power for almost 1,000 years, since Edward the Confessor built his 'West Minster' and palace on marshy Thorney Island; in the 14th century the country's first Parliament met in **Westminster Abbey**. The area contains much of what the folks back home will expect you to see, including **Buckingham Palace**, the **Houses of Parliament** and **Nelson's Column**, along with major national cultural institutions. By its nature, Westminster is imposing rather than atmospheric; St James's, paticularly the lovely park, has a little more charm – in a very stately fashion, of course.

Sights & museums

Banqueting House

Whitehall, Westminster, SW1A 2ER (7930 4179/www.hrp.org.uk). Westminster tube/Charing Cross tube/rail. **Open** 10am-5pm Mon-Sat. Last entry 4.30pm. May close at short notice. **Admission** £4.50; free-£3.50 reductions. **Map** p147 E1 ❶
Designed by Inigo Jones in 1622, the exterior's austerity belies Rubens's sumptuous ceiling inside; call to check the hall is open before you visit. Charles I was beheaded just outside in 1649.

Buckingham Palace & Royal Mews

St James's, SW1A 1AA (7766 7300/ Royal Mews 7766 7302/www.royal collection.org.uk). Green Park or St James's Park tube/Victoria tube/rail. **Open** *State Rooms* late July-late Sept 9.45am-3.45pm daily. *Queen's Gallery* 10am-4.30pm daily. Closed during Ascot & state occasions. *Royal Mews* Mar-Oct 11am-3.15pm Mon-Thur, Sat, Sun (last entry 4.15pm when palace is open); late July-late Sept 10am-5pm daily (last entry 4.15pm). **Admission** *Palace* £14; free-£12.50 reductions. *Queen's Gallery* £7.50; free-£6 reductions. *Royal Mews* £6.50; free-£5.50 reductions. **Map** p146 C2 ❷

The world's most famous palace, built in 1703, started life as a grand house for the Duke of Buckingham, but George III liked it so much he bought it. His son, George IV, hired John Nash to convert it into a full-on palace, and work on the 600-room residence began in 1825. But the project was beset with disaster from the start. Nash was fired after George IV's death – he was too flighty, apparently – and the reliable but unimaginative Edward Blore was given the job to finish. After critics saw the result, they dubbed him 'Blore the Bore'. What's more, Queen Victoria, who was the first royal to live here, hated the place, calling it 'a disgrace to the country'.

Judge for yourself. During August and September, while the Windsors are on their holidays, the ostentatious State Apartments – used for banquets and investitures – open to the public. We reckon that after the initial thrill of being inside it's not all that interesting.

The Queen's Gallery contains highlights of Liz's decorative and fine art collection: Old Masters, Sèvres porcelain and the Diamond Diadem (familiar from millions of postage stamps) and other glittering baubles. Further along Buckingham Palace Road, the Royal Mews holds horses (when they're not out Trooping the Colour) and fabulous royal carriages.

Cabinet War Rooms & Churchill Museum

Clive Steps, King Charles Street, Westminster, SW1A 2AQ (7930 6961/www.iwm.org.uk). St James's Park or Westminster tube. **Open** 9.30am-6pm daily. Last entry 5pm. **Admission** £11; free-£8.50 reductions. **Map** p147 E2 ❸

This small underground set of rooms was Churchill's bunker during World War II. Every book, chart and pin in the map room remains where it was in 1945, as does the microphone Churchill used to broadcast to the nation. An impressive new museum charts his life with state-of-the-art displays.

Changing of the Guard

Buckingham Palace, St James's, SW1A 1AA (7321 2233/www.royal.gov.uk). Green Park or St James's Park tube/ Victoria tube/rail. **Ceremonies** *May-July* 11.30am daily. *Aug-Apr* alternate days. **Map** p146 C2 ❹

Scarlet coats and bearskin hats line up in the forecourt of Wellington Barracks from 10.45am; at 11.27am the soldiers march, accompanied by their band, to relieve the sentries in the forecourt of Buckingham Palace in an impressive 45-minute ceremony (cancelled in heavy rain). If there are four sentries at the front rather than two, it means HM is in residence. The guard is also changed at Horse Guards Parade, which links St James's Park with Whitehall, at 10am daily (11am Sundays).

Clarence House

St James's, SW1A 1AA (7766 7303/ www.royalcollection.org.uk). Green Park tube. **Open** *Aug-early Oct* 10am-5.30pm daily (last entry 4.30pm). **Admission** £7; free-£4 reductions. All tickets must be pre-booked. **Map** p147 D1 ❺

Standing austerely beside St James's Palace, Clarence House was erected between 1825 and 1827. The house has been much altered by its many royal inhabitants, among them the Queen Mother, who lived there until she died in 2002. Prince Charles and his sons have since moved in, but parts of the house are open to the public in summer:

LONDON BY AREA

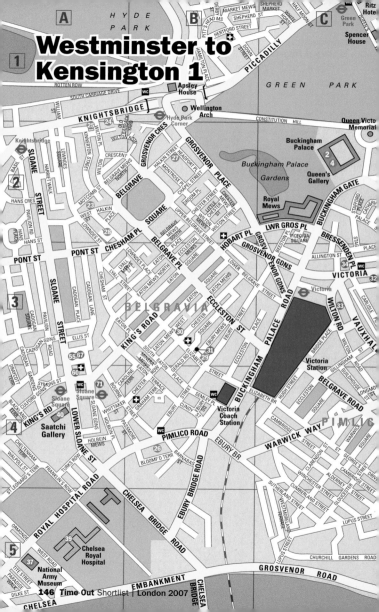

Westminster to Kensington 1

HYDE PARK

HYDE PARK

GREEN PARK

GREEN PARK

PICCADILLY

KNIGHTSBRIDGE

CONSTITUTION HILL

Apsley House
Wellington Arch
Hyde Park Corner

Ritz Hotel
Green Park
Spencer House

Queen Victoria Memorial

Buckingham Palace

Buckingham Palace Gardens

Queen's Gallery

Royal Mews

BELGRAVE SQUARE

BELGRAVIA

GROSVENOR PLACE

HOBART PL

LWR GROS PL

BUCKINGHAM GATE

VICTORIA

BRESSENDEN PL

VAUXHALL

SLOANE STREET

BELGRAVE PL

CHESHAM PL

PONT ST

SLOANE STREET

KING'S ROAD

ECCLESTON ST

GROSVENOR GDNS

BUCKINGHAM PALACE ROAD

WILTON RD

Victoria Station

Victoria Coach Station

Saatchi Gallery

KING'S RD

LOWER SLOANE ST

PIMLICO ROAD

EBURY BR

WARWICK WAY

BELGRAVE ROAD

PIMLICO

ROYAL HOSPITAL ROAD

CHELSEA BRIDGE ROAD

EBURY BRIDGE ROAD

Chelsea Royal Hospital

National Army Museum

GROSVENOR ROAD

CHELSEA EMBANKMENT

CHELSEA BRIDGE

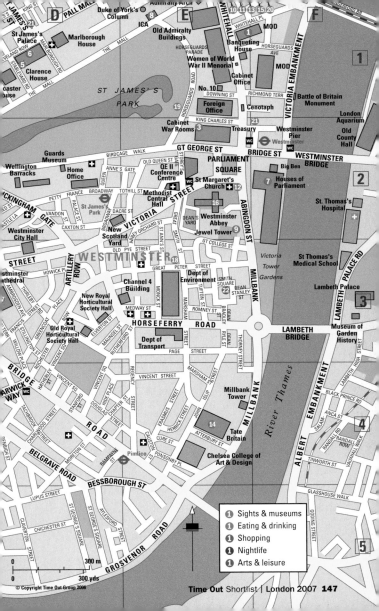

1 Sights & museums
1 Eating & drinking
1 Shopping
1 Nightlife
1 Arts & leisure

© Copyright Time Out Group 2006

ICA

five receiving rooms and the small but significant art collection, strong in 20th-century British art. Tickets tend to sell out by the end of August.

Gun Salutes

Green Park, St James's, W1, & Tower of London, The City, EC3. **Dates** 6 Feb (Accession Day); 21 Apr & 17 June (Queen's birthdays); 2 June (Coronation Day); 10 June (Duke of Edinburgh's birthday); 17 June (Trooping the Colour); State Opening of Parliament; 11 Nov (Lord Mayor's Show); 12 Nov (Remembrance Sunday); & state visits. **Map** p147 D1 ⑥

For the State Opening of Parliament soldiers set up huge guns in Green Park and unleash a fusillade. The other dates see a mounted charge through Hyde Park in time for a 41-gun salute at noon (or 11am on the Queen's birthday); another company fires a 62-gun salute at the Tower of London at 1pm.

Houses of Parliament

Parliament Square, Westminster, SW1A 0AA (Commons 7219 4272/ Lords 7219 3107/tours 7219 4206/ www.parliament.uk). Westminster tube. **Open** in session only; phone for details. **Admission** *Visitors' Gallery free.*

Tours summer only £7; free-£5 reductions. **Map** p147 F2 ⑦

Completed in 1860, this neo-Gothic extravaganza was the creation of architect Charles Barry, who won the competition to replace the original Houses of Parliament, which were destroyed by fire in 1834. Augustus Pugin designed the gorgeous interiors. The only remaining parts of the original palace are the Jewel Tower (below) and Westminster Hall, one of the finest medieval buildings in Europe. There is a visitors' cafeteria and you can watch MPs and lords in session from the galleries. Parliament goes into recess in summer, when there are public tours of the main ceremonial rooms, including Westminster Hall and the two Houses.

ICA

The Mall, St James's, SW1Y 5AH (box office 7930 3647/www.ica. org.uk). Piccadilly Circus tube/Charing Cross tube/rail. **Open** *Galleries* noon-7.30pm daily. **Membership.** **Map** p147 E1 ⑧

The Institute of Contemporary Arts is best known for uncompromising exhibitions, but it also has an art cinema and a performance space that puts on very decent gigs. The Beck's Futures exhibition and prize (mid March-mid May) is a regular here. There's a small daily membership charge.

Jewel Tower

Abingdon Street, Westminster, SW1P 3JY (7222 2219/www.english-heritage.org.uk). Westmintster tube. **Open** Apr-Oct 10am-5pm daily. Nov-Mar 10am-4pm daily. **Admission** £2.60; free-£2 reductions. **Credit** MC, V. **Map** p147 E2 ⑨

The storehouse for the monarch's personal valuables, the Jewel Tower was the only part of the original medieval Palace of Westminster to survive the fire of 1834. It houses various displays and archaeological finds.

National Gallery

Trafalgar Square, St James's, WC2N 5DN (7747 2885/www.nationalgallery. org.uk). Charing Cross tube/rail. **Open**

LONDON BY AREA

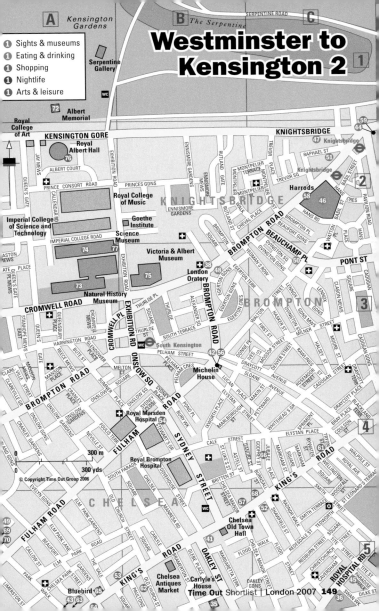

A Kensington Gardens
B The Serpentine
C

SERPENTINE ROAD

- **1** Sights & museums
- **1** Eating & drinking
- **1** Shopping
- **1** Nightlife
- **1** Arts & leisure

Serpentine Gallery

WC

72 Albert Memorial

Royal College of Art

KENSINGTON GORE

Royal Albert Hall

KNIGHTSBRIDGE

59
47 Knightsbridge
51

JAY MEWS
ALBERT COURT

PRINCE CONSORT ROAD

CALLENDAR RD

QUEEN'S GATE

76

EXHIBITION ROAD

ENNISMORE MEWS

PRINCES GDNS

ENNISMORE GARDENS

RUTLAND GATE

TREVOR PL
MONTPELIER TERRACE
MONTPELIER PLACE
TREVOR SQ

RAPHAEL ST

BASIL ST

Knightsbridge

Royal College of Music

K N I G H T S B R I D G E

Harrods

58
46

HANS CRES

PAVILION ROAD

2

Imperial College of Science and Technology

Goethe Institute

ENNISMORE GARDENS

Science Museum

CHEVAL PLACE

RUTLAND ST

BROMPTON ROAD

BEAUCHAMP PL

BROMPTON PL
BEAUFORT GDNS

HANS RD
HANS PL

PONT ST

IMPERIAL COLLEGE ROAD

74 **77**

73

Natural History Museum

75

Victoria & Albert Museum

38
London Oratory

OVINGTON GDNS

OVINGTON SQ

50

YEOMAN'S ROW

49
EGERTON TERR

EGERTON GDNS

LENNOX GDNS

CADOGAN SQUARE

3

CROMWELL ROAD

EXHIBITION RD
CROMWELL PL

THURLOE PL

THURLOE ST

ALEXANDER SQ

BROMPTON ROAD

EGERTON CRES

EGERTON GDNS

B R O M P T O N

WALTON STREET

HASKER ST

FIRST ST

MILNER ST

OVINGTON GDNS MWS

MOORE ST

CADOGAN GDNS

SOUTH TERRACE

South Kensington

WC

42 56

Michelin House

PELHAM ST
PELHAM CRES
PELHAM PLACE

SOUTH TERRACE

DENYER ST
DRAYCOTT AVENUE

SLOANE AVENUE

DONNE PL

HALSEY ST

RAWLINGS STREET

ROSEMOOR STREET

DRAYCOTT PLACE

BRAY PLACE

COULSON ST

4

BROMPTON ROAD

ONSLOW SQUARE

ONSLOW GDNS

SUMNER PLACE

SYDNEY PLACE

FULHAM ROAD

Royal Marsden Hospital

SYDNEY STREET

BURY WK

LUCAN PLACE

MARLBOROUGH STREET

MAKINS ST

WHITEHEAD'S GRO

SPRIMONT PLACE

ELYSTAN PLACE

MARKHAM SQUARE

WELLINGTON SQ

BYWATER ST

TRYON ST

WALPOLE ST

ROYAL AVE

WOODFALL ST

SMITH

KING'S ROAD

Royal Brompton Hospital

CALE STREET

BRITTEN ST

ST LUKE'S ST

ASTELL ST

SOUTH PARADE

TANCRED ST

GODFREY ST

JUBILEE PL

BURNSALL ST

66

61

5

C H E L S E A

EVELYN GDNS

FULHAM ROAD

OLD CHURCH STREET

CHELSEA MANOR STREET

DOVEHOUSE STREET

SYDNEY STREET

CHELSEA SQUARE

MANRESA RD

THE VALE OF HEALTH

CHELSEA MANOR

57
68
WC

RADNOR WALK

SMITH TERRACE

BRAMERTON ST

52

Chelsea Old Town Hall

FLOOD ST

REDESDALE ST

TEDWORTH

TITE ST

ST LEONARD'S TERRACE

49
69
70

ELM PARK GARDENS

BEAUFORT ST

ELM PARK ROAD

THE VALE

CHELSEA PARK GARDENS

CARLYLE SQUARE

OLD CHURCH STREET

PAULTONS SQUARE

53

KING'S ROAD

MARGARETTA TERR

OAKLEY GARDENS

OAKLEY STREET

GLEBE PLACE

41

Chelsea Antiques Market

Carlyle's House

CHRISTCHURCH STREET

REDBURN STREET

SHAWFIELD ST

FLOOD WALK

CHELSEA MANOR GDNS

RADNOR WALK

ROYAL HOSPITAL RD

CAVERSHAM ST

SWAN WK

45

5

Bluebird **65**

43 63
64

LIMERSTON ST

BEAUFORT ST

CALOW ST

ELM PK

CHELSEA PARK GDNS

WALK

THE VALE

KING'S ROAD

OLD CHURCH ST

PAULTONS

36

0 — 300 m
0 — 300 yds

© Copyright Time Out Group 2006

Trafalgar Square

10am-6pm Mon, Tue, Thur-Sun; 10am-9pm Wed. *Tours* 11.30am, 2.30pm daily; additionally 6pm, 6.30pm Wed; 11.30am, 12.30pm, 2.30pm, 3.30pm Sat. **Admission** free. *Special exhibitions* prices vary. **Map** p147 E1 ⑩

One of the greatest art collections in the world, with more than 2,000 western European pieces, starting with 13th-century religious works and approaching our time via da Vinci, Raphael, Rubens, Rembrandt, Van Dyck, Caravaggio, Turner, Constable, Gainsborough, Cézanne and Picasso. The stars, however, are Impressionist and post-Impressionist: Monet's *Water Lilies* series and Van Gogh's *Chair*.

Event highlights 'Cézanne in Britain' (4 Oct 2006-7 Jan 2007), Velázquez (18 Oct 2006-21 Jan 2007).

National Portrait Gallery

2 St Martin's Place, St James's, WC2H 0HE (7306 0055/tours 7312 2483/www.npg.org.uk). Leicester Square tube/Charing Cross tube/rail. **Open** 10am-6pm Mon-Wed, Sat, Sun; 10am-9pm Thur, Fri. *Tours* times vary, phone for details. **Admission** free. *Special*

exhibitions prices vary. **Map** p147 E1 ⑪

The famous faces range from Tudor royalty to present-day celebrities. Highlights include the only known contemporary portrait of William Shakespeare and a painting of Henry VIII by Holbein. Dickens, Darwin and Disraeli are on the first floor. There's a good restaurant on the top floor.

Event highlights Photographer Angus McBean's portraits from the 1930s to the '60s (to 22 Oct 2006). David Hockney portraits, including new works specially created for the show (12 Oct 2006-21 Jan 2007). 'Portraits in Fashion' 22 Feb-28 May 2007; 'Daily Encounters' (photojournalism) July-Oct 2007.

St Margaret's Church

Parliament Square, Westminster, SW1P 3PL (7654 4840/www. westminster-abbey.org/stmargarets). St James's Park or Westminster tube. **Open** 9.30am-3.45pm Mon-Fri; 9.30am-1.45pm Sat; 2-5pm Sun. *Services* 11am Sun. **Admission** free. **Map** p147 E2 ⑫

Built from 1486 to 1523, Westminster Abbey's neighbour has some of the best pre-Reformation stained glass in London. Later windows celebrate explorer Sir Walter Raleigh, executed in Old Palace Yard in 1618, and poet John Milton, who was married here.

St Martin-in-the-Fields

Trafalgar Square, St James's, WC2N 4JJ (7766 1100/www.stmartin-in-the-fields.org). Leicester Square tube/Charing Cross tube/rail. **Open** *Church* 8am-6.30pm daily. *Evening concerts* 7.30pm Thur-Sat & alternate Tue. **Admission** free. **Map** p147 F1 ⑬

A church has stood here since the 13th century, 'in the fields' between Westminster and the City; this one dates from 1726. Best known for its classical music concerts, it also has a brass-rubbing centre and a good café in the crypt. A refurbishment project should be finished in 2007.

Tate Britain

Millbank, Westminster, SW1P 4RG (7887 8000/www.tate.org.uk). Pimlico tube. **Open** 10am-5.50pm daily. *Late*

Old-school dinners

The British food movement, kick-started by Fergus Henderson with the opening of St John (p88) in 1994, has moved squarely into the mainstream. More British restaurants (most recently Roast, p65, and Canteen, p175) and a renewed interest in indigenous ingredients and recipes followed. And now the National Gallery has collaborated with restaurateur Oliver Peyton to unleash a no-holds-barred Brit experience in the form of the National Dining Rooms (p153). This isn't the first time Peyton has masterminded a British menu: in 2005 he opened Inn the Park (in St James's Park, p153). But with the National Dining Rooms he'll reach – and have to please – a far wider audience.

We went along just after it opened to see how things were going. We loved the British retro-chic look (care of über-designer David Collins), but it was the menu that really blew us away. This is trad English fare at its best: oxtail soup accompanied by bone marrow-stuffed dumplings (£7.50), say, or pork belly and pease pudding (£14.50). Puddings are hearty (treacle tart or lemon posset, for example) and the choice of cheeses splendid: Blackstick Blue, from Lancashire, is just one of many intriguing options.

There's a very affordable café as well, offering snacks such as smoked mackerel pâté and apple and sage sausage roll. Best of all is the baking: Bakewell tarts, Victoria sponges and gingerbread men are all present and correct. And you will rarely see such a wide selection of quality British drinks anywhere.

So let's hope the revival of the nation's cuisine continues – but regardless of that, the National Dining Rooms should be on every visitor's must-try list.

opening to 10pm last Fri of mth. *Tours*
11am, noon, 2pm, 3pm Mon-Fri; noon,
3pm Sat, Sun. **Admission** free. *Special
exhibitions* prices vary. *Tours* free.
Map p147 E4 ⑭

The original Tate has London's second
greatest collection of historical art,
after the National Gallery. Here it's all
made in Britain: Hogarth, William
Blake, Gainsborough, Constable,
Reynolds, Bacon and Moore, and a
whole lot of Turner. There are living
artists, too, with works by Peter Blake,
Howard Hodgkin, Lucian Freud and
David Hockney. You can see both
Tates in one trip thanks to the boat service between here and Tate Modern.
Event highlights Annual show for the
contemporary art Turner Prize (17 Oct
2006-7 Jan 2007).

Trafalgar Square

Westminster. Charing Cross tube/rail.
Map p147 E1 ⑮

The centrepiece of London, Trafalgar
Square was begun in 1820s and named
after Admiral Horatio Nelson's great
1805 victory. It's where big demonstrations often finish up, with speech-
es from the base of Nelson's Column,
and was hugely improved by a partial
pedestrianisation a few years ago. One-
off entertainment events are common,
and it's a boisterous spot on New
Year's Eve. The plinth at the square's
north-western corner was empty for
over 150 years until it began to host a
series of temporary works. The current
one, by leading Britartist Marc Quinn,
is a statue of a pregnant woman who
born with no arms and shortened legs.
Event highlights In April 2007 the
fourth plinth sculpture will be changed
to Thomas Schütte's perspex acrylic
structure *Hotel for the Birds*.

Westminster Abbey

*20 Dean's Yard, Westminster, SW1P
3PA (7222 5152/tours 7654 4900/
www.westminster-abbey.org). St James's
Park or Westminster tube.* **Open** *Nave
& Royal Chapels* 9.30am-3.45pm Mon,
Tue, Thur, Fri; 9.30am-7pm Wed; 9am-
1.45pm Sat. *Abbey Museum & Chapter
House* 10.30am-4pm Mon-Sat. *Cloisters*

Inn the Park

8am-6pm Mon-Sat. *Garden* Apr-Sept
10am-6pm Tue-Thur; Oct-Mar 10am-
4pm Tue-Thur. Last entry 1hr before
closing. **Admission** £10; free-£6
reductions. *Abbey Museum & Chapter
House* free. **Map** p147 E2 ⑯

Since Edward the Confessor built a
church here just in time for his own
funeral in 1066, a 'who's who' of mon-
archy has been buried here, and, with
two exceptions (Edwards V and VIII),
every ruler since William the Conqueror
(1066) has been crowned in the abbey.
Of the original church, only the Pyx
Chamber (the one-time royal treasury)
and the Norman undercroft remain: the
Gothic nave and choir were rebuilt in
the 13th century, the Henry VII Chapel,
with its spectacular fan vaulting, was
added in 1503-12, and Nicholas
Hawksmoor's west towers in 1745.

The interior is cluttered with monuments to statesmen, scientists, musi-
cians and poets. The centrepiece of the
octagonal Chapter House is its faded
13th-century tiled floor, while the Little
Cloister, with its pretty garden, offers

respite from the crowds, especially during free lunchtime concerts (call for details). Come early, late, or on midweek afternoons to avoid the crowds.

Westminster Cathedral

Victoria Street, Westminster, SW1P 1QW (7798 9055/tours 7798 9064/ www.westminstercathedral.org.uk). St James's Park tube/Victoria tube/rail. **Open** 7am-7pm Mon-Fri, Sun; 8am-7pm Sat. *Campanile* Apr-Nov 9.30am-12.30pm, 1-5pm daily. Dec-Mar 9.30am-12.30pm, 1-5pm Thur-Sun. **Admission** free; donations welcome. *Campanile* £3; £1.50 reductions. No credit cards. **Map** p147 D3 **⓱**

This neo-Byzantine confection is Britain's premier Catholic cathedral, built between 1895 and 1903. The inside remains unfinished, but you can get a taste of what's planned from the magnificent marble columns and mosaics. Eric Gill's Stations of the Cross sculptures (1914-18) are world renowned: simple and objective, they were controversial at the time of installation. Dark wood floors and flickering candles add to the drama. The view from the bell tower is superb: best of all, it's got a lift.

Eating & drinking

Cinnamon Club

Old Westminster Library, 30-32 Great Smith Street, Westminster, SW1P 3BU (7222 2555/www.cinnamonclub.com). St James's Park or Westminster tube. **Open** 7.30-9.30am, noon-2.30pm, 6-10.45pm Mon-Fri; 6-10.45pm Sat. **£££ Modern Indian.** **Map** p147 E2 **⓲**

Housed in a converted 19th-century library, this elegant and spacious restaurant has the feel of an exclusive gentlemen's club. Chef Vivek Singh's regularly changing menu is a show-stopper from beginning to end; be sure to save room for dessert.

Inn the Park

NEW *St James's Park, St James's, SW1A 2BJ (7451 9999/www.innthe park.co.uk). St James's Park tube.* **Open** 8am-11am, noon-3pm, 5-10pm Mon-Fri; 9-11am, noon-4pm, 5-10pm Sat, Sun. **££. British/café.** Map p147 E1 **⓳**

Nudging the lakefront and surrounded by leafy greens, Inn The Park makes a pleasant oasis for weary tourists in St James's Park. Simple yet striking menus complement the relaxed atmosphere: as well as full-on lunch and dinner menus, there are informal teas and breakfasts available.

National Dining Rooms

NEW *Sainsbury Wing, The National Gallery, Trafalgar Square, St James's, WC2N 5DN (7747 2525). Charing Cross tube/rail.* **Open** 10am-5.30pm Mon, Tue; 10am-8.30pm Wed; 10am-5.30pm Thur-Sun. **£-£££. British. Map** p147 F1 **⓴**
See box p151.

Red Lion

48 Parliament Street, Westminster, SW1A 2NH (7930 5826). Westminster tube. **Open** 11am-11pm Mon-Fri; 11am-9.30pm Sat; noon-7pm Sun. **Pub. Map** p147 E2 **㉑**

No (public) bar sums up Westminster as well as this famous boozer, just yards from the Houses of Parliament. Upstairs is a grill room, and the cellar (not always open) has a decent enough bar; but the handsome, skinny ground floor, which comes complete with a division bell to summon absentee MPs to the vote, a TV tuned to BBC Parliament and walls lined with memorabilia, is where the action is.

Shopping

Berry Bros & Rudd

3 St James's Street, St James's, SW1A 1EG (7396 9600/www.bbr.com). Green Park tube. **Open** 10am-6pm Mon-Fri; 10am-4pm Sat. **Map** p147 D1 **㉒**

Berry's has been operating as a wine merchant in St James's since the middle of the 17th century, and traditional wine regions still rule the roost. Off the gorgeously rickety wood-panelled main room there are three chambers showing just part of the company's vast selection.

LONDON BY AREA

Arts & leisure

St John's, Smith Square

Smith Square, Westminster, SW1P 3HA (7222 1061/www.sjss.org.uk). Westminster tube. **Open** box office 10am-5pm Mon-Fri. **Map** p147 E3 ㉒

This elegant 18th-century former church hosts a nightly programme (except during summer) of orchestral and chamber concerts, with occasional vibrant recitals on its magnificent Klais organ. There's also a wonderfully secluded restaurant in the crypt, open whether or not any music is scheduled.

Victoria to Pimlico

It's a bit of a comedown from the grandeurs of Westminster to the everyday offices and shops of Victoria. There are a few handsome houses and squares but this is typical rail (and coach) station hinterland, grotty B&Bs and all. Pimlico is a mixed residential area not without its charms; Belgravia is a step or three upmarket.

Eating & drinking

Amaya

NEW *Halkin Arcade, Belgravia, SW1X 8JT (7823 1166/www.realindianfood. com). Knightsbridge tube.* **Open** 12.30-2.15pm, 6-11.15pm Mon-Fri; 12.30-2.30pm, 6-11.15pm Sat; 12.45-2.45pm, 6-10.15pm Sun. **£££. Modern Indian**. **Map** p146 A2 ㉓

Amaya is doing for Indian food what Nobu did for Japanese – namely making it cool, even fashionable. It's the acclaimed – and highly swish – newish venture from the Panjabi sisters, and specialises in kebabs.

Blue Bar

The Berkeley, Wilton Place, SW1X 7RL (7235 6000/www.the-berkeley.co.uk). Hyde Park Corner tube. **Open** 4pm-1am Mon-Fri, Sun; 3pm-1am Sat. **Map** p147 A1 ㉔

This deeply stylish venue is located by the lobby of the Berkeley hotel. The drinks list offers a large selection of high-end champagnes, classic and contemporary cocktails, wines by the glass, and 50 whiskies. Bar snacks include upscale 'oriental tapas'.

Boxwood Café

The Berkeley, Wilton Place, Belgravia, SW1X 7RL (7235 1010/www.gordon ramsay.com). Hyde Park Corner or Knightsbridge tube. **Open** noon-3pm, 6-11pm Mon-Fri; noon-4pm, 6-11pm Sat, Sun. **£££. Modern British**. **Map** p147 A2 ㉕

The posh Berkeley hotel might be old-school, but the Boxwood Café feels young and individualistic. Staff are easy-going, the dining room comfortable and the menu stuffed with indulgent and cheekily conceived food.

Hunan

51 Pimlico Road, Pimlico, SW1W 8NE (7730 5712). Sloane Square tube. **Open** 12.30-2.30pm, 6.30-11.30pm Mon-Sat. **££-££££. Chinese**. **Map** p147 B4 ㉖

This eccentric establishment remains one of the most delightful Chinese restaurants in London. Let staff decide what to feed you, then wait for a procession of small and delicious dishes to arrive. The standard of cooking is high.

Nahm

The Halkin, Halkin Street, Belgravia, SW1X 7DJ (7333 1234/www.nahm. como.bz). Hyde Park Corner tube. **Open** noon-2.30pm, 7-10.30pm Mon-Fri; 7-10.30pm Sat; 7-10pm Sun. **£££. Thai. Map** p146 B2 ㉗

Kitchen maestro David Thompson serves inspired modern Thai cooking at this stylish restaurant, in the exclusive Halkin hotel. When the thought-provoking menu works – royal Thai classics made with first-rate ingredients – it's simply spectacular.

Star Tavern

6 Belgrave Mews West, Belgravia, SW1X 8HT (7235 3019/www. fullers.co.uk). Hyde Park Corner or Knightsbridge tube/Victoria tube/rail. **Open** 11am-11pm Mon-Sat; noon-10.30pm Sun. **Pub. Map** p146 A2 ㉘

Amaya

Behind the heavily fortified German Embassy, the Star was once a honey-pot for London's gangsters and film stars, who would frequent the tiny bar area, expansive lounge and first-floor room. These days Fuller's ales and two welcoming fires draw locals and an after-work crowd.

Thomas Cubitt

NEW *44 Elizabeth Street, Belgravia, SW1W 9PA (7730 6060/www.the thomascubitt.co.uk). Hyde Park Corner tube/Victoria tube/rail.* **Open** noon-11pm daily. **Pub. Map** p146 B3 **29**

This is how a pub renovation should be done. The new oak panelling, new wooden floor, fireplaces and sturdy bar are perfectly in keeping with the Grade II-listed building. The ground floor bustles with people enjoying Old Speckled Hen and Marston's Pedigree, or bar snacks such as oysters or posh sausage and mash. The first floor is occupied by a more ambitious dining room.

Shopping

Elizabeth Street in Victoria is blessed with boutiques, beauty shops and foodie havens.

Baker & Spice

54-56 Elizabeth Street, Victoria, SW1W 9PD (7730 3033/www.bakerand spice.com). Sloane Square tube/Victoria tube/rail. **Open** 8am-7pm Mon-Sat. **Map** p146 B3 **30**

Despite being a chain, Baker & Spice is a byword for quality in breads, pastries, cakes and tarts. Breads include rye, chollah and San Francisco sourdough. Soups and savouries are also available, and you can eat in or take away.

Poilâne

46 Elizabeth Street, Victoria, SW1W 9PA (7808 4910/www.poilane.fr). Sloane Square tube/Victoria tube/rail. **Open** 7.30am-7.30pm Mon-Fri; 7.30am-6pm Sat. **Map** p146 B3 **31**

This popular bakery's sourdough might be the most famous bread in the world. Pesticide-free wheat and spelt flour is mixed with salt from the violet-scented marshes of Guérande in western France; then, after fermentation, the loaves are baked in wood-fired ovens for an hour.

Nightlife

Pacha London

Terminus Place, Victoria, SW1V 1JR (7833 3139/www.pachalondon.com). Victoria tube/rail. **Open** 10pm-5am Fri; 10pm-6am Sat. *Bar* 10pm-3am Fri, Sat. **Admission** £15-£20. **Map** p146 C3 **32**

This lavish outpost of the Ibiza club giant was truly made for lording it. A heady mix of chandeliers, oak panels and a stained-glass ceiling ensure a chic experience, despite the fact it's located in a bus depot. Glammed-up clubbers shake their booty to rocking house beats courtesy of Hed Kandi, among others.

Arts & leisure

Apollo Victoria Theatre

Wilton Road, Pimlico, SW1V 1LL (7834 6318/www.apollovictoria.co.uk). Pimlico tube. **Map** p146 C3 **33**

From September 2006, *Wicked* will be in residence. A smash hit stateside, the musical tells the story of the good and wicked witches from before *The Wizard of Oz* began.

Victoria Palace Theatre

Victoria Street, Pimlico, SW1E 5EA (0870 895 5577/www.victoriapalace theatre.co.uk). Victoria tube/rail. **Map** p146 C3 **34**

The Palace secured the prestigious Time Out Live Award for Best Musical in 2006 with a tremendous version of the hit film *Billy Elliot*, scored by Elton John, and directed by Stephen Daldry.

Knightsbridge & Chelsea

Knightsbridge is where the money comes out to play: in strings of designer shops and fashionable restaurants where your credit card had better be gold. It's for all that neither hip nor particularly stylish: it's largely old-school money, which makes for great people-watching. South Kensington is more of the same, with a slightly lower stuffiness rating.

Money talks in Chelsea, too. The heart of both 1960s Swinging London and 1970s punk, it now epitomises the city's take on café society. The cost of living has seen off all but the most successful painters and punks. A redevelopment of Sloane Square promises well, but for the time being means construction works are in progress at the top of the enjoyable artery of King's Road.

Sights & museums

Carlyle's House

24 Cheyne Row, Chelsea, SW3 5HL (7352 7087/www.nationaltrust.org.uk). Sloane Square tube. **Open** 2-5pm Wed-Fri; 11am-5pm Sat, Sun. Closed Nov-late Mar. **Admission** £4.20. No credit cards. **Map** p149 B5 ⸬
Thomas Carlyle and his wife Jane moved to this four-storey house in 1834. Later it was preserved as a museum, giving a snapshot of Victorian life from the basement kitchen, with its little bed for the maid, up to Carlyle's attic office.

Chelsea Physic Garden

66 Royal Hospital Road (entrance on Swan Walk), Chelsea, SW3 4HS (7352 5646/www.chelseaphysicgarden. co.uk). Sloane Square tube. **Open** Apr-Oct noon-5pm Wed; 2-6pm Sun. **Admission** £6.50; free-£4 reductions. *Tours* free. **Map** p149 C5 ⸬
The garden was set up in 1673, but the key phase of development was in the 18th century. The grounds are filled with beds of healing herbs and rare trees, dye plants and medicinal vegetables.

National Army Museum

Royal Hospital Road, Chelsea, SW3 4HT (7730 0717/www.national-army-museum.ac.uk). Sloane Square tube. **Open** 10am-5.30pm daily. **Admission** free. **Map** p146 A5 ⸬

Eccentric exhibits and displays make this museum far more entertaining than the modern exterior might suggest. The collection runs from Agincourt in 1415 to National Service in the 1950s. Major Michael 'Bronco' Lane, who climbed Everest, has kindly donated his frostbitten fingertips.

Oratory Catholic Church (Brompton Oratory)

Thurloe Place, Brompton Road, South Kensington, SW7 2RP (7808 0900/ www.bromptonoratory.com). South Kensington tube. **Open** 6.30am-8pm daily. *Services* phone for details. **Admission** free; donations appreciated. **Map** p149 B3 ⸬
The second-biggest Catholic church in the country (after Westminster Cathedral) was completed in 1884 but feels older – partly from its Baroque Italianate style, but also because many of its marbles, mosaics and statuary pre-date the structure. The interior is vast, magnificent and ornate.

Royal Hospital Chelsea

Royal Hospital Road, Chelsea, SW3 4SR (7881 5200/www.chelsea-pensioners.org.uk). Sloane Square tube. **Open** *Oct-Apr* 10am-noon, 2-4pm Mon-Sat. *May-Sept* 10am-noon, 2-4pm Mon-Sun. **Admission** free. **Map** p146 A5 ⸬
About 350 Chelsea Pensioners (retired soldiers) live here. The Hospital was founded in 1682 by Charles II and designed by Sir Christopher Wren, with additions by Robert Adam and Sir John Soane. There's a museum about the history of the pensioners.

Saatchi Gallery

NEW *Duke of York's HQ, off King's Road, Chelsea, SW3 4RY (www.saatchi-gallery.co.uk). Sloane Square tube.* **Open/admission** contact for details before visiting. **Map** p146 A4 ⸬
Charles Saatchi, the godfather of BritArt, has found an imposing new home for his collection. In spring 2007 it will be on show once more at the Duke of York's HQ, by then transformed into 50,000 square feet of rectilinear white space with a café/bar attached.

Event highlights 'The Triumph of Painting': the epic cycle of contemporary painting shows restarts with Part 3.

Eating & drinking

Apartment 195

195 King's Road, Chelsea, SW3 5ED (7351 5195/www.apartment195.co.uk). Sloane Square tube. **Open** 4-11pm Mon-Sat. **Bar. Map** p149 B5 ④

Apartment 195 is a lovely space, its wood panelling and battered leather seats sexed up with bright pop art and uptempo sounds. Saucily clad female mixologists serve stunning cocktails, while the decent bar menu is tailored to deep pockets.

Bibendum

Michelin House, 81 Fulham Road, Chelsea, SW3 6RD (7581 5817/ www.bibendum.co.uk). South Kensington tube. **Open** noon-2.30pm, 7-11.30pm Mon-Fri; 12.30-3pm, 7-11.30pm Sat; 12.30-3pm, 7-10.30pm Sun. **££-£££. Modern European. Map** p149 B4 ④

If you go for Bibendum's three-course prix-fixe menu at £28.50, you'll feel decidedly pleased at what good value it is. Meals here – one of Conran's finest establishments – are usually faultless, and you get to eat in a glorious room.

Chutney Mary

535 King's Road, Fulham, SW10 0SZ (7351 3113/www.realindianfood.com). Fulham Broadway tube. **Open** 6.30-11.30pm Mon-Fri; 12.30-3pm, 6.30-11.30pm Sat; 12.30-3pm, 6.30-10.30pm Sun. **£££. Indian. Map** p149 A5 ④

Run by the Panjabi sisters – of Amaya and Masala Zone fame – this fine-dining restaurant boasts an airy conservatory, decorated in colonial style, contrasting with a more formal dining area. Spicing is well balanced and the wine list strong.

Fifth Floor

Harvey Nichols, Knightsbridge, SW1X 7RJ (7235 5250/www.harveynichols. com). Knightsbridge tube. **Open** *Café 8am-10pm Mon-Sat; 10am-6pm Sun. Restaurant noon-3pm, 6-11pm Mon-Thur; noon-3.30pm, 6-11pm Fri; noon-11pm Sat; noon-3.30pm Sun. ££ café. £££ restaurant.* **Modern European. Map** p149 C2 ④

The Fifth Floor recently had a revamp that brought in a new chef – both have proved to be successful changes. From the pale blue, rounded space to the staff's professionalism, everything now seems spot on again. The main courses are perhaps a little small, but the density of flavours compensates.

Gordon Ramsay

68 Royal Hospital Road, Chelsea, SW3 4HP (7352 4441/3334/www.gordon ramsay.com). Sloane Square tube. **Open** noon-2pm, 6.30-10.15pm Mon-Fri. **££££. Modern European. Map** p149 C5 ④

Winning the lottery is easier than getting a table at the home base of Britain's most talented restaurateur, but if you manage it, you'll be bowled over by the experience. A perky three-course set lunch menu is a viable option for those of us who aren't millionaires, and dishes are generous, faultlessly prepared and rewarding.

Ladurée

NEW *Harrods (Hans Road entrance), Knightsbridge, SW1X 7XL (7893 8293). Knightsbridge tube.* **Open** 9am-9pm Mon-Sat; noon-6pm Sun. **££. Café. Map** p149 C2 ④

Ladurée is a fantasy of macaroons, couverture and delicate pastry, enough to satisfy the cravings of a sweet-tooth fairy. There's also a little bar, immaculate hot dishes and a room that's stunning, even by Harrods' standards.

Mr Chow

151 Knightsbridge, Knightsbridge, SW1X 7PA (7589 7347/www.mrchow. com). Knightsbridge tube. **Open** 12.30-3pm, 7pm-midnight daily. **£££. Chinese. Map** p149 A2 ④

Mr Chow is the Ivy of Chinese restaurants: long-established, much loved and fabulously glamorous in a lived-in way. The food is surprisingly good and authentic, given that the ambience and clientele are decidedly Western.

Get the concept?

Where can you find a pair of pristine post-war Lady armchairs designed by Marco Zanuso, Dosa silk pyjamas, Rupert Sanderson heels, a facsimile of Sylvia Plath's *Ariel* manuscript and a mini Rolleiflex under one roof? Part lifestyle boutique, part design gallery, the Shop at Bluebird (p164) is making the King's Road rock again.

Shop at Bluebird moved into Terence Conran's restaurant/café/deli complex at the end of 2005, occupying the ground floor of the art deco Bluebird garage. The capacious space is an ever-shifting showcase of clothing for men, women and children, lingerie, shoes and accessories, furniture, books and gadgets.

Owners John and Belle Robinson (the people behind the Jigsaw chain) cite European 'concept' stores such as Colette in Paris as inspiration, but there is none of the froideur associated with such temples to avant-garde design.

Staff have been vetted for friendliness and the constantly changing displays have a sense of fun: the book section is illuminated by a ceiling installation of over 1,000 lightbulbs, and art T-shirts and niche denim sit in disembowelled TVs.

Fashion-wise the house style is more understated than edgy and embraces a huge variety of labels from recent St Martin's graduates to the likes of Sharon Wauchob, Emma Cook and Eley Kishimoto. Not everything is expensive: you can pick up a top for as little as £35. Exclusive collaborations, such as a range of limited-edition retro-cool Bluebird shirts designed by Jermyn Street traditionalists Turnbull & Asser, mean you can pick up something truly unique.

By the time this guide hits the shelves, a spa and a music section (manned by guest DJs at weekends) should have opened, and there are also plans for a programme of art events.

Sloane Street

Racine

239 Brompton Road, Brompton, SW3 2EP (7584 4477). Knightsbridge or South Kensington tube. **Open** noon-3pm, 6-10.30pm Mon-Fri; noon-3.30pm, 6-10.30pm Sat; noon-3.30pm, 6-10pm Sun. **£££. French. Map** p149 B3 ㊽

Racine brings a slice of chic Parisian style to stuffy old Knightsbridge. Push past the heavy curtain into a dark room – sleek dark leather, smoked mirrors, immaculate white tablecloths – and settle in for an indulgent array of French bourgeois classics.

Sea Cow

NEW *676 Fulham Road, Fulham, SW6 5SA (7610 8020/www.theseacow.co.uk). Parsons Green tube.* **Open** noon-10.30pm Mon-Sat; noon-10pm Sun. **££. Fish and chips. Map** p149 A5 ㊾

We like this Sea Cow a lot. The south London mini-chain has low prices, chirpy service and excellent fish and chips, with batter that's pale but crisp, chips that are hand-cut and firm, and minted mushy peas. A display case allows you to inspect the day's catch.

Townhouse

31 Beauchamp Place, Brompton, SW3 1NU (7589 5080/www.lab-townhouse.com). Knightsbridge tube. **Open** 4pm-midnight Mon-Sat; 4-11.30pm Sun. **Bar. Map** p149 C2 ㊿

From the street, Townhouse is little more than a discreet sign and a doorway. Get past the bouncer and you'll find a sleek, narrow bar, and a tiny seating area at the back. The cocktail list is as big as a phonebook, the crowd is a Chanel ad come to life.

Zuma

5 Raphael Street, Knightsbridge, SW7 1DL (7584 1010/www.zumarestaurant.com). Knightsbridge tube. **Open** noon-2.30pm, 6pm-midnight Mon-Fri; 12.30-3pm, 6pm-midnight Sat; 12.30-3pm, 6-10pm Sun. **£££. Japanese. Map** p149 C2 (51)

Many diners seem to be here for the scene, which shows how silly they are, because the Japanese food is seriously good. If you come for the food, do lunch, as the hubbub at the bar can get tiresome at night.

Glamour kittens are scampering to this eclectic white-painted boudoir, filled with iridescence and clothes by exclusive designers from Australia, New Zealand and New York, and SPANK and Julianne French lingerie. The shop is also a great source of jeans from not-yet ubiquitous US labels.

Butler & Wilson

189 Fulham Road, Chelsea, SW3 6JN (7352 8255/www.butlerandwilson. co.uk). South Kensington tube. **Open** 10am-6pm Mon, Tue, Thur-Sat; 10am-7pm Wed; noon-6pm Sun. **Map** p149 B4 **54**

Fans of costume jewellery have been snapping up Simon Wilson's flamboyant baubles for 25 years; less well known is that the Fulham Road shop has a treasure trove of vintage clothes upstairs. The stock includes Victorian crocheted tops and shawls, sequinned 1920s dresses and '60s mini dresses, plus beautiful antique jewellery.

Chloé

152-153 Sloane Street, Chelsea, SW1X 9BX (7823 5348/www.chloe. com). Sloane Square tube. **Open** 10am-6pm Mon, Tue, Thur-Sat; 10am-7pm Wed. **Map** p146 A3 **55**

Hip and sassy London gal Phoebe Philo injects more of her cool, laid-back urban sense of style into this label each season. Philo hits the right note every time, balancing good-quality classics (those high-waisted, wide-leg trousers) with a dash of humour.

Conran Shop

Michelin House, 81 Fulham Road, Chelsea, SW3 6RD (7589 7401/ www.conran.com). South Kensington tube. **Open** 10am-6pm Mon, Tue, Fri; 10am-7pm Wed, Thur; 10am-6.30pm Sat; noon-6pm Sun. **Map** p149 B3 **56**

One of the first retailers to embody the term 'lifestyle' by introducing shoppers to the notion of buying everything for their home from one place . The company hand-picks pieces that are already, or destined to become, design classics, although it's not afraid to throw in newer, more eye-catching items.

Shopping

Knightsbridge is home to famous department stores Harrods and Harvey Nichols. Designer flagships line Sloane Street, and King's Road is good for general browsing and antiques.

Antiquarius

131-141 King's Road, Chelsea, SW3 5EB (7351 5353/www.antiquarius. co.uk). Sloane Square tube then 11, 19, 22 bus. **Open** 10am-6pm Mon-Sat. **Map** p149 C5 **52**

This well-kept antiques arcade is a good source of Arts and Crafts and Aesthetic Movement objects, Baccarat glass, clocks, jewellery and watches. The Art Deco Pavilion has stylish furniture, photo frames and cigarette accessories. Prices are negotiable.

Austique

330 King's Road, Chelsea, SW3 5UR (7376 3663/www.austique.co.uk). Sloane Square tube, then 11, 19, 49 bus. **Open** 10.30am-6.30pm Mon-Sat; noon-5pm Sun. **Map** p149 A5 **53**

LONDON BY AREA

Found objects

The V&A's Surrealism expo promises to be another blockbuster

Hot on the heels of its hugely successful 2006 exhibition 'Modernism', the V&A – which does, after all, bill itself 'the world's greatest museum of art and design' – is putting on a show that maps the intersections of the canonic art movement with numerous design fields. 'Surreal Things' is already generating an expectant buzz.

Typically canny, the V&A will be taking a new angle on Surrealism, tracing its influence on architecture, commercial design, graphics and film, from the 1920s to the years after World War II. The exhibition will be object-led, rather than focusing on the usual run of paintings and literary works. One of the core pieces of the collection is Salvador Dalí's Mae West Lips sofa. Lascivious, suggestive and not a little bizarre, its fleshy pink voluptuousness encapsulates the Surrealists' fixation on desire as a driving force. By the time Dalí collaborated with Elsa Schiaparelli on a silk evening dress with a lobster print in 1937, the theatrical aesthetics of Surrealism had begun their process of osmosis beyond the perimeter of fine art into other design disciplines. Another of Schiaparelli and Dalí's creations in partnership, the Tear dress, will also be on display.

■ 'Surreal Things: Surrealism and Design', V&A, 29 Mar-22 July 2007

Duke of York Square

King's Road, Chelsea, SW3 4LY. Sloane Square tube. Map p147 B5 ⑤⑦
West London's first new public square for over a century is a former barracks transformed into a tastefully landscaped, tree-lined pedestrian area. A combination of listed and modern buildings houses high-end high-street clothes stores including All Saints, Ted Baker, GAS, Agnès b and – in the central glass-walled pavilion – Joseph, Myla and Suede. A branch of Pâtisserie Valerie has lots of outdoor tables.

Harrods

87-135 Brompton Road, Knightsbridge, SW1X 7XL (7730 1234/www.harrods. com). Knightsbridge tube. **Open** 10am-8pm Mon-Sat; noon-6pm Sun. **Map** p149 C2 ⑤⑧
The mother of all upscale department stores, with floor after floor of expensive designer clothing overseen by surprisingly friendly staff who know if you can't afford to buy but don't mind you looking. And looking is fab – it costs nothing to soak up the ambience in the ground-floor Room of Luxury with accessories by the likes of Gucci, Dior and Hermès. Those who go beyond browsing can avail themselves of the new free personal shopping service. The legendary food halls are the biggest attractions; the Urban Retreat spa is also highly rated.

Harvey Nichols

109-125 Knightsbridge, Knightsbridge, SW1X 7RJ (7235 5000/www.harvey nichols.com). Knightsbridge tube. **Open** 10am-8pm Mon-Sat; 10am-6pm Sun. **Map** p149 C2 ⑤⑨
Harvey Nicks is an elegant and urban one-stop shop for front-line fashion. New collections from the likes of Giambattista Valli, Luella and Kris van Assche maintain the store's reputation for eclectic ready-to-wear pieces for both sexes. The ground floor is a cosmetics junkie's paradise, and also houses Pout and Bliss concessions, as well as the holistic Beyond Beauty area. For refreshment is the light-suffused Fifth Floor bar, café and restaurant (p158).

Traditional Toys p164

Jo Malone

*150 Sloane Street, Knightsbridge,
SW1X 9BX (7730 2100/www.jo
malone.co.uk). Sloane Square tube.*
Open 9.30am-6pm Mon, Tue, Sat;
9.30am-7pm Wed-Fri; noon-5pm Sun.
Map p146 A4 ⑥⓪

In the 11 years since Jo Malone
launched her luxurious fragrance
brand, the business has been a run-
away international success. Her coveted range of scents, candles, skincare
and bodycare products is sleekly pack-
aged, mainly in glass bottles or jars
with simple cream-and-black labels.
Pricey but worth it.

Korres

*124 King's Road, Chelsea, SW3 4TR
(7581 6455/www.korres.com). Sloane
Square tube.* **Open** 10am-7pm Mon-Sat;
noon-6pm Sun. **Map** p149 C4 ⑥①

This Athens-based company produces
a line of gorgeous products based on
kitchen ingredients such as coriander,
lemon, nutmeg and vanilla, and avoid-
ing mineral oils (thought to clog the
skin and prevent the elimination of tox-
ins), silicones or propylene glycol.

Manolo Blahnik

*49-51 Old Church Street, Chelsea, SW3
5BS (7352 3863). South Kensington
tube.* **Open** 10am-5.30pm Mon-Fri;
10.30am-4.45pm Sat. **Map** p149 B5 ⑥②

Given the master cobbler's reputation,
it's surprisingly low-key here (although
you do have to ring a bell to be buzzed
in). The shop is usually busy with
women happy to part with £300-plus for
a pair of shoes; the timeless lines, creative use of materials (reptile skins are a
perennial feature) and colours mean they
will see you through several seasons.

Megan's Delicatessen

*571 King's Road, Chelsea, SW6 2EB
(7371 7837/www.megansdeli.com).
Parsons Green or Fulham Broadway
tube then 11, 14, 22 bus.* **Open** 8am-
6pm Mon-Fri; 9am-6pm Sat. **Map**
p149 A5 ⑥③

This attractive King's Road deli sells
Poilâne bread, cheeses, olives, sauces
and own-made jams. All the products
are GM- and additive-free, and cakes
and muffins are baked on the premises. Home-style hot dishes can been-
joyed in the 'secret garden' at the back.

Victoria & Albert Museum p166

Rococo

*321 King's Road, Chelsea, SW3 5EP
(7352 5857/www.rococochocolates.
com). Sloane Square tube then 11, 19,
22 bus.* **Open** 10am-6.30pm Mon-Sat;
noon-5pm Sun. **Map** p149 A5 ⑥④
The beautiful Rococo offers fruit and
flower fondants, caramels and gingers.
Chocolate bars come in flavours like
orange and geranium, rosemary and
lavender; truffles and chocolates are
similarly exotic. Sugar-free, dairy-free
and organic are also sold.

Shop at Bluebird

NEW *350 King's Road, Chelsea, SW3
5UU (7351 3873. Sloane Square tube
then 11, 19, 22 bus.* **Open** 10am-7pm
Mon, Tue, Fri, Sat; 9am-7pm Wed,
Thur; noon-6pm Sun. **Map** p149 A5 ⑥⑤
See box p159.

Traditional Toys

*53 Godfrey Street, Chelsea, SW3 3SX
(7352 1718/www.traditionaltoy.com).
Sloane Square tube then 11, 19, 22
bus.* **Open** 10am-5.30pm Mon-Fri;
10am-6pm Sat. **Map** p149 C4 ⑥⑥

Every nook and cranny of this terrific
little shop is filled with games, books
and toys. For pocket-money budgets
there are farm animals, stickers, skip-
ping ropes and the like. Don't miss the
fantastic fancy dresses.

Arts & leisure

Cadogan Hall

*5 Sloane Terrace, Chelsea, SW1X 9DQ
(7730 4500/www.cadoganhall.com).
Sloane Square tube.* **Map** p146 A3 ⑥⑦
This former church reopened in June
2004 as a light and airy auditorium. It
seats around 900 people and sightlines
are excellent, whether from the raked
ground-floor seating or an an impressive horseshoe balcony. The English
Chamber Orchestra plays regularly, and
the Royal Philharmonic is resident until
Royal Festival Hall has been renovated.

Chelsea Cinema

*206 King's Road, Chelsea, SW3 5XP
(7351 3742/www.artificial-eye.com).
Sloane Square tube then 11, 19, 22, 319
bus.* **Map** p149 C5 ⑥⑧

Run by film distributor Artificial Eye, CC specialises in world cinema.

Chelsea Football Club

Stamford Bridge, Fulham Road, Fulham, SW6 1HS (0870 300 1212/ www.chelseafc.co.uk). Fulham Broadway tube. **Map** p149 A5 ⑥⑨

Chelsea were led to successive Premiership victories in 2004/5 and 2005/6 by their testily charismatic Portuguese manager Jose Mourinho. Forget about watching a league match, but tickets for European or domestic cup ties can sometimes be had.

Fulham Football Club

Craven Cottage, Stevenage Road, Fulham, SW6 6HH (0870 442 1234/ www.fulhamfc.com). Putney Bridge tube. **Map** p149 A5 ⑦⓪

Owned by Mohammad al-Fayed of Harrods fame, this reliable mid-table team has played at this friendly ground since the 1890s; extensive refurbishments were completed in 2004.

Royal Court

Sloane Square, Chelsea, SW1W 8AS (7565 5000/www.royalcourt theatre.com). Sloane Square tube. **Map** p146 A4 ⑦①

The emphasis at the RC is always on new, uncompromising voices in British theatre – from John Osborne's *Look Back in Anger* in the inaugural year, 1956, to numerous discoveries over the past decade, Sarah Kane, Joe Penhall and Conor McPherson among them. Recently redeveloped, it now has two stages: Upstairs (a studio theatre) and Downstairs (the main stage).

South Kensington

Welcome to London's intellectual hub, an area where it's hard to walk 100 paces without chancing upon some august museum or institute. Three heavyweight museums (**Natural History Museum**, **Science Museum** and **Victoria & Albert Museum**), three lofty colleges (Imperial College London, the Royal College of Art and the Royal College of Music) and the ginormous Royal Albert Hall dominate the area once known as Albertopolis, in honour of the prince who oversaw their founding.

Sights & museums

Albert Memorial

Kensington Gardens (opposite Royal Albert Hall), South Kensington, SW7 (tours 7495 0916). South Kensington tube or bus 9, 10, 52. **Map** p149 A1 ⑦②

One of the great sculptural achievements of Queen Victoria's age, the memorial centres on her gilded husband, enshrined in a white marble frieze of poets and painters; bronze statues and intricate mosaics represent the sciences and arts. The 180ft (55m) spire is inlaid with semi-precious stones.

Natural History Museum

Cromwell Road, South Kensington, SW7 5BD (information 7942 5725/ switchboard 7942 5000/www.nhm. ac.uk). South Kensington tube or bus 9, 10, 52. **Open** 10am-5.50pm Mon-Sat; 11am-5.50pm Sun. **Admission** free; charges apply for special exhibitions. **Map** p149 A3 ⑦③

This cathedral to the wonders of creation is impressive in itself, even before you get to the giant Diplodocus skeleton cast in the main hall of the Life Galleries. If you come with children, you may not see much more than the Dinosaur gallery, with its star turn, the animatronic T. rex, roaring in its enclosure. Some of the galleries are pretty static and dry; others, like Creepy Crawlies, so beloved of children you can hardly get near the exhibits. In the Earth Galleries there's scary fun in Restless Surface, whose most famous exhibit is a mock-up of a Kobe supermarket, where the floor shakes to video coverage of the 1995 earthquake. Outside, the Wildlife Garden (open Apr-Oct, £1.50) is the museum's living exhibit, with a range of British habitats. **Event highlights** Annual Wildlife Photographer of the Year show (21 Oct-Apr 2007). 'Dino Jaws': which uses nine animatronic dinos to investigate the giant reptiles' eating habits (to 15 Apr 2007). Antartica exhibition, covering wildlife and science: expect stunning imagery and mini-environments to explore (from May 2007).

Science Museum

Exhibition Road, South Kensington, SW7 2DD (7942 4454/booking & information line 0870 870 4868/ www.sciencemuseum.org.uk). South Kensington tube. **Open** 10am-6pm daily. **Admission** free; charges apply for special exhibitions. **Map** p149 A3 ⓴

The Science Museum shows how science filters down through daily life, with displays on engines, cars, planes, ships, the home, medicine and computers. The vast collection contains such landmark inventions such as Stephenson's Rocket, Whittle's turbo-jet engine, Arkwright's spinning machine and the Apollo 10 command module celebrated in the Making the Modern World gallery. The Wellcome Wing has an IMAX cinema (below) and the Who Am I? gallery, which explores discoveries in genetics and brain science. The temporary exhibition 'Inside the Spitfire' runs until spring 2007. The new-look Energy Hall now includes a gallery about power and energy saving.

Victoria & Albert Museum

Cromwell Road, South Kensington, SW7 2RL (7942 2000/www.vam.ac.uk). South Kensington tube. **Open** 10am-5.45pm Mon, Tue, Thur-Sun; 10am-10pm Wed & last Fri of mth. **Admission** free; charges apply for special exhibitions. **Map** p149 B3 ⓻

The grand galleries of the 150-year old V&A contain about four million pieces of furniture, textiles, ceramics, sculpture, paintings, posters, jewellery, glass and metalwork from cultures across the world. The museum boasts the finest collection of Italian Renaissance sculpture outside Italy; home-grown treasures include the Great Bed of Ware, Canova's *The Three Graces* and Henry VIII's writing desk. The Fashion galleries run from 18th-century court dress right up to a summer chiffon number for 2005; temporary exhibition 'The Golden Age of Couture' in late 2007 will highlight fashion from the 1940s and 1950s. The Architecture Gallery and study centre has videos, models, plans and descriptions of various architectural styles, while the famous photography collection, started in 1852, holds over 500,000 images. A fine area for contemplation is the John Madejski Garden, with its beds of lilies and lemon trees. The museum has enjoyed 94% more visitors since admission charges were abolished in 2001. **Event highlights** 'Leonardo da Vinci: Experience, Experiment and Design' (14 Sept 2006-7 Jan 2007). 'At Home in Renaissance Italy' (5 Oct 2006-7 Jan 2007). 'James Athenian Stuart: Neoclassical Pioneer' (22 Mar-24 Jun 2007). 'Surreal Things: Surrealism and Design' (29 Mar-22 Jul 2007; see box p162). 'Lee Miller' (2 Aug 2007-6 Jan 2008). 'The Golden Age of Couture 1947-1957' (27 Sept 2007-6 Jan 2008).

Arts & leisure

Royal Albert Hall

Kensington Gore, South Kensington, SW7 2AP (box office 7589 8212/www. royalalberthall.com). South Kensington tube. **Open** Box office 9am-9pm daily. **Map** p149 A2 ⓰

This grand rotunda, seating up to 5,200 people, is the home of classical music's Proms every summer, and assorted events year round. Built as a memorial to Queen Victoria's husband, it has hosted opera, rock, jazz, boxing, tennis, circus, fashion shows, conventions and awards ceremonies. A refurbishment in 2004 installed air-conditioning, modernised the backstage area and moved the main entrance to the south side.

Science Museum IMAX

Exhibition Road, South Kensington, SW7 2DD (0870 870 4868/www. sciencemuseum.org.uk). South Kensington tube. **Map** p149 A3 ⓱

This huge screen shows 3-D films, often about natural world.

Kenwood House p168

Neighbourhood London

LONDON BY AREA

Central London is not, by and large, residential. So some of the city's most interesting areas, where people live, rest and play, and scenes develop, are at its edges. This chapter focusses on the more notable and close-in of these, all of which will merit a morning's exploration. It also picks out individual sights, museums and other venues that are notable enough to be worth travelling to, particularly new openings.

North London

Islington's main drag isn't much to look at but there are enough Georgian squares and terraces in its hinterland to ensure a reliable stream of patrons for its gift, clothes and antiques shops. It's also developed a nightlife scene, though it's a bit school-age. **Camden** is known for its market, one of London's biggest tourist draws, but has little else to merit a visit. It was famously a cradle of Britpop, still in evidence here, and remains musically active. **Hampstead** is a prettily leafy, well-off village – the term is descriptive rather than estate-agent-speak – known for its artistic and celebrity residents and gorgeous Heath.

Sights & museums

Camden Market

Camden Market *Camden High Street, junction with Buck Street, NW1 (7485 5473)*. **Open** 9.30am-5.30pm daily.
Camden Canal Market *off Chalk Farm Road, south of junction with Castlehaven Road, NW1 9XJ (7485 8355/www.camdenlock.net)*. **Open** 9.30am-6.30pm daily.
Camden Lock *Camden Lock Place, off Chalk Farm Road, NW1 8AF*

(7284 2084/www.camdenlockmarket. com). **Open** 10am-6pm Mon-Wed, Fri-Sun; 10am-7pm Thur.
Electric Ballroom *184 Camden High Street, NW1 8QP (7485 9006/www. electric-ballroom.co.uk).* **Open** 10am-6pm Sat, Sun before bank hols; record & film fairs occasional Sats throughout the year.
Stables *off Chalk Farm Road, opposite junction with Hartland Road, NW1 8AH (7485 8355/www.camdenlock.net).* **Open** 9.30am-5.30pm daily (reduced stalls Mon-Fri).
All *Camden Town or Chalk Farm tube.* Camden Market heaves with locust-plague numbers of people (mostly tourists), particularly at weekends when most stalls are open. And as a market, it's far from inspiring. The section advertised as Camden Market, just next to the tube station, flogs cheap sunglasses and cut-price interpretations of current fashions; the rest bears little resemblance to the cutting-edge place it was years ago. The Electric Ballroom sells second-hand clothes and young designers' wares, but it's neither cheap nor particularly exciting. Camden Lock Market, set around a courtyard next to Regent's Canal, is nicer. Crafty shops and stalls sell funky lighting, contemporary fashion, ethnic homewares, arts, antiques and more. These days, the Stables Market has permanent clothes and food huts, rather like an alternative shopping mall, set to become more entrenched with the opening of the glass-wrapped Triangle's shops and entertainment venues. In the railway arches, upmarket retro stalls and clubwear outlets have taken over – the freaky day-glo clubwear and cool T-shirts at Cyberdog are worth a peek. Head to the further end, around the Horse Hospital, for outlets selling antiques and 20th-century furniture.

Hampstead Heath

It was the inspiration for CS Lewis's Narnia, and the Heath's charming contours and woodlands make it feel far larger and more rural than it is (something over a mile in each direction): you can quite easily get lost here. The views of London from the top of Parliament Hill are stunning; on hot days, the murky open-air bathing ponds (men's, women's and mixed, open daily all year) are a godsend. There's also a great lido at Gospel Oak (7485 3873). The information points can tell you about concerts held on summer Sundays.

Highgate Cemetery

Swains Lane, Highgate, N6 6PJ (8340 1834/www.highgate-cemetery.org). Archway tube/143, 210, 271 bus. **Open** *East Cemetery* Apr-Oct 10am-5pm Mon-Fri; 11am-5pm Sat, Sun. Last entry 4.30pm. Nov-Mar 10am-4pm Mon-Fri; 11am-4pm Sat, Sun. Last entry 3.30pm. *West Cemetery tours* Apr-Oct 2pm Mon-Fri; hourly 11am-3pm Sat, Sun. Nov-Mar hourly 11am-3pm Sat, Sun. **Admission** *East Cemetery* £2. *West Cemetery tours* £5; £1 reductions; prior booking advisable. *Camera permit* £1. No video cameras. No under-8s. No credit cards.
London's most famous graveyard is best known for the Karl Marx and George Eliot memorials in the East Cemetery, but the West Cemetery (accessible only on guided tours) is the real highlight, with gloomy catacombs and elaborate funerary architecture (plus poet Christina Rossetti and chemist Michael Faraday).

Keats House

Keats Grove, Hampstead, NW3 2RR (7435 2062/www.cityoflondon.gov. uk/keats). Hampstead Heath rail/ Hampstead tube/24, 46, 168 bus. **Open** 1-5pm Tue-Sun. **Admission** £3.50; free-£1.75 reductions.
The Romantic poet lived here from 1818 to 1820. As well as mooching through the rooms, you can attend events in the poetry reading room. Industrial carpets ruin the ambience rather, but the garden in which Keats famously wrote 'Ode to a Nightingale' is a pleasant place to wander.

Kenwood House/ Iveagh Bequest

Hampstead Lane, Hampstead, NW3 7JR (8348 1286/www.english-

Sporting giant

By the time you read this, the new Wembley Stadium should have opened for business. But at press time William Hill bookmakers were offering odds of only 8 to 1 on the ground being ready for the FA Cup Final in June 2007. Plans to hold the 2006 event there were dropped following construction delays, each chewed over with relish by the press – the project has not exactly been taken to the public bosom. The previous 1923 stadium with its iconic twin towers is still mourned, and the location and financing of the new national stadium were highly controversial.

However, we predict a bit of an about-turn in public opinion when the venue does finally open – still officially due some time in 2006. The old stadium was historic, but the new one is looking firmly to the future. It will be the largest football stadium in the world, with capacity for 90,000 people. Visitors will be able to refuel from a choice of a reputed 688 food and drink outlets, and 2,618 toilets will outdo the amenities of any other world stadium. Those twin towers have been replaced by a bigger, bolder feature – an enormous latticed steel arch bestriding the whole stadium, the largest single-span roof structure in the world. At 133 metres tall, it is so big that the entire London Eye could be rolled underneath it. Dozens of grass varieties were tested for their suitability on the pitch, and even the stadium's acoustics were calculated meticulously to ensure optimum atmosphere.

Wembley will remain the national stadium for football – what it's most famous for – but in 2012 it will also become a key venue in London's Olympic Games. And by generating thousands of new jobs and millions of pounds of income for the area, it should accelerate the redevelopment of a decidedly run-down corner of the capital.

Wembley Arena, seating a relatively more modest 12,750 successfully opened in spring 2006 after a revamp of its own.
■ www.whatsonwembley.com

Holly Bush

are all made with the French *steak haché* in mind, using high-quality Aberdeen Angus beef and with an emphasis on flavour over gimmicky toppings. Presentation is prioritised, the restaurant itself is just as tasteful, and staff are friendly. Plenty of joints call their burgers gourmet; Haché has earned that distinction.

Holly Bush

22 Holly Mount, Hampstead, NW3 6SG (7435 2892/www.hollybushpub.com). Hampstead tube. **Open** noon-11pm Mon-Sat; noon-10.30pm Sun. *Food served* 12.30-4pm, 6.30-10pm Mon-Fri; 12.30-10pm Sat; 12.30-9pm Sun. **Pub**.
London's best country pub, complete with real ales and a log fire to warm yourself after rambles on Hampstead Heath. Little has changed here since the 1880s; it's a local institution.

Keston Lodge

131 Upper Street, Islington, N1 1QP (7354 9535/www.kestonlodge.com). Angel tube/Highbury & Islington tube/rail. **Open** noon-midnight Mon-Wed, Sun; noon-1am Thur; noon-2am Fri, Sat. *Food served* noon-3pm, 5-10pm Mon-Fri; noon-5pm, 6-10pm Sat, Sun. **Admission** £3 after 10.30pm Fri, Sat. **Bar**.
Exposed pipework, raw concrete and pegboard pitch for, and hit, industrial urban chic, softened by capacious booths and sofas. City types and a contingent of older locals come for their fix of berry Martinis, decent inexpensive food and relatively muted soundtrack.

Lock Tavern

35 Chalk Farm Road, Camden, NW1 8AJ (7482 7163/www.lock-tavern.co.uk). Camden Town or Chalk Farm tube. **Open** noon-midnight Mon-Thur; noon-1am Fri, Sat; noon-11pm Sun. *Food served* noon-3pm, 5-10pm Mon-Fri; noon-5pm, 6-9pm Sat; noon-5pm Sun. **Pub**.
Don't be intimidated. The punters may be fiercely fashionable, the staff icily gorgeous and the music almost too tasteful, but this is a brilliant boozer in a prime location. Dark but cosy decor, ace pies and regular DJ sessions.

heritage.org.uk). Hampstead tube/ Golders Green tube then 210 bus. **Open** *Apr-Oct* 11am-5pm daily. *Nov-Mar* 11am-4pm daily. *Tours* by appointment only. **Admission** free; donations appreciated. *Tours* £3; £1.50-£2 reductions.
Built in 1616, the house was remodelled by Robert Adam in the 18th century. Brewing magnate Edward Guinness bought it in 1925 and filled it with his art collection: old masters now on display include a Rembrandt self-portrait. Outside, the landscaped grounds remain mostly unchanged from their creation in 1793, with a terrace giving lovely views over the lake. In July and August there are lakeside concerts.

Eating & drinking

Haché

24 Inverness Street, Camden, NW1 7HJ (7485 9100/www.hacheburgers. com). Camden Town tube. **Open** noon-10.30pm Mon-Sat; noon-10pm Sun. **£**. **Burger bar**.
Haché is the pick of a new crop of gourmet burger restaurants. Its burgers

Ottolenghi

Ottolenghi

*287 Upper Street, Islington, N1 2TZ
(7288 1454/www.ottolenghi.co.uk).
Angel tube/Highbury & Islington
tube/rail.* **Open** 8am-11pm Mon-Sat;
9am-7pm Sun. **££. Café**.

This divine deli/café is a sleek, minimalist affair, but, provided you don't
mind communal tables, you'll feel
spoiled rotten when you visit. There's
just such a good range of choices – the
soups, salad dishes, meats, artisanal
breads, cakes and pastries are all
equally irresistible. Portions are on the
small side, but the quality of cooking
is beyond reproach.

S&M Café

*4-6 Essex Road, Islington N1 8LN
(7359 5361/www.sandmcafe.co.uk).
Angel tube.* **Open** 7.30am-11.30pm
Mon-Thur; 7.30am-midnight Fri;
8.30am-midnight Sat; 8.30am-10.30pm
Sun. **£. Café**.

The premises occupied by this good
value but superior sausage and mash
café are listed, so the lovely 1950s
exterior of the *Quadrophenia*-featured
Alfredo's caff remains. Inside doesn't

disappoint either: it's still all formica
and squeezy ketchup bottles, with no
Nouveau Islington airs and graces.

Shopping

After Noah

*121 Upper Street, Islington, N1 1QP
(7359 4281/www.afternoah.com).
Angel tube/Highbury & Islington
tube/rail.* **Open** 10am-6pm Mon-Sat;
noon-5pm Sun.

A large part of After Noah's appeal is
its retro ambience and charming layout: half of the ground floor is devoted
to old-fashioned kids' toys, retro sweets
and pocket-money trinkets, the rest is
a whimsical array of new gifts and
homewares, plus some original Arts
and Crafts pieces.

Camden Passage

*Camden Passage, off Upper Street,
Islington, N1 5ED (7359 0190/www.
antiquesnews.co.uk/camdenpassage).
Angel tube.* **Open** *General market* 7am-
4pm Wed; 7am-5pm Sat. *Book market*
8.30am-6pm Thur.

Held in a pedestrianised backstreet
near Angel, this market majors in

KOKO

costume jewellery, silver plate and downright junk – but that doesn't mean you can't find rare items at good prices. More interesting are the dealers in the surrounding arcades, who open to coincide with the market.

Diverse
294 Upper Street, Islington, N1 2TU (7359 8877/www.diverseclothing.com). Angel tube. **Open** 10.30am-6.30pm Mon-Sat; noon-5.30pm Sun.
The women's clothing shop lives up to its name, with an excellent selection of luxe labels. Expect the likes of Marc by Marc Jacobs, Matthew Williamson, Chloé, Rick Owens and Missoni. There's also a healthy stock of hip jeans from Paper Denim & Cloth, Rogan, Earnest Sewn and Notify.

Nightlife

Barfly
49 Chalk Farm Road, Camden, NW1 8AN (7691 4244/www.barfly club.com). Camden Town or Chalk Farm tube. **Open** 7.30pm-midnight Mon-Thur; 7.30pm-3am Fri, Sat; 7.30-11pm Sun. **Admission** £5-£8. No credit cards.

Sure, it's part of the Barfly chain, but cast away any thought of All Bar One: it's a small-gig venue that goes all out to support new talent. This being Camden, expect balding once-were-rockers moshing against girls in designer vintage and skinny jeans in two rooms with the essential bare-brick walls and odd tattered posters. Club nights feature plenty of squealing guitar action, some of the best you'll find in town.

Elbow Room
89-91 Chapel Market, Islington, N1 9EX (7278 3244/www.theelbowroom. co.uk). Angel tube. **Open** 5pm-2am Mon; noon-2am Tue-Thur; noon-3am Fri, Sat; noon-midnight Sun.
Elbow Room follows a well-established, slick, good-time formula that wins it many friends around these parts. A pool room and bar by day, it becomes more clubby by night, retro-chic style. Two-for-one cocktails of a lurid nature between 5pm and 8pm.

Jazz Café
5 Parkway, Camden, NW1 7PG (information 7916 6060/box office 0870 150 0044/www.jazzcafe.co.uk).

Camden Town tube. **Open** 7pm-1am Mon-Thur; 7pm-2am Fri, Sat; 7pm-midnight Sun. *Gigs* 9pm daily.
Admission varies.

Jazz is only a small piece in the jigsaw of events here, which also takes in funk, hip hop, soul, R&B, singer-songwriters and much more besides. It's a slick, modern venue with a balcony eating area (you'll need to book).

KOKO

1A Camden High Street, Camden, NW1 9JE (7388 3222/box office 0870 145 1115/www.koko.uk.com). Mornington Crescent tube. **Open** 9.30pm-4am Fri; 10pm-4am Sat. Phone to check other days. **Admission** free-£15. Credit at bar only.

Opulent in an old-fashioned way – gloss claret and gold paint, balconies, plenty of Greek gods holding up columns – KOKO interior is all about vertical levels. The sound system works for both DJs and live shows. Friday is all about Club NME, with some scream-worthy bands; Saturdays is a mix of Sunday Best, Guilty Pleasures and hard dance raves.

Luminaire

NEW *311 Kilburn High Road, Kilburn, NW6 7JR (7372 7123/8558/www.the luminaire.co.uk) Kilburn or Kilburn Park tube.*

This excellent retro indie venue has really come to prominence in the last year, and won *Time Out*'s 2006 Live Award for best music venue. It's cool and comfortable, with impressive sound, imaginative bookings and a decently priced bar that can make a cocktail or two.

Wembley Arena

Empire Way, Wembley, Middx HA9 0DW (8902 8833/box office 0870 060 0870/www.whatsonwembley.com). Wembley Park tube/Wembley Central tube/rail.

At the time of writing, the stadium, a 12,500-capacity hangar of a place, was being refurbished, but the arena itself reopened in April 2006, with Depeche Mode among the early attractions.

Arts & entertainment

Almeida

Almeida Street, Islington, N1 1TA (7359 4404/www.almeida.co.uk). Angel tube.

The well-groomed Almeida theatre turns out thoughtfully crafted theatre for grown-ups. Besides frequent casting coups it also commands loyalty from top directors such as Howard Davies and Sir Richard Eyre. Productions seldom disappoint.

Roundhouse

NEW *Chalk Farm Road, Camden, NW1 8EH (7424 9991/www.round house.org.uk). Camden Town or Chalk Farm tube.*

This iconic Camden performance venue, a legendary player in 1960s counter culture, reopened in summer 2006 after 15 dark years. It comprises an 1,800-seater auditorium, a studio venue and a creative centre for young people. The programme promises to be an eclectic and challenging schedule of musical and dramatic performance.

Sadler's Wells

Rosebery Avenue, Islington, EC1R 4TN (box office 0870 737 7737/www.sadlers wells.com). Angel tube.

One of the premier dance venues in the world, with the most exciting line-up in town. Top companies from Pina Bausch and William Forsythe to notable British troupes such as Rambert Dance Company and Birmingham Royal Ballet are showcased throughout the year.

East London

On the doorstep of the City of London, **Shoreditch** (sometimes erroneously called Hoxton, which is a little further north) has for the past decade been picking up press as London's latest happening area. It's now London's 'Nightlife Central', and although inevitably the buzz has been diluted, it is still there. Don't, by the way, expect Shoreditch to look like much; all

LONDON BY AREA

the fun goes on indoors. Its inner-city patchwork is part of its appeal.

Despite its proximity to the greedy City, **Spitalfields**, unorthodox to its core, retains a non-conformist character. Brick Lane, an urban ley line if there ever was one, is at once Cockney market street, clubland nexus and Bengali community centre. For a walk around this area, see p48.

Bethnal Green, slightly further out, is inevitably picking up some of the fabulousness overflow (and people can still afford to live there), so there are several interesting venues opening here.

We have also included venues that may be of use to delegates of conferences at the ExCel centre on the fascinating Isle of Dogs (within the Thames's big loop).

Sights & museums

Bethnal Green Museum of Childhood

Cambridge Heath Road, Bethnal Green, E2 9PA (8983 5200/recorded information 8980 2415/www.museum ofchildhood.org.uk). Bethnal Green tube/rail/Cambridge Heath rail. **Open** 10am-5.50pm daily. **Admission** free; donations appreciated.

A branch of the Victoria and Albert, the museum has a huge collection of children's toys, games and costumes, with a special collection of moving and optical toys such as zoetropes. It's been closed for renovation but should reopen in November 2006 with plenty of hands-on activities.

Dennis Severs' House

18 Folgate Street, Spitalfields, E1 6BX (7247 4013/www.dennissevershouse. co.uk). Liverpool Street tube/rail. **Open** 2-5pm 1st & 3rd Sun of mth; noon-2pm Mon following 1st & 3rd Sun of mth; Mon eves (times vary). **Admission** £8 Sun; £5 noon-2pm Mon; £12 Mon eves. Booking essential. No under-10s.

This Huguenot house recreates, down to the smallest detail, life in Spitalfields

between 1724 and 1914. As its creator Dennis Severs wanted, hearth and candles burn, smells linger, and objects are scattered haphazardly, as if the inhabitants had left just moments before. This is art, not mere historic reconstruction.

Geffrye Museum

136 Kingsland Road, Shoreditch, E2 8EA (7739 9893/www.geffrye-museum.org.uk). Liverpool Street tube/rail then 149, 242 bus or Old Street tube/rail then 243 bus. **Open** 10am-5pm Tue-Sat; noon-5pm Sun. **Admission** free; donations appreciated. *Almshouse* £2; free-£1 reductions.

A physical history of the English interior, housed in a set of converted almshouses, the Geffrye recreates quintessential English living rooms from the 17th century to the present day and also has gardens designed on similar chronological lines. There's an airy restaurant and special exhibitions are mounted throughout the year.

Museum in Docklands

No.1 Warehouse, West India Quay, Hertsmere Road, E14 4AL (recorded information 0870 444 3856/box office 0870 444 3857/www.museum indocklands.org.uk). Canary Wharf tube/West India Quay DLR. **Open** 10am-6pm daily. Last entry 5.30pm. **Admission** £5; free-£3 reductions.

This huge museum explores much of the history of London's docklands over two millennia, from Roman times through their imperial heyday to their post-shipping present. Many exhibits are narrated by eyewitnesses: the Docklands at War section is particularly harrowing.

Eating & drinking

Canteen

NEW *2 Crispin Place, Spitalfields E1 6DW (0845 686 1122/www.canteen. co.uk). Liverpool Street tube/rail.* **Open** 11am-11pm Mon-Fri; 9am-11pm Sat, Sun. **££. British**. Crispin Place is that spanking new development next to Old Spitalfields

Market. It's airy, light and modern, with shared blond wood tables. Yet the food is old school, and pleasingly so. There are caff favourites like bacon sarnies and macaroni cheese; good pies; rib-sticking puds and proper sophisticated mains on a versatile menu that the kitchen turns out well given the keen pricing. Home-made crumpets a must.

E Pellicci

332 Bethnal Green Road, Bethnal Green, E2 0AG (7739 4873). Bethnal Green tube/rail. **Open** *6.15am-4.45pm Mon-Sat.* **£. Café**. No credit cards.
This 105-year-old East End masterpiece now has Grade II-listed status. Maria Pellicci's range of own-cooked Italian specials, such as liver and bacon butties and steak pie, is unrivalled.

Fifteen

15 Westland Place, Hoxton, N1 7LP (0871 330 1515/www.fifteen restaurant.com). Old Street tube/rail. **Open** *noon-4.30pm, 6.30-11.30pm daily.* **££££. Modern European**.
The aim of Jamie Oliver's Fifteen Foundation is to change the lives of 30 youngsters each year by training them to become 'the next generation of star chefs'. In our experience, the food ranges from good to excellent, though wines start at a hefty £20 a bottle.

Grapes

76 Narrow Street, Limehouse, E14 8PP (7987 4396). Limehouse or Westferry DLR. **Open** *noon-3pm, 5.30-11pm Mon-Fri; noon-11pm Sat; noon-10.30pm Sun. Food served noon-2.30pm, 7-9pm Mon-Sat; noon-3.30pm Sun.* **Pub**.
A historic riverside pub almost too appealing to be true, dating back to 1720. Cosy, crooked and rickety, it does all the proper pub stuff – beer and Sunday roasts – perfectly. And no mobile phones are allowed. A balcony extends over the Thames.

Great Eastern Dining Room

54-56 Great Eastern Street, Shoreditch, EC2A 3QR (7613 4545/www.great easterndining.co.uk). Old Street tube/ rail. **Open** *Below 54 bar* 7.30pm-1am Fri, Sat. *Ground-floor bar* noon-midnight Mon-Fri; 6pm-midnight Sat. *Restaurant* noon-3pm, 6.30pm-midnight Mon-Fri; 6.30pm-midnight Sat. Bars **££**. Restaurant **£££**. **International**.
The Great Eastern Dining Room is a stylish and spacious venue, with dark wood floors and striking contemporary chandeliers. The menu lists a modish range of pan-Asian dishes, so you'll find sushi sitting alongside curries, spicy soups, salads and noodle dishes. The puddings are almost too pretty to eat – but we're sure you'll find a way.

Green & Red Bar & Cantina

NEW *51 Bethnal Green Road, Bethnal Green, E1 6LA (7749 9670/www.green red.co.uk). Liverpool Street or Old Street tube/rail.* **Open** *5pm-midnight Mon-Fri; noon-midnight Sat; noon-11.30pm Sun. Food served* 6-11pm Mon-Fri; noon-11pm Sat; noon-10.30pm Sun. **Tequila bar**.
In some ways Green & Red is very much a typical Shoreditch bar with its warehouse DJ chic, yet it differs in that the people behind it really care about the drinks they serve. Or, specifically, about tequila, which they treat very seriously indeed, to the extent of offering 'flights' – samplers that allow you to compare and contrast their admirably broad range. Add a great tequila-based cocktail list, engaged and engaging staff, and good Mexican food from tequila-producing area Jalisco, and you've got a bar that deserves the buzz it's generating.

Gun

27 Coldharbour, Isle of Dogs, E14 9NS (7515 5222/www.thegundocklands.com). Canary Wharf tube/DLR/South Quay DLR. **Open** *11am-midnight Mon-Sat; noon-11pm Sun. Food served* noon-3pm, 6-10.30pm Mon-Fri; noon-4.30pm, 6-10.30pm Sat; noon-4.30pm, 6-9.30pm Sun. **££-£££. Gastropub**.
Once a waterside drinking den for seafarers and dockers from the adjacent West India Docks, the Gun is now a far

London's best club? Probably

Bethnal Green Working Men's Club takes the cabaret crown.

There's a soft mist of rain in the air on this Friday night, but the queue still stretches round the corner of the East End Victorian building. Guys in skinny jeans and cravats stroll in with pretty young things corseted into dresses their grandmothers might have worn. A girl on rollerskates sweeps past pouring Earl Grey tea, while a trestle table heaves with home-made sandwiches and cakes. On stage, a rock 'n' roll band warms up, and the DJ puts on a Chuck Berry record. Welcome to the coolest joint in town.

Sound a bit avant-garde for a working men's club? Rest assured that the old-timers have not been booted out into the streets. The basement remains the inner sanctum for members. The parties happen in the school hall-styled main room upstairs. The place is the antithesis of superclubs like Fabric, and party-goers love the fact that bottles of beer are £2.50 as opposed to nearer a fiver in the West End. Members, meanwhile, are overjoyed that their beloved club is close to paying off its crippling £40,000 debt, and is able to afford essential works to the building – the club's last overhaul was in the early 1970s.

Semi-spontaneous 'happenings' like Viva Cake, the Karminsky Experience, Oh My God I Miss You, XXXX and the Whoopee Club are the most exciting phenomenon in clubland right now. Promoters barely out of school are lining up circus acts, tarot readers, hot new bands, jive instructors and DJs whose music collections go far beyond the latest top ten sellers from the Soho record shops. Make no mistake: this shabby East End working men's club is the centre of London clubland. Go now. It's probably already too late. Bethnal Green Working Men's Club, 42 Pollard Row, E2 6NB (7739 2727).

Sosho

Les Trois Garcons is a splendid venue for a big night out. It's a handsomely converted former pub – 'Edwardian high camp' pretty accurately describes the interior – run with warmth and verve. Food is ambitious but well realised, with some wonderful splurging options. Very much a one-off, and all the more fun for that.

Loungelover

1 Whitby Street, Shoreditch, E2 7DP (7012 1234/www.loungelover.co.uk). Liverpool Street tube/rail. **Open** 6pm-midnight Tue-Thur; 6pm-1am Fri; 7pm-1am Sat; 4-10.30pm Sun. *Food served* 6-11.30pm Tue-Fri; 7-11.30pm Sat; 4-10pm Sun. **Cocktail bar**.
Loungelover's decor is wonderfully and divinely decadent: its chaotic mix of extravagantly theatrical fixtures is genuinely eye-popping. We do love the place but noted a slightly snooty attitude and an unadvertised service charge on our last visit.

Plateau

Canada Place, Canada Square, Isle of Dogs, E14 5ER (7715 7100/www.conran.com). Canary Wharf tube/DLR. **Open** *Bar & grill* noon-11pm Mon-Sat; noon-3.45pm Sun. *Restaurant* noon-3pm, 6-10.30pm Mon-Fri; 6-10.30pm Sat. **£££**. **French**.
Plateau's space-age look is exactly right for Canary Wharf, with walls of glass, great views and groovy designer furniture (it's a Conran joint) that make everyone look good. Good food; high prices; good service.

Sông Quê

134 Kingsland Road, Shoreditch, E2 8DY (7613 3222). Old Street tube/rail. **Open** noon-3pm, 5.30-11pm Mon-Sat; noon-11pm Sun. **£**. **Vietnamese**.
With fake ivy and plastic lobsters on the walls, Sông Quê might not look a likely venue for exquisite food. Like a culinary excursion through Vietnam, though, the assortment of dishes covers specialities from all regions – and the results are delicious. As they are in many of the other Vietnamese cafés scattered around here.

classier option, with a restored original oak bar, Georgian-style fireplaces and a riverside terrace favoured with great views. There's a fine-dining Modern British menu, cooked with flair, plus earthier pub choices.

Lebanese Lounge

NEW *50-52 Hanbury Street, Spitalfields, E1 5JL (7539 9200). Aldgate East tube.* **Open** 11am-11pm daily. **££**. **Lebanese**.
On one side of small courtyard is a convivial smoking lounge, on the other a formal dining room. The menu is gimmick-free, with the standard mix of hot and cold meze and mains from the charcoal grill. Food and service here are far superior to many of the restaurants in the traditional Middle Eastern enclave of Queensway and the Edgware Road.

Les Trois Garcons

1 Club Row, Shoreditch, E1 6JX (7613 1924/www.lestroisgarcons.com). Liverpool Street tube/rail. **Open** 7-10.30pm Mon-Thur; 7-11pm Fri, Sat. **£££**. **French**.

Sosho

2 Tabernacle Street, EC2A 4LU (7920 0701/www.sosho3am.com). Moorgate or Old Street tube/rail. **Open** noon-10pm Mon; noon-midnight Tue; noon-1am Wed, Thur; noon-3am Fri; 7pm-4am Sat; 9pm-4am Sun. *Food served* noon-9.30pm Mon; noon-10.30pm Tue-Fri; 7-11pm Sat. **Admission** £3-£5 after 9pm Thur-Sun. **Cocktail bar.**
Once hip, Sosho's look – dark floor, exposed brickwork, squashy sofas – is now tuppence plain, but it's agreeable for all that. And anyway, you're here for Dale DeGroff's peerless cocktails.

Shopping

@work

156 Brick Lane, Spitalfields, E1 6RU (7377 0597/www.atworkgallery.co.uk). Aldgate East tube/Liverpool Street tube/rail. **Open** 11am-6pm Mon-Sat; 11am-4pm Sun.
This little workshop and gallery is a great place to come looking for quirky, notice-me jewellery. You're looking at prices from £25 to many thousands of pounds for bespoke items.

Beyond Retro

112 Cheshire Street, Spitalfields, E2 6EJ (7613 3636/www.beyondretro. com). Liverpool Street tube/rail. **Open** 10am-6pm daily.
Off Brick Lane, this is a great one-stop shop for some fashion-conscious retro clothing at palatable prices. The vast, yellow-walled warehouse space has plenty of vintage wardrobe staples, including denim, tutus and leather jackets. You'll also find flight bags, old-skool trainers and much more.

Junky Styling

12 Dray Walk, Old Truman Brewery, 91-95 Brick Lane, Spitalfields, E1 6RF (7247 1883/www.junkystyling.co.uk). Liverpool Street tube/rail. **Open** 10.30am-6.30pm daily.
Owners Kerry Seager and Anni Saunders take two or more items of formal clothing (a pinstripe suit, a men's shirt and a tweed jacket, for example) and recycle them into an entirely new garment (skirts £50-£200; jackets £120-£350), always sharply tailored, usually with a hint of grunge. Alternatively, bring your own clothes to be transformed into a new garment of your choice in two to four weeks.

Shelf

40 Cheshire Street, Spitalfields, E2 6EH (7739 9444/www.helpyourshelf. co.uk). Liverpool Street tube/rail. **Open** 1-6pm Sat; 11am-6pm Sun.
A top place to visit for individual gifts, at Shelf you'll find mugs, lamps, unusual notebooks and stationery, postcards, prints and tableware by local artists and designers.

Smallfish

NEW *329 Old Street, Hoxton, EC1V 9LE (7739 2252/www.smallfish.co.uk). Liverpool Street or Old Street tube/rail.* **Open** noon-8pm Mon; 11am-8pm Tue-Fri; 10.30am-7.30pm Sat; 10.30am-6.30pm Sun.
Smallfish deals primarily in new vinyl and CDs, with electronica, experimental and mainstream dance being the genres of choice. The number of labels verges on the ridiculous, and staff appear to know every disc intimately.

Start

42-44 Rivington Street, Shoreditch, EC2A 3BN (7729 3334/www.start-london.com). Old Street tube/rail. **Open** 10.30am-6.30pm Mon-Fri; 11am-6.30pm Sat; 1-5pm Sun.
This spacious boutique has a defined and slick New York feel. Just across the road from the original premises, which now house menswear, the two-level double shop is like a mini department store. A Becca cosmetics counter complements carefully selected pieces by Cacharel, Alberta Ferretti and Miu Miu. The daywear collection boasts an excellent range of premium jeans; striking accessories include Scott Stephen's jewellery.

Timothy Everest

32 Elder Street, Spitalfields, E1 6BT (7377 5770/www.timothyeverest.co.uk). Liverpool Street tube/rail. **Open** 9am-6pm Mon-Fri; 9am-4pm alternate Sat.

What do Jarvis Cocker, Tom Cruise and David Beckham have in common? A fondness for handmade suits by the charming Timothy Everest, who rejects conventionally classic cuts. A made-to-measure suit can cost as little as £695.

Nightlife

Big Chill Bar

Old Truman Brewery, off Brick Lane, Spitalfields, E1 6QL (7392 9180/www. bigchill.net). Aldgate East tube/ Liverpool Street tube/rail. **Open** noon-midnight Mon-Thur; noon-1am Fri, Sat; 11am-11.30pm Sun. *Food served* noon-11pm Mon-Sat; noon-10.30pm Sun.

It's hard to imagine a more convivial crowd in the whole of London's thriving bar scene. The prestige of the Big Chill's annual festival plus fine artistic touches such as low-slung leather seating, a chandelier and a bison head all add to its allure. See box p100.

Cargo

83 Rivington Street, Shoreditch, EC2A 3AY (7749 7844/www.cargo-london.com). Old Street tube/rail. **Open** 6pm-1am Mon-Thur; 6pm-3am Fri, Sat; 6pm-midnight Sun. **Admission** £6-£10.

While much of Shoreditch concerns itself primarily with *how* you look while you're dancing, this railway-arch space is really only concerned with what you're dancing to. Which could be locally grown hip hop at Friends & Family or grooves to world moves at Ross Clarke's Destination Out. There's a small restaurant, plus summertime barbecues.

Comedy Café

66-68 Rivington Street, Shoreditch, EC2A 3AY (7739 5706/www.comedy cafe.co.uk). Liverpool Street or Old Street tube/rail. **Open** 7pm-midnight Wed, Thur; 6pm-1am Fri, Sat.

Most nights feature strong bills with three to four stand-ups plying their trade – expect to see the likes of Dan Antopolski, Julia Morris and Rob Rouse. Wednesday is open mike night. Attracts large parties.

Favela Chic

NEW *91-93 Great Eastern Street, Shoreditch, EC2A 3HZ (7613 5228/www.favelachic.com).Old Street tube/rail.* **Open** 6pm-1am Mon-Thur, Sun; 6pm-2am Fri, Sat. *Food served* 7pm-midnight daily.

There's a Favela Chic in Paris; this is the new London branch, already drawing queues (book dinner to guarantee a seat). For food and drink Favela Chic is merely adequate, but that's not the reason people come: that would be the modern Brazilian beats, funk carioca (sometimes called baile funk), samba 'n' bass and all the other great sounds coming out of Brazil. Loud and fun.

Medicine

89 Great Eastern Street, Shoreditch, EC2A 3HX (7739 5173/www. medicinebar.net). Old Street tube/rail. **Open** 5-11pm Mon-Wed; 5pm-2am Thur, Sat; 4pm-2am Fri. **Admission** £4-£6 after 9pm Fri, Sat.

A perfect example of when a bar is also a club. This ground floor space heaves with the post-work City crowd before making room later on for the cooler Shoreditch lot who come for Little Issst, the pint-sized electro happening once a month, Norman Jay's regular all nighters, and Tim Deluxe's AT. It works at keeping its music policy on the right side of cool.

93 Feet East

150 Brick Lane, Spitalfields, E1 6QN (7247 3293/www.93feeteast.co.uk). Aldgate East tube/Liverpool Street tube/rail. **Open** 5-11pm Mon-Thur; 5pm-1am Fri; noon-1am Sat; noon-10.30pm Sun. **Admission** £5-£10 after 9pm Fri, Sat. Credit at bar only.

We'd sell our granny to get this place a late licence, but till the devil says 'hell yeah', 93 Feet East continues to be slightly hampered by having to close at 1am. Still, it makes the most of what it's got – a great courtyard that wraps right around the back, a large balcony terrace, a bar crammed full of squishy sofas, a loft and a main space that works well as a cinema, gig venue or club.

333

Plastic People

*147-149 Curtain Road, Shoreditch,
EC2A 3QE (7739 6471/www.plastic
people.co.uk). Liverpool Street or Old
Street tube/rail.* **Open** 10pm-2am Thur;
10pm-3.30am Fri, Sat; 7.30pm-midnight
Sun. Times vary, check website. No
credit cards.

Plastic People subscribes to the old-
school line that says all you need for a
kicking party is a dark basement and
a sound system. But what it lacks in
size and decor it makes up for in sound
quality and some of London's most
progressive club nights.

333

*333 Old Street, Hoxton, EC1V 9LE
(7739 5949/www.333mother.com). Old
Street tube/rail.* **Open** *Bar* 8pm-3am
Mon-Wed; 8pm-4am Thur, Sun; 8pm-
1am Fri, Sat. *Club* 8pm-3am Wed; 10pm-
4am Thur, Sun; 10pm-5am Fri, Sat.
Admission £5-£10. Credit at bar only.

The queues still form at this landmark
Hoxton club thanks to constantly
evolving programming that, recently,
has taken in grime in the form of
Straight Outta Bethnal and given a
home to the Queens of Noize noisy
guitar bashes most Fridays. Three

floors (dark basement, big main,
Mother bar upstairs, all filled with oh-
so-cool party people) lay on everything
from Jamaican dancehall to jazz-tinged
house and electro-disco.

T-Bar

NEW *56 Shoreditch High Street,
Shoreditch, E1 6JJ (7729 2973/www.
tbarlondon.com). Liverpool Street or
Old Street tube/rail.* **Open** 9am-
midnight Mon-Wed; 9am-1am Thur;
9am-2am Fri; 8pm-2am Sat; 11am-
midnight Sun. *Food served* 9am-3pm,
5-9pm Mon-Fri; 11am-10pm Sun.

Housed inside the huge Tea Building
(home also to a gallery, studios and
design agency), T may be quiet early on
a Tuesday night but, come midnight at
the weekend, it will be rammed to the
rafters with young revellers. They're
here because there's plenty of room to
dance and no admission charged to hear
the name DJs who often play. 1960s-
styled warehouse decor, decent food and
a good, not too pricey, cocktail list.

Vibe Bar

*Old Truman Brewery, 91-95 Brick
Lane, Spitalfields, E1 6QL (7377 2899/
www.vibe-bar.co.uk). Aldgate East*

Vibe Bar p181

South London

Other than the riverside attractions described in our South Bank chapter, south London's primary area of interest for visitors is Greenwich, laden with the heritage of centuries as a royal and maritime centre. With several museums and historic buildings, enjoyable weekend markets and a lovely park, you can happily spend a day here.

Sights & museums

Cutty Sark

King William Walk, Greenwich, SE10 9HT (8858 3445/www.cuttysark. org.uk). Cutty Sark DLR/Greenwich DLR/rail. **Open** 10am-5pm daily. Last entry 4.30pm. **Admission** £5; free-£3.90 reductions.

Launched in 1869, the *Cutty Sark* brought tea from China to London, and, later, wool from Australia, and is now moored up in a riverside dry dock. The lower hold contains the largest collection of merchant figureheads in the country. But the handsome old ship is in danger of falling apart, so it will be closed for restoration from October 2006 to April 2007. After that you can take a 'hard hat' tour while the work goes on.

National Maritime Museum

Romney Road, Greenwich, SE10 9NF (8858 4422/information 8312 6565/ tours 8312 6608/www.nmm.ac.uk). Cutty Sark DLR/Greenwich DLR/rail. **Open** *July, Aug* 10am-6pm daily. *Sept-June* 10am-5pm daily. *Tours* phone for details. **Admission** free; donations appreciated.

Of the permanent galleries, 'Explorers' includes a chilling *Titanic* video display, while 'Passengers' has a cruise liner cabin mock-up and hilarious old footage. 'Art of the Sea' in Queen's House (see below) is the world's largest maritime art collection. The All Hands gallery provides interactive learning for children.

tube/Liverpool Street tube/rail. **Open** 11am-11.30pm Mon-Thur, Sun; 11am-1am Fri, Sat. **Admission** £3.50 after 8pm Fri, Sat.

Rotating DJs and a full book of live acts play diverse styles (reggae to hip hop, proper songs to experimental leftfield). In the summer, folk hang in the fairy-lit courtyard, a convenient stumble across the road from 93 Feet East.

Arts & entertainment

Rich Mix

NEW *35-47 Bethnal Green Road, Bethnal Green, E1 6LA (7613 7490/www.richmix.org.uk). Liverpool Street tube/rail.*

A rich mix of artforms are promoted at this exciting new centre, which houses a gallery, performance space, three cinemas, recording and broadcast studios, and considers fashion, food, communication, sport, design, technology and digital arts to fall within its brief. State of the arts, in the best, most inclusive way, and a great building, too.

Old Royal Naval College

King William Walk, Greenwich, SE10 9NN (8269 4747/tours 8269 4791/ www.greenwichfoundation.org.uk). Cutty Sark DLR/Greenwich DLR/rail. **Open** 10am-5pm daily (last entry 4.15pm). *Tours* by arrangement. **Admission** free.

Sir Christopher Wren's 1696 buildings were first a hospital, then a naval college and are now university premises. You can visit the rococo chapel and 18th-century Painted Hall. The chapel has free organ recitals on the first Sunday of each month. There's an ice rink outside in winter.

Queen's House

Romney Road, Greenwich, SE10 9NF (8312 6565/www.nmm.ac.uk). Cutty Sark DLR/Greenwich DLR/rail. **Open** Jan-June, Sept-Dec 10am-5pm daily. July, Aug 10am-6pm daily. Last entry 30 mins before closing. *Tours* daily; phone to check. **Admission** free; occasional charge for temporary exhibitions. *Tours* free.

This handsome Palladian abode by Inigo Jones was completed in 1640. The beautiful entrance hall, with its gallery, elaborate painted ceiling and panels, and an elegant, spiral staircase, segue into the Orangery, which affords sweeping views over Greenwich Park. The house contains the National Maritime Museum's art collection, which includes paintings by Reynolds, Hogarth and Gainsborough. A delightful colonnade connects it to the museum.

Royal Observatory & Planetarium

Greenwich Park, Greenwich, SE10 9NF (8312 6565/www.rog.nmm.ac.uk). Cutty Sark DLR/Greenwich DLR/rail. **Open** 10am-5pm daily. Last entry 4.30pm. *Tours* phone for details. **Admission** free. *Tours* free.

It's a healthy climb uphill through Greenwich Park to reach the observatory, built by Sir Christopher Wren in 1675. When you get there, though, you can straddle the Prime Meridian Line, with one foot in each of the planet's hemispheres. The dome houses the largest refracting telescope in the country, while the hilltop terrace gives the unaided eye one of the best points from which to survey London.

Four 'Time' galleries explore the standardisation of global time, which is based on the Greenwich meridian. 'Time and Longitude' covers much the same ground as Dava Sobel's bestseller *Longitude*, with the advantage that here you can actually clap eyes on some of John Harrison's extraordinary 18th-century marine clocks, among other beautiful artefacts. Other galleries focus on GPS and time-related technology down the ages.

Until the new planetarium opens (planned for 2007) visitors can see shows in a temporary planetarium back down the hill in the National Maritime Museum, with live commentary from a real astronomer.

Event highlights In spring, a new planetarium in a striking new building is scheduled to open. Shows will be live, and astronomers will commentate and answer your questions: they say every show will be different. At the same time the new 'Time and Space' gallery should open, covering astronomy past and present. A new education centre will also be opening.

Eating & drinking

Rivington

NEW *178 Greenwich High Road, Greenwich, SE10 8NN (8293 9270/ www.rivingtongrill.co.uk). Greenwich rail/DLR.* **Open** 9-11am, noon-3pm, 6.30-11pm Mon-Fri; 9-11am, noon-4pm, 6.30-11pm Sat; 9-11am, noon-4pm, 6.30-10pm Sun. **£££. British**.

Rivington is the offshoot of a well-reputed Shoreditch operation run by the company behind the Ivy, but early indications when it opened in spring 2006 were that it had some ground to make up. The service wasn't yet good enough, and the food – rootsy Brit with a modern sensibility – variable in quality and, we thought, too expensive. However, with this pedigree we expect things will improve.

Trafalgar Tavern

Park Row, Greenwich, SE10 9NW (8858 2909/www.trafalgartavern. co.uk). Cutty Sark DLR/Maze Hill rail. **Open** noon-1am Mon-Thur; noon-2am Fri, Sat; noon-midnight Sun. *Food served* noon-10pm Mon-Sat; noon-5pm Sun. **££**. **Gastropub**.

The Trafalgar Tavern celebrated the anniversary of its namesake battle by proudly adding a statue of Nelson to the riverside cobblestones by the pub's entrance. It's a landmark, thanks to the River Thames lapping against the wall, but it wears its status with low-key grandeur as well as pleasing, unpretentious food and prices. Several large rooms with, unsurprisingly, nautical decoration.

Shopping

The Emporium

330-332 Creek Road, Greenwich, SE10 9SW (8305 1670). Cutty Sark DLR. **Open** 10.30am-6pm Tue-Sun.

For vintage fans, the main attraction in Greenwich is this shop, where prices are more reasonable than they are in central London. The emphasis is slightly more on menswear than it is on womenswear, and most items are from the 1950s, '60s and '70s. The Emporium is famous for its vintage sunglasses.

Essential Music

16 Greenwich Market, Greenwich, SE10 9HZ (8305 1876). Greenwich rail/DLR. **Open** 10am-6pm daily.

Hidden in the shroud of Greenwich's covered market, Essential is home to a strong selection of CDs: rock, pop, electronica, jazz, blues, soul and 1970s.

Flying Duck Enterprises

320-322 Creek Road, Greenwich, SE10 9SW (8858 1964/www.flying-duck.com). Cutty Sark DLR. **Open** 11am-6pm Mon-Fri; 10.30am-6.30pm Sat, Sun.

This colourful shop stocks a plethora of reasonably priced original pieces from the 1950s, '60s and '70s. Kitsch '50s bar culture is well represented.

Greenwich Market

Off Greenwich High Road, Greenwich, SE10 (www.greenwichmarket.net). Greenwich rail/DLR/Cutty Sark DLR. **Open** *Antiques & collectibles* 7.30am-5pm Thur; 9.30am-5pm Fri. *Village Market, Stockwell Street* 7am-5pm Sat, Sun. *Arts & crafts* 9.30am-5pm Sat, Sun. *Food court* 10am-4pm Sat, Sun.

Heading into the town centre from the station, you come first to the antiques market, a collection that varies from tat to treasures. Next along is the Village Market, where a second-hand clothes mingle with Chinese silk dresses, cheap trendy clothes, ethnic ornaments and CDs. Passing the food court you reach the covered Crafts Market, ideal for gift-hunting. The central hub of stalls sells a delicious selection of olives, breads, jam doughnuts and brownies.

Arts & leisure

Carling Academy Brixton

211 Stockwell Road, Brixton, SW9 9SL (information 7771 3000/box office 08707 712 000/www.brixton-academy.co.uk). Brixton tube/rail.

Excellent sightlines, decent sound and a glorious, cod-Gothic interior ensure that shows at this 4,700-capacity institution are real events.

West London

The triangle made by the tube stations of Notting Hill Gate, Ladbroke Grove and Westbourne Park contains some lovely squares, houses and gardens along with the fashionable shops, bars and restaurants that serve their not-so-poor, but stylishly boho, residents. Notting Hill Gate isn't an attractive high street, but a turn north into Pembridge Road takes you towards the boutique streets of Westbourne Grove and Ledbury Road. Don't miss the enjoyable market street of Portobello Road. Market day is Saturday, but it's a proper shopping artery during the week, too.

Sights & museums

Kensal Green Cemetery

Harrow Road, Kensal Green, W10 4RA (8969 0152/tours 7402 2749/www. kensalgreen.co.uk). Kensal Green tube. **Open** *Apr-Sept* 9am-6pm Mon-Sat; 10am-6pm Sun. *Oct-Mar* 9am-5pm Mon-Sat; 10am-5pm Sun. **Admission** free. *Tours £5 donation; £4 reductions. No credit cards.*

Behind the neo-classical gate is a green oasis of the dead. The resting place of both the Duke of Sussex, sixth son of King George III, and his sister, HRH Princess Sophia, was the place to be buried in the 19th century. Wilkie Collins, Anthony Trollope and William Makepeace Thackeray all lie here, but it is the mausoleums of lesser folk that make the most eye-catching graves (bring a torch).

Museum of Brands, Packaging & Advertising

NEW *2 Colville Mews, Lonsdale Road, Notting Hill, W11 2AR (7908 0880/ www.museumofbrands.com). Notting Hill Gate tube.* **Open** 10am-6pm Tue-Sat; 11am-4pm Sun. *Last admission 1hr before closing.* **Admission** £5.80; free-£3.50 reductions.

Robert Opie began collecting the sort of things most of us throw away when he was 16. Over the years the collection has grown to include everything from milk bottles to vacuum cleaners through posters advertising milk and vacuum cleaners. The museum's emphasis is on British consumerism over the last century or so, though there are items as old as an ancient Egyptian doll. The greatest interest is for British nostalgists, even of the modern day, from Crunchie bars to Kia-ora orange squash.

Eating & drinking

Clarke's

124 Kensington Church Street, Kensington, W8 4BH (7221 9225/ www.sallyclarke.com). Notting Hill Gate tube. **Open** 12.30-2pm Mon; 12.30-2pm, 7-10pm Tue-Fri; 11am-2pm, 7-10pm Sat. **£££**. **Modern European**.

For more than 20 years Sally Clarke's restaurant has produced fresh, simple cooking with seasonal and meticulously sourced ingredients. Influences dip in and out of France, the Med and California. Dinner is a no-choice set menu (£49.50 for four courses, or you can have fewer).

The Cow

89 Westbourne Park Road, Westbourne Park, W2 5QH (7221 0021). Royal Oak or Westbourne Park tube. **Open** noon-11pm Mon-Thur; noon-midnight Fri, Sat; noon-10.30pm Sun. *Food served* noon-3.30pm, 6-10.30pm Mon-Sat; noon-3.30pm, 6-10pm Sun. **£££**. **Gastropub**.

It may be just a small 1950s-styled room over a pub, but Tom Conran's Cow is surely one of the best restaurants in Notting Hill. The mix of classical and inventive on the short menu is admirable, and service is relaxed. Guinness and oysters a speciality, the crowd west London arty-trendy.

Dove

19 Upper Mall, Hammersmith, W6 9TA (8748 5405). Hammersmith or Ravenscourt Park tube. **Open** 11am-11pm Mon-Sat; noon-10.30pm Sun. *Food served* noon-2.30pm, 5-9pm Mon-Sat; 12.30-4.30pm Sun. **Pub**.

We include the Dove because of its terrace overlooking the Thames (packed out for the Boat Race), but it would be a great pub whatever its location: dripping with historic and literary connections, it is sumptuously scruffy and has good wine, beer and food.

Galicia

323 Portobello Road, Ladbroke Grove, W105SY (8969 3539). Ladbroke Grove tube. **Open** Tue-Sun noon-11.30pm. **££**. **Spanish**.

A family restaurant that's a permanent part of the scenery for the Iberian community in the area. Munch on authentic tapas dishes and wash them down with Galician wine or beer surrounded by (mainly) Spanish voices.

LONDON BY AREA

E&O

14 Blenheim Crescent, Notting Hill,
W11 1NN (7229 5454/www.eando.nu).
Ladbroke Grove or Notting Hill Gate
tube. **Open** noon-3pm, 6-10.30pm
Mon-Sat; 12.30-3pm, 6-10pm Sun.
£££. Oriental.
This hip New York-style venue pulls
in Prada-clad A-listers by the limo-
load. The design is suffused with
understated cool (striking dark wood
contrasts with cream walls) and staff
are welcoming and efficient. The chilli-
salt squid is a must-try.

Earl of Lonsdale

277-281 Westbourne Grove, Notting
Hill, W11 2A (7727 6335). Notting Hill
or Ladbroke Grove tube. **Open** noon-
11pm Mon-Fri; 10am-11pm Sat; noon-
10.30pm Sun. *Food served* noon-3pm
and 6-9.15pm daily. **Pub**.
This Samuel Smith pub has had an
unusually sensitive refurbishment
recently which has retained all that is
wonderful about an old boozer (plenty
of etched glass and a host of little dark-
panelled snugs) while sprucing it up
for the 21st century. There's also very
cheap beer, one of the best pub gardens
in the area and a friendly bunch of
locals to chat to.

Electric Brasserie

191 Portobello Road, Ladbroke Grove,
W11 2ED (7908 9696/www.the-
electric.co.uk). Ladbroke Grove tube.
Open 8am-12.30am Mon-Wed; 8am-
1am Thur-Sat; 8am-midnight Sun.
££. Brasserie.
Next to the Electric Cinema, this hip
brasserie is a cool place to hang out
with friends, and has proved a major
hit with local celebrities. There's a
noisy, bustling bar at the front with
communal tables and benches, and a
quieter, more formal dining area at the
back. Good cocktails.

The Ledbury

127 Ledbury Road, Notting Hill, W11
2AQ (7792 9090/www.theledbury.com).
Westbourne Park tube. **Open** noon-
2.30pm, 6.30-11pm Mon-Sat; noon-
2.30pm, 6.30-10pm Sun. **£££. French**.

The Ledbury represents a distinct
culinary step up for Notting Hill. The
talented chef is Australian Brett
Graham, and, small niggles aside, his
handsome restaurant is winning
deserved accolades.

River Café

Thames Wharf, Rainville Road,
Hammersmith, W6 9HA (7386
4200/www.rivercafe.co.uk).
Hammersmith tube. **Open** 12.30-
2.15pm, 7-9pm Mon-Thur; 12.30-
2.30pm, 7-9.15pm Fri, Sat; noon-3pm
Sun. **££££. Italian**.
While it's all too easy to be disen-
chanted by the restaurants of celebrity
chefs (in this case Rose Gray and Ruth
Rogers), the River Café rarely disap-
points. This operation seems only to
improve with age, continuing to rely on
top-notch ingredients, simply cooked,
to produce excellent, memorable meals
time after time.

Shopping

As well as the wonderful, winding
Portobello Road, there are plenty
of shopping opportunities around
Golborne Road (antiques),
Ladbroke Grove and Westbourne
Grove (jewellers and boutiques).

Aimé

32 Ledbury Road, Notting Hill, W11
2AB (7221 7070/www.aimelondon.
com). Notting Hill Gate tube. **Open**
10.30am-7pm Mon-Sat.
French-Cambodian sisters Val and
Vanda Heng Vong bring a slice of
understated Parisian cool to Notting
Hill, showcasing designers such as
Isabel Marant and Claudie Pierlot.
Aimé is the main London stockist of
chic French basics line APC, and sells
the sweet Repetto ballet flats sported
by Brigitte Bardot.

Appleby

95 Westbourne Park Villas,
Westbourne Park, W2 5ED (7229
7772/www.applebyvintage.com).
Westbourne Park tube. **Open**
11am-6pm Mon-Sat.

Only the most immaculate pieces make it onto the rails of Jane Appleby-Deen's shop. Her stock is an interesting mix of pieces from the early 1920s through to the 1980s. Most customers come here to look for something special and while most clothes are over £80, cheaper items have been introduced.

Books for Cooks

4 Blenheim Crescent, Ladbroke Grove, W11 1NN (7221 1992/www.books forcooks.com). Ladbroke Grove tube. **Open** 10am-6pm Tue-Sat.

The lovely smells that emanate from this traditional-looking shop ensure its continued popularity: every day, staff cook treats from the limitless recipes to hand in the smart test kitchen/coffee shop at the back. Cookery workshops take place upstairs.

The Cross

141 Portland Road, Holland Park, W11 4LR (7727 6760). Holland Park tube. **Open** 11am-5.30pm Mon-Sat.

Still one of London's most successful boutiques. The eclectic compilation of designers takes in Easton Pearson, Gharani Strok and Clements Ribeiro. American imports include environmentally friendly celeb-fave Dosa from LA. There's also casualwear from Ella Moss, Juicy Couture and Splendid, great sweaters from Tania

and the shop's own luscious cashmere. Cross The Road – at No.139 – sells homewares.

Paul Smith

122 Kensington Park Road, Notting Hill, W11 2EP (7727 3553/www.paul smith.co.uk). Notting Hill Gate tube. **Open** 10am-6pm Mon-Fri; 10am-6.30pm Sat.

Sir Paul Smith's popularity as the doyen of British style shows little sign of waning. The collections – including women's, kids', accessories and furniture – are spread over four floors. The place is dotted with Sir Paul's collection of art and other objects, providing a fascinating insight into the vision behind his colourful yet refined suits, tailoring, luxe knits, preppy casualwear and outerwear.

Portobello Road Market

Portobello Road, W10, W11; Golborne Road, W10. Ladbroke Grove, Notting Hill Gate or Westbourne Park tube (www.portobelloroad.co.uk). **Open** *General* 8am-6.30pm Mon-Wed, Fri, Sat; 8am-1pm Thur. *Antiques* 4am-6pm Sat.

Starting at the Notting Hill end are mainly antiques stalls. Further down the hill you come to the food stalls, ranging from traditional fruit and veg to tasty cheeses, stuffed olives, bratwurst and crêpes. Next up come

Portobello Road Market

clothes and jewellery (from cheap trendy club- and casual wear to craft bracelets and earrings). The cafés under the Westway are a good place to have some refreshment before plunging into the new designers' clothes and vintage wear off to the left.

Rellik

8 Golborne Road, Ladbroke Grove, W10 5NW (8962 0089/www. relliklondon.co.uk). Westbourne Park tube. **Open** 10am-6pm Tue-Sat.

Arguably the trendiest of London's retro shops, Rellik counts models, designers and fashion journalists among its loyal customers. Clothes range from the 1920s to the 1980s, taking in pieces by Vivienne Westwood, Pucci, Yves Saint Laurent, Bill Gibb, Ossie Clark and Zandra Rhodes among many others.

Themes & Variations

231 Westbourne Grove, Notting Hill, W11 2SE (7727 5531/www.themesand variations.com). Notting Hill Gate tube. **Open** 10am-1pm, 2-6pm Mon-Fri; 10am-6pm Sat.

Liliane Fawcett's enduringly chic gallery has always had a strong focus on Scandinavian and Italian decorative arts and furniture. Stylish post-war and contemporary furniture is her speciality, and the place also has very good lighting.

Nightlife

Ruby & Sequoia

6-8 All Saints Road, Ladbroke Grove, W11 1HH (7243 6363/www. ruby.uk.com). Westbourne Park tube. **Open** 6pm-12.30am Mon-Thur; 6pm-2am Fri; 11am-2am Sat; 11am-12.30am Sun. *Food served* 6-11pm Mon-Fri; noon-11pm Sat, Sun.

This latest bar and restaurant from the Ruby Lounge folks is ace. The fun ground floor bar is impressive enough; the dining area offers an ambitious menu and prices to match; but it's as a bar that R&S is best. After 9pm DJs work the decks in the bigger and more elegant basement full of studied cool.

Arts & leisure

Carling Apollo Hammersmith

Queen Caroline Street, Hammersmith, W6 9QH (8563 3800/box office 0870 606 3400/www.getlive.co.uk). Hammersmith tube.

A 5,000-capacity music venue about which there's little else to say.

Porchester Spa

The Porchester Centre, Queensway, W2 5HS (7792 3980). Bayswater tube. **Open** *Women only* 10am-10pm Tue, Thur, Fri; 10am-4pm Sun. *Men only* 10am-10pm Mon, Wed, Sat. *Mixed couples* 4-10pm Sun. Last entry 2hrs before closing. **Admission** £20.35; £28.25 couples.

The Porchester is quite unlike any other spa you'll visit. Forget air-conditioning and tinkly music: this place feels like a municipal swimming pool, just with original art deco architectural touches. The therapies here are as good as many of those costing three times as much in more luxurious surroundings.

Riverside Studios

Crisp Road, Hammersmith, W6 9L (8237 1111/www.riversidestudios. co.uk). Hammersmith tube.

Originally a film and TV studio since before the war (this was once the set for Quatermass), nowadays you'll see a different calibre of artistic endeavour at the Riverside Studios. Its theatre, film and exhibition spaces present a consistently innovative, challenging and broad progamme of events which has kept the Riverside Studios, in their latest incarnation, fresh for more than 30 years.

Shepherd's Bush Empire

Shepherd's Bush Green, Shepherd's Bush, W12 8TT (8740 1515/box office 0870 771 2000/www.shepherds-bush-empire.co.uk). Shepherd's Bush tube.

This 2,000-capacity former BBC theatre is London's best mid sized venue. The sound is usually splendid, the atmosphere warm, the staff friendly and the booking policy eclectic.

Royal Botanic Gardens p193

Day Trips

Scattered around the more elegant reaches of outer London are a wealth of landmark museums, parks and royal residences that easily merit a trip. Thanks to London's efficient commuter rail network and its extensive tube lines, all are well within an hour's journey from central London. For information on train services call 08457 484950, and for tube and bus services 7222 1234.

Note that between April and September, a riverboat service runs from Westminster Pier to Kew Gardens and Hampton Court, allowing you to combine these two destinations in one long day out.

Eltham Palace

Court Yard, off Court Road, SE9 5QE (8294 2548/www.elthampalace.org.uk). Eltham rail. **Open** *Apr-Oct* 10am-5pm Mon-Wed, Sun. *Nov-Mar* 10am-4pm Mon-Wed, Sun. Closed 22 Dec-31 Jan. **Admission** *House & grounds* (incl audio tour) £7.60; free-£5.70 reductions. *Grounds* £4.80; free-£3.60 reductions.

Eltham is not one of London's more celebrated suburbs, so this place comes as a surprise: a magnificent royal residence dating back to the 13th century, outstandingly rebuilt in high style in the 1930s, with broad, beautiful gardens.

The royal palace fell out of favour in Henry VIII's reign, and its Great Hall was used as a barn for many years. But in 1931 it was reborn, thanks to millionaire patrons Stephen and Virginia Courtauld. They commissioned a thoroughly modern house adjoining the relics of the old palace; its luxurious art deco interior has been preserved and furnished by English Heritage.

The Great Hall, with its stained glass and intricate hammer-beam roof, plus a 15th-century stone bridge over the moat and various medieval ruins, are all that's left of the royal original. The 1930s interiors are expensive, elegant and glossy, all polished veneer and chunky marble, with centuries of

European design heritage seen through a Deco optic. The Courtaulds engaged an international posse of designers to show what could be done with a brief to dazzle and a budget to disbelieve, and specced many high-tec touches such as piped music and a clock that took its time signal direct from Greenwich.

The couple and their pet lemur Mah-Jongg enjoyed entertaining lavishly in their palace for only eight years before handing it over to the army in 1944. By the time English Heritage took over in the 1980s and '90s, the original furniture was gone: what is there now are painstakingly precise reproductions.

The extensive grounds are beautifully restored and the traditional tea room and shop have a 1930s flavour.

Firepower

Royal Arsenal, SE18 6ST (8855 7755/www.firepower.org.uk). Woolwich Arsenal rail. **Open** *Nov-Mar* 10.30am-5pm Fri-Sun. *Apr-Oct* 10.30am-5pm Wed-Sun. Last entry 4pm. **Admission** £5; free-£4.50 reductions.

This army museum traces artillery from catapults to nuclear warheads. Sounds, smoke and searchlights lend realism, and there's all sorts of weaponry to look at. An interactive demonstration uses table-tennis balls for ammunition. Kids love the first-floor Command Post, with its climbing wall, air-raid shelters and paintball gallery. In 2006 there's a fireworks exhibition (20 Oct-31 Dec, including a grand display on Bonfire Night).

Ham House

Ham Street, Ham, Richmond, Surrey TW10 7RS (8940 1950/www.national trust.org.uk/hamhouse). Richmond tube/rail, then 371 bus. **Open** *Gardens* 11am-6pm or dusk if earlier Mon-Wed, Sat, Sun. *House* 1-5pm Mon-Wed, Sat, Sun. Closed Nov-Mar. **Admission** *House & gardens* £8; free-£4 reductions. *Gardens only* £4; free-£2 reductions.

Built in 1610 for one of James I's courtiers, this lavish red-brick mansion is an outstanding Stuart property, filled with period furnishings, rococo

mirrors and ornate tapestries. The detailing is exquisite, down to a table in the dairy with sculpted cows' legs. The formal grounds attract the most attention: there's a trellised Cherry Garden dominated by a statue of Bacchus. The tea room in the old orangery turns out historic dishes (lavender syllabub, for instance) using ingredients from the kitchen gardens. From Ham House you can take a small passenger ferry across the river to Marble Hill house.

Hampton Court Palace

East Molesey, Surrey KT8 9AU (0870 751 5175/information 0870 752 7777/www.hrp.org.uk). Hampton Court rail/riverboat from Westminster or Richmond to Hampton Court Pier (Apr-Oct). **Open** *Palace* Mar-Oct 10am-6pm daily. Nov-Feb 10am-4.30pm daily (last entry 1hr before closing). *Park* dawn-dusk daily. **Admission** *Palace, courtyard, cloister & maze* £12.30; free-£10 reductions. *Maze only* £3.50; £2.50 reductions. *Gardens only* £4; free-£3 reductions.

Primarily remembered for chopping off Anne Boleyn's head, having six wives and bringing about the Reformation, Henry VIII is one of history's best-known monarchs. This Tudor palace is a suitably spectacular monument to him. It was built in 1514 by Cardinal Wolsey, Henry's high-flying lord chancellor, but Henry liked it so much he seized it for himself in 1528. For the next 200 years it was a focal point in English history: Elizabeth I was imprisoned in a tower here by her elder sister Mary I; Shakespeare gave his debut performance to James I here in 1604; and after the Civil War, Oliver Cromwell was so besotted with the building that he ditched his puritanical principles and moved in.

Centuries later, the rosy walls of the palace still dazzle. Its vast size can be daunting, so you could take advantage of the costumed guided tours. If you do decide to go it alone, it's probably best to start with Henry VIII's State Apartments, which include the Great

Hall, noted for its splendid hammer-beam roof, beautiful stained-glass windows and elaborate religious tapestries; in the Haunted Gallery, the ghost of Catherine Howard – Henry's fifth wife, executed for adultery in 1542 – can reputedly be heard shrieking and forever trying to flee. The King's Apartments, added in 1689 by Sir Christopher Wren, are notable for a splendid mural of Alexander the Great, painted by Antonio Verrio. The Queen's Apartments and Georgian Rooms feature similarly elaborate paintings, chandeliers and tapestries. The Tudor Kitchens are great fun, with their giant cauldrons, fake pies and blood-spattered walls (no vegetarians in those days).

More spectacular sights await outside, where the exquisitely landscaped gardens include perfectly sculpted trees, peaceful Thames views, and the famous maze (in which, incidentally, it's virtually impossible to get lost).

Horniman Museum

100 London Road, Forest Hill, SE23 3PQ (8699 1872/www.horniman. ac.uk). Forest Hill rail/122, 176, 185, 312, P4 bus. **Open** 10.30am-5.30pm daily. **Admission** free; donations appreciated.

It's a little out of the way, but there are many curiosities in this jolly art nouveau museum. In the Natural History gallery, a plump stuffed walrus on a plinth presides over skeletons, pickled animals, stuffed birds and insect models in glass cases; on the gallery above is the Apostle clock, with a delightful animated chime at 4pm. The African Worlds gallery has Egyptian mummies, ceremonial masks and an Ijele masquerade costume. Outside, there is a spacious café and lovely gardens. An aquarium opened in 2006 to explore endangered ecosystems, with more than 250 species of animals and plants.

Marble Hill House

Richmond Road, Twickenham, Middlesex, TW1 2NL (8892 5115/ www.english-heritage.org.uk). Richmond tube/rail/St Margaret's rail/33, 90, 490, H22, R70 bus. **Open** *Apr-Nov* 10am-2pm Sat; 10am-5pm Sun; group visits Mon-Fri by request. *Oct* 10am-4pm daily. *Nov-Mar* by request. *Tours* noon, 3pm Tue, Wed. **Admission** (includes tour) £4; free-£3 reductions.

Eltham Palace p189

Ah, royal love. King George II spared no expense to please his mistress, Henrietta Howard. Not only did he build this perfect Palladian house (1724) for his lover, he almost dragged Britain into a war while doing so: by using Honduran mahogany to construct the grand staircase, he sparked a diplomatic row with Spain. In retrospect, it was worth it. Over the centuries, this stately mansion has welcomed the great and the good: luminaries such as Alexander Pope, Jonathan Swift and Horace Walpole were all entertained in the opulent Great Room. Picnic parties are welcome; so are athletes (there are tennis, putting and cricket facilities). Ferries regularly cross the river to neighbouring Ham House.

Royal Botanic Gardens (Kew Gardens)

Kew, Richmond, Surrey TW9 3AB (8332 5655/information 8940 1171/www.kew.org). Kew Gardens tube/rail/Kew Bridge rail/riverboat to Kew Pier. **Open** *Late Mar-Aug* 9.30am-6.30pm Mon-Fri; 9.30am-7.30pm Sat, Sun. *Sept, Oct* 9.30am-6pm daily. *Late Oct-early Feb* 9.30am-4.15pm daily. *Early Feb-late Mar* 9.30am-5.30pm daily. Last entry 30mins before closing. *Tours* 11am, 2pm daily. **Admission** £11.75; free-£8.75 reductions.

Kew's lush, landscaped beauty represents the pinnacle of the English gardening obsession. From the early 1700s until 1840, when the gardens were given to the nation, these were the grounds for two royal residences, the White House and Richmond Lodge. Eighteenth-century residents King George II and Queen Caroline were enthusiastic gardeners; Caroline was fond of exotic plants, and had a series of temples built. In the mid 1700s, Lancelot 'Capability' Brown began designing an organised layout for the property.

At 300 acres, Kew is enormous, so pick up a map at the ticket office, and follow the signs. The tourist train from Victoria Gate provides a 35-minute tour of the gardens' highlights (£3.50;

What the Dickens?

A £62-million project, **Dickens World** is part of a regeneration scheme for the Medway town of Chatham, 35 miles south-east of London, and home to Dickens during his childhood. Due to open in April 2007, the park aims to deliver commercial 'edutainment'. Within a covered Victorian London setting, with cobbled pavements, dim lighting and faux Dickensian architecture, the planned park will combine shops, restaurants and a multiplex cinema, rides based on the novels (anyone for the Oliver Twister?) and employees parading in costume.

Critics will doubtless home in on the 'dumbing down' element: it's hard to imagine how theme park characters can be anything other than one-dimensional or how the complexities of the plots will be represented. And while Dickens himself wouldn't necessarily have been against the project (his own magazine was a profit-making enterprise), the melding of financial ambition with great literature isn't going to sit that well with purists.

Yet, if Dickens World helps us to celebrate one of England's finest and most prolific writers, it's not to be scoffed at; and if it regenerates an area long in need of socio-economic rejuvenation (the dockyard that employed Dickens's father closed in the 1980s), then perhaps the great novelist and social commentator just might have approved.

■ www.dickensworld.co.uk

£1 reductions). Any visit to Kew should take in the two huge 19th-century greenhouses filled to the roof with plants, some as old as the fanciful glass structures that house them. The high-tech Princess of Wales Conservatory houses ten climate zones under one roof, and the elegantly arched Davies Alpine House opened in March 2006 to provide a homely climate for high-altitude native plants.

Queen Charlotte's Cottage has a dazzling springtime bluebell garden and the Rose Garden and Woodland Garden are the stuff of fairy tales, while Redwood Grove has a treetop walkway 33 feet above the ground. For an interesting perspective on 17th-century life, head to Kew Palace, the smallest royal palace in Britain, a lovely structure that was due to reopen in 2006 after years of renovation.

You can see Syon House (below) from Kew, but transport is difficult (the river's in the way).

Syon House

Syon Park, Brentford, Middx TW8 8JF (8560 0881/www.syonpark.co.uk). Gunnersbury tube/rail then 237, 267 bus. **Open** *House mid Mar-Oct 11am-5pm Wed, Thur, Sun. Gardens year-round 10.30am-dusk daily. Tours by arrangement.* **Admission** *House & gardens £7.50; £6.50 reductions. Gardens £3.75; £2.50 reductions. Tours free.*

The Percys, Dukes of Northumberland, sure know a film tie-in when they see one. Their Northumbrian home, Alnwick Castle, stood in for Hogwarts in *Harry Potter and the Philosopher's Stone*, while Syon House took a starring role in *Gosford Park*. The house stands on the site of a Bridgettine monastery. During the Dissolution of the Monasteries the nuns' father confessor, Richard Reynolds, refused to accept King Henry VIII as head of the church and was executed. The building was turned into a house in 1547 for the Duke of Northumberland, and its neo-classical interior was created by Robert Adam in 1761. The gardens were designed by Lancelot 'Capability' Brown. Paintings by Van Dyck, Gainsborough and Reynolds hang inside. Other attractions include the London Butterfly House (8560 7272), the Tropical Experience (8847 4730), an indoor adventure playground and a trout fishery.

Thames Barrier Information & Learning Centre

1 Unity Way, SE18 5NJ (8305 4188/ www.environment-agency.gov.uk). North Greenwich tube/Charlton rail/riverboats to & from Greenwich Pier & Westminster Pier/177, 180 bus. **Open** *Apr-Sept 10.30am-4.30pm daily. Oct-Mar 11am-3.30pm daily. Closed 24 Dec-2 Jan.* **Admission** *Exhibition £1.50; free-£1 reductions.*

The key player in London's flood defences is the world's largest adjustable dam. Since it was built in 1982 it has saved London from flooding nearly 70 times. The small Learning Centre shows which parts of London would be submerged if it stopped working. Time your visit to see it in action (there's not in fact a lot to see at other times): every September there's a full-scale test closure, with a partial test once a month (ring for dates). The best views are from a boat: Campion Cruises (8305 0300) runs trips from Greenwich (Mar-Oct only).

WWT Wetland Centre

Queen Elizabeth's Walk, SW13 9WT (8409 4400/www.wwt.org.uk). Hammersmith tube then 283 bus/33, 72, 209 bus. **Open** *Mar-Oct 9.30am-6pm daily. Nov-Feb 9.30am-5pm daily. Last entry 1hr before closing.* **Admission** *£7.25; free-£6 reductions.*

A mere four miles from central London, the Wetland Centre feels worlds away. Quiet ponds, rustling reeds and wildflower gardens teem with bird life – 150 species at last count. Botanists ponder its 27,000 trees and 300,000 aquatic plants; naturalists swoon at the 300 varieties of butterfly, 20 types of dragonfly, four species of bat and the endangered water voles. There's a decent café with an outdoor terrace.

Essentials

Hotels

There's a hotel boom in London at the moment, expected to continue till the 2012 Olympics, by which time at least 20,000 rooms will have been added. You might hope that this would result in a competitive market, but in the short-term, at least, it ain't so: Deloitte estimates that in 2006 rates will have climbed year on year by an average of 7 to 8 per cent. Just as well, then, that London's budget to mid range hotels have recently raised their game, with lots of renovations and facility upgrades and the arrival of more and more chains – not everyone's first choice, but a boon in this town if you want to keep your night rate in double figures. That's not to say there aren't also more characterful options, but you should steer clear of booking blind: there's a depressingly large amount of dross masquerading as country charm.

Now boutique minimalism has filtered down to corporate digs and the better mid range properties offer facilities like CD players and robes as standard, the top end has to offer something special. Few of the newer offerings have shown enough cachet or imagination to justify their prices, given that the well-established players generally remain on top of their game. The sector seems in thrall to the rise of hotel queen Kit Kemp (see box p204), who plans to open the Haymarket in late 2006.

Money matters

Hotels are constantly offering special deals, particularly for

Claridge's p203

Hotels

S H O R T L I S T

Best new
- Haymarket (box p204)
- New Linden (p211)
- Base2stay (p209)
- Yotel (p210)

Best for hipsters
- Hotel 167 (p211)
- Zetter (p201)

Glossy mag favourites
- Brown's (p201)
- Soho Hotel (p207)

Most stellar restaurants
- Claridge's (p203)
- Halkin (p209)
- Metropolitan (p204)

Best residents' bar
- Claridge's Macanudo bar (p203)
- Sanderson's Purple bar (p207)

Cheap as chips
- Generator (p203)
- Piccadilly Backpackers (p207)

Cheap for the location
- Mad Hatter (left)
- Premier Travel Inn Metro (p199)

Best afternoon tea
- Claridge's (p203)
- The Savoy (p207)

Superior B&Bs
- B&B Belgravia (p209)
- Number Sixteen (p211)
- 22 York Street (p207)

Budget style
- Harlingford Hotel (p203)
- New Linden (p211)

All-round winners
- Baglioni (p209)
- Great Eastern Hotel (p199)
- Malmaison (p200)
- Rookery (p200)
- Soho Hotel (p207)
- One Aldwych (p207)

weekends: always check websites or ask about special rates when booking. Also check discount hotel websites – for example www.alpharooms.com and www.london-discount-hotel.com – for prices that can fall well below the rack rates listed here.

Many high-end hotels quote room prices exclusive of VAT. Always check.

The South Bank

Mad Hatter

3-7 Stamford Street, South Bank, SE1 9NY (7401 9222/www.fullershotels. com). Southwark tube/Waterloo tube/rail. £.

Owned by the Fuller's pub chain, the Mad Hatter has recently ditched the 'Ye Olde England' pastiche in its non-smoking rooms for contemporary colour schemes and modern wall-mounted headboards. They don't exactly ooze character, but they're

ESSENTIALS

Time Out Shortlist | London 2007 **197**

Luxury London Hotels
at lowest prices available - guaranteed

call *freephone* 0800-LONDON
that's 0800-566-366 if you don't have letters on your phone.
If you are outside of the UK call +44 800 566 366

0800 LONDON®
LONDON'S FREE TELEPHONE BOOKING SERVICE

We can also arrange your seats at the theatre, opera,
football, rock and pop concerts, private sightseeing tours
or a chauffeur to pick you up from the airport.
Open every day until midnight

London hotels, hostels, B&Bs & apartments, all at guaranteed lowest rates

London hotels
FROM
£50
per double room per night

All deals are subject to availability so check online now or call 0207 437 4370

Plus, you can now get LondonTown.com's great internet rates over the phone

You can call us every day until midnight on
0207 437 4370

LONDONTOWN.com™
Your Best Friend in London™

Zetter p201

large and well kept, and the attached Fuller's pub offers a decent selection of English ales. Tate Modern and the South Bank theatres are nearby.

Premier Travel Inn Metro

County Hall, Belvedere Road, South Bank, SE1 7PB (0870 238 3300/www. travelinn.co.uk). Waterloo tube/rail. **£**.
A room in a landmark building on the Thames, next to the London Eye, for less than £90? County Hall's former tenant, the Greater London Council, has been gone for over two decades, but the prices at this outpost of the Premier Travel Inn chain are still more in line with the 1980s. Just don't expect the opulence of the exterior to carry on inside, or any river views.

Southwark Rose

NEW *Southwark Bridge Road, Southwark, SE1 9HH (7015 1480/ www.southwarkrosehotel.co.uk). London Bridge tube/rail.* **££**.
It may sound like a dodgy faux-Tudor guesthouse, but the Southwark Rose (handily placed for Tate Modern, Borough Market and Shakespeare's Globe) is the antithesis: a slick, purpose-built, budget-conscious property with the elements that have become shorthand for 'modern luxury hotel'.

The City

Great Eastern Hotel

40 Liverpool Street, The City, EC2M 7QN (7618 5000/www. great-eastern-hotel.co.uk). Liverpool Street tube/rail. **££££**.
Once a faded railway hotel, the Great Eastern is now a mammoth urban style mecca, with a design sympathetic to the glorious Victorian building. Bedrooms wear the regulation style mag uniform: Eames chairs, chocolate shagpile rugs and white Frette linens. And you'll never go hungry or thirsty – the hotel has seven restaurants and bars, of generally impressive quality, though they're no longer Conran-run. The hotel has recently become a Hyatt.

Ibis

NEW *5 Commercial Street, The City, E1 6BF, (7422 8400/www.ibishotel. com). Aldgate East tube.* **£**.

ESSENTIALS

Mandeville p204

This is a cheap and cheerful chain, so don't expect character or luxury, but the location is well placed for nightlife, the prices keen and the rooms newly done out, with all the basic facilities, including TV and wireless internet. There's a brasserie attached.

Malmaison

Charterhouse Square, Clerkenwell, EC1M 6AH (7012 3700/www. malmaison.com). Farringdon tube/rail. **££**.

The 'Mal' charges rates well below anything comparable for its thoughtfully specced rooms (24-hour room service, CD players and free broadband access), non-institutional public areas and atmospheric restaurant. It's a lovely building (an old nurses' home) with a buzz to it, but as with any chain you are aware it is a formula.

Rookery

12 Peter's Lane, Cowcross Street, Clerkenwell, EC1M 6DS (7336 0931/www.rookeryhotel.com). Farringdon tube/rail. **£££**.

Hidden down an alleyway, the infinitely charming Rookery has been converted from a row of 18th-century buildings and crammed full of glorious antiques: Gothic oak beds, plaster busts and clawfoot bathtubs. It's equipped with the full range of modern creature comforts too. Rooms vary in size, and all are characterful.

Saint Gregory

100 Shoreditch High Street, Shoreditch, E1 6JQ (7613 9800/ www.saintgregoryhotel.com). Shoreditch tube/Old Street or Liverpool Street tube/rail. **£££**.

The Saint Gregory feels a bit like a Holiday Inn masquerading as a style hotel. But that's not such a bad thing. The location's great, and the rates, particularly special weekend deals, are reasonable. The rooms – decorated in a game attempt at retro chic – are spacious and comfortable with swanky Villeroy & Boch bathrooms. The airy Globe Restaurant on the seventh floor boasts mesmerising views of the City.

Threadneedles

5 Threadneedle Street, The City, EC2R 8AY (7657 8080/www.theeton collection.com). Bank tube/DLR. **£££**.

from the huge industrial windows and cosied up with such homely comforts as hot-water bottles. Prices beat the West End hands down.

The West End

Academy Hotel

21 Gower Street, Bloomsbury, WC1E 6HG (7631 4115/www.theeton collection.com). Goodge Street tube. **££**. Comprising five Georgian townhouses, the Academy has a tastefully restrained country-house style. Both conservatory and library open onto fragrant walled gardens, where drinks and breakfast are served in summer, and windows are double-glazed to keep out the noise.

Arosfa

83 Gower Street, Bloomsbury, WC1E 6HJ (tel/fax 7636 2115/www.arosfa london.com). Goodge Street tube. **£**. Arosfa means 'place to stay' in Welsh, but we reckon this townhouse B&B sells itself short. Yes, the accommodation is fairly spartan, but it's spotless, and all the rooms have en suite shower/ WC (albeit tiny). It has a great location – in the heart of Bloomsbury, opposite a huge Waterstone's – and a pleasing walled garden.

Ashlee House

261-265 Gray's Inn Road, Bloomsbury, WC1X 8QT (7833 9400/www.ashlee house.co.uk). King's Cross tube/rail. **£**. Ashlee House is a rare beast: a youth hostel with a bit of style. The funky lobby is decorated with sheepskin-covered sofas and arty mesh wallpaper digitally printed with London scenes. It's got all the handy hostel stuff on site: internet, TV room, luggage storage, laundry and kitchen, and there's no curfew.

Brown's

NEW *Albemarle Street, Mayfair, W1S 4BP (7493 6020/www.roccoforte hotels.com). Green Park tube.* **££££**. Brown's was the quintessential London hotel, opened in 1837 by Lord Byron's butler, James Brown. In 2003

Occupying the former HQ of the Midland Bank, Threadneedles successfully integrates modern design with a monumental space, complete with an exquisite stained-glass ceiling dome in the lobby. The decor is soothingly neutral, with Korres toiletries in the serene limestone bathrooms. Stress-busting comforts include a scented candle lit at turn-down and a 'movie treats' menu of popcorn, ice-cream and Coke (albeit at a price that may raise your blood pressure). There are weekend deals to tempt non-execs.

Zetter Restaurant & Rooms

86-88 Clerkenwell Road, Clerkenwell, EC1M 5RJ (7324 4444/www.thezetter. com). Farringdon tube/rail. **££**. A bona fide loft hotel in a converted warehouse, with a soaring atrium, exposed brick and funky 1970s furniture. There's a refreshing lack of attitude – the place is comfortable and fun. Instead of minibars, vending machines in the corridors dispense everything from champagne to disposable cameras. Rooms are bathed in natural light

Rocco Forte added it to his portfolio and embarked on a top-to-toe refurb; it reopened in December 2005. Forte's sister, Olga Polizzi, was charged with the design, and like her Hotel Tresanton in Cornwall, Brown's has the feel of a chic private home.

Charlotte Street Hotel

15-17 Charlotte Street, Fitzrovia, W1T 1RJ (7806 2000/www.firmdale.com). Goodge Street, Oxford Circus, Tottenham Court Road or Warren Street tube. **£££**.

Another member of Kit and Tim Kemp's Firmdale hotel group, oozing non-stuffy tradition, comfort and class. Resident or non-resident, you can visit on a Sunday night and you can combine a three-course set meal with a screening of a classic film in the mini cinema for just £35 (booking advisable).

Clarendon

NEW *34-37 Bedford Place, Bloomsbury, WC1B 5JR (7307 1575/www.grange hotels.com). Holborn or Russell Square tube.* **££**.

The Grange Hotels chain seems to be taking over this street with its 'Townhouse Collection' occupying several terraced properties. No bad thing, as all four hotels offer smart, affordable accommodation around the corner from the British Museum. At this, the newest, free quality dailies are piled in the airy lobby opening on to a patio garden. The style is subtly traditional and the grand proportions of deluxe rooms are worth the upgrade, though standard doubles aren't cramped. Summer visitors: there's no air-con. Neighbouring Buckingham and Portland have kitchenettes.

Claridge's

55 Brook Street, Mayfair, W1A 2JQ (7629 8860/www.claridges.co.uk). Bond Street tube. **££££**.

Claridge's is a byword for upper-class English lodgings, but though it remains traditional it's neither stuffy nor backward-looking: its bar and restaurant (Gordon Ramsay) are both actively fashionable, the decor has distinctly stylish modern touches, afternoon tea is divinely presented and guests include a sprinkling of hipsters. It deserves its landmark status.

Cumberland

NEW *Great Cumberland Place, Marylebone, W1A 4RF (0870 333 9280/www.guoman.com). Marble Arch tube.* **£££**.

The sheer scale of this recently revamped hotel takes your breath away. It has 900 rooms and a lobby you could land a plane in, with striking modern decor. Rooms are fairly minimalist, with huge plasma TVs: comfortable, yes, but lacking personality. The place seems to be doing a roaring trade, though. Celebrity chef Gary Rhodes oversees the brasserie kitchen.

Generator

37 Tavistock Place, Bloomsbury, WC1H 9SE (7388 7666/www.generator hostels.com). Russell Square tube. **£**.

This industrially styled backpacker palace has no curfew, and the massive bar hosts karaoke nights and happy hours galore. There's also a games room, a movie lounge, a travel agent, a shop and an internet room. Oh, we almost forgot: there are beds, too, 837 of them, should you ever want to get some sleep.

Harlingford Hotel

61-63 Cartwright Gardens, Bloomsbury, WC1H 9EL (7387 1551/ www.harlingfordhotel.com). Russell Square tube/Euston tube/rail. **££**.

On the corner of a Georgian crescent lined with cheap hotels, the Harlingford is a stylish trailblazer. But don't expect a porter to carry your bags upstairs, and do turn a blind eye to the odd suitcase scuff on the paintwork. The adjacent garden and tennis court are available to guests.

Hazlitt's

6 Frith Street, Soho, W1D 3JA (7434 1771/www.hazlittshotel.com). Tottenham Court Road tube. **£££**.

Named after the 18th-century essayist William Hazlitt, this idiosyncratic

Kemp class

Husband and wife team Tim and Kit Kemp (aka Firmdale Hotels) have launched five hugely successful hotels in as many years. They pulled off country-goes-urban with panache at the warehouse-style Soho Hotel in 2004 ('the most glamorous hotel in the world' according to *Tatler*). But can they cap it all with their most ambitious project to date, the transformation of a prestigious John Nash terrace?

Firmdale has such a fine track record of playing off quintessential English style against bold statements – to immensely appealing effect – that we have allowed ourselves to get excited about the new Haymarket Hotel. Due to open in early 2007, it will be the most luxurious of the Kemp hotels – a five-star with a 20-metre swimming pool and all the trimmings – but we're more intrigued by its architectural pedigree. Occupying prestigious Grade II listed property, the hotel will take up the length of John Nash's striking, colonnaded Suffolk Place off Haymarket. Previously the London HQ for American Express, the 19th-century building has been empty since it was gutted by fire in 2002. Only the monumental Shooting Room escaped the flames and the Kemps' architects have been required to work painstakingly around it. This is Crown Estate, after all.

The hotel will comprise 50 individually designed bedrooms and suites, plus – aptly – three exclusive townhouses.

■ www.firmdale.com

Georgian townhouse hotel has an impressive literary pedigree. Rooms are as true to period as possible, with fireplaces, massive carved wooden beds and clawfoot bathtubs. But don't worry, you don't have to sacrifice 21st-century comforts – the electronics are hidden away in antique cupboards.

Jenkins Hotel

45 Cartwright Gardens, Bloomsbury, WC1H 9EH (7387 2067/www.jenkins hotel.demon.co.uk). Russell Square tube/Euston tube/rail. **££.**
The Jenkins has been a hotel since the 1920s, so it's fitting that an episode of Agatha Christie's *Poirot* was filmed in room nine. But although it's traditional, don't expect a period look – just tidy, freshly painted en suite rooms furnished with pretty bedspreads, crisp, patterned curtains and, unusually, a small fridge. Guests have access to the garden and tennis court.

Mandeville

NEW *Mandeville Place, Marylebone, W1U 2BE (7935 5599/www. mandeville.co.uk). Bond Street tube.* **£££.**
Increasingly chi-chi Marylebone has lacked a hotel to match its fashion status – until now. Spotting a gap in the market, the owners of the Mandeville commissioned interior designer Stephen Ryan to turn an unremarkable traditional hotel into a style statement. The public areas carry it off, and the rooms are nice, with faux leather headboards, Versace-esque classical-print curtains and Italian marble bathrooms, but we're quite not convinced that they have the extras or the glam factor to justify the rates.

Metropolitan

19 Old Park Lane, Mayfair W1K 1LB (7447 1000/www.metropolitan.co.uk). Green Park or Hyde Park Corner tube. **££££.**
The Met's minimalist rooms are less of a draw than they used to be, and the standard doubles are actually quite small (although the hotel has an upgrade policy when larger ones are

22 York Street p207

B&B Belgravia p209

available). Still, they've recently been refurbished, so everything is pristine. Upstairs, Nobu is an unchallenged destination dining spot, and there's a good spa. You can still recapture something of the hotel's A-list heyday in the refurbished Met Bar.

Morgan Hotel

24 Bloomsbury Street, Bloomsbury, WC1B 3QJ (7636 3735/www.morgan hotel.co.uk). Tottenham Court Road tube. **££**.

Imagine *EastEnders* transplanted to Bloomsbury. The three Shoreditch-bred Ward siblings have been running this cheap and cheerful hotel since the 1970s. While it doesn't aspire to boutique status, rooms have extras beyond basic B&B standard: modern headboards with inbuilt reading lamps, air-con, new bathrooms with granite sinks and – as in the best hotels, darling – a phone by the loo.

One Aldwych

1 Aldwych, Covent Garden, WC2B 4RH (7300 1000/www.onealdwych.com). Covent Garden or Temple tube/Charing Cross tube/rail. **££££**.

One Aldwych is a modern classic. It's housed in a magnificent Edwardian newspaper HQ, but the contemporary rooms come equipped with up-to-date gadgetry and an ecologically sound water system. There's a private cinema with sumptuous Italian seats (dinner-and-a-movie packages are available), a spa, two great restaurants and a well-equipped gym, but the *pièce de résistance* is undoubtedly the shimmering 18m pool, complete with music piped into the water.

Piccadilly Backpackers

12 Sherwood Street, Soho, W1F 7BR (7434 9009/www.piccadillybackpackers. com). Piccadilly Circus tube. **£**.

Piccadilly Backpackers has two things going for it: rates (from £12 per night in pod-style dorms) and location. The accommodation is basic, although there are good common facilities including a widescreen TV lounge, laundrette and 24-hour internet café.

Sanderson

50 Berners Street, Fitzrovia, W1T 3NG (7300 1400/www.morganshotel group.com). Oxford Circus tube. **££££**.

Design hotels may be two a penny in London these days, but this Schrager and Starck creation is still a knock-out, partly because it combines modern minimalism with a playful, theatrical style. The pricey Long Bar and Spoon+ restaurant fill nightly with fashionable types; also downstairs is the quieter Purple Bar, open to guests only. There's also a suitably fashiony spa.

The Savoy

Strand, Covent Garden, WC2R 0EU (7836 4343/www.fairmont.com). Covent Garden or Embankment tube/Charing Cross tube/rail. **££££**.

Less ostentatious than the Ritz, the still-supreme Savoy mixes neo-classical, art deco and gentlemen's club aesthetics. Choose a traditional, modern English or art deco bedroom: all have watering-can showerheads and the latest technology. The rooftop gym, with a small pool, is another asset. The property was bought by Fairmont Hotels in 2005, and a £30 million room restoration is under way.

Soho Hotel

4 Richmond Mews (off Dean Street), Soho, W1D 3DH (7559 3000/ www.firmdale.com). Tottenham Court Road tube. **£££**.

Kit Kemp gave her sixth hotel her signature contemporary country-house style, but it has a smidgeon of urban edge, in keeping with its location in a Soho alleyway and its red-brick warehouse style. In keeping with the Firmdale formula are the trademark facilities: extensive lounging areas with honesty bar, buzzy bar/restaurant Refuel, two luxurious screening rooms and gym and treatment rooms. A hit from the week it opened.

22 York Street

22-24 York Street, Marylebone, W1U 6PX (7224 2990/www.22york street.co.uk). Baker Street tube. **££**.

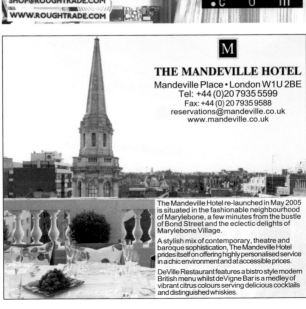

There's no sign on the door; people usually discover Liz and Michael Callis's immaculately kept B&B by word of mouth. Unpretentious and comfortable, it's perfect for those who loathe hotels and are uncomfortable in designer interiors. Breakfast is an occasion, served at a huge, curving wooden table in the traditional kitchen.

Westminster to Kensington

Aster House

3 Sumner Place, Chelsea, SW7 3EE (7581 5888/www.asterhouse.com). South Kensington tube. **££**.

This award-winning B&B bravely attempts to live up to its upmarket address. In reality, the lobby – with its pink faux marble and gold chandeliers – is more kitsch than glam, but the effect is still charming. So is the lush garden, with its pond and wandering ducks, and the palm-filled conservatory, where guests eat breakfast. The bedrooms are comfortable, if floral, with smart marble bathrooms (ask for one with a power shower).

B&B Belgravia

NEW *64-66 Ebury Street, Westminster, SW1W 9QD (7823 4928/www.bb-belgravia.com). Victoria tube/rail.* **££**.

B&B Belgravia is one of the most attractive B&Bs we've seen, almost to *Elle Deco* levels, and it's liveable as well as lovely: there's a laptop equipped with free internet connection, high-tech coffee machine, games and toys for the kids and a collection of DVDs. Bedrooms are chic and predominantly white, with flat-screen TVs and sleek bathrooms with power showers.

Baglioni

60 Hyde Park Gate, South Kensington, SW7 5BB (7368 5700/www.baglioni hotellondon.com). High Street Kensington/Gloucester Road tube. **££££**.

The Baglioni is hard to beat for exciting designer style. Occupying a Victorian mansion just across from Kensington Palace, it has none of the sniffy formality of some of its deluxe English counterparts. The Baglioni has brought a welcome touch of bling to the boutique scene – we predict the new guests- and members-only basement bar could prove to be the long-overdue successor to the Met Bar.

Base2Stay

NEW *25 Courtfield Gardens, Earl's Court, SW5 0PG (0845 262 8000/ www.base2stay.com). Earl's Court tube.* **£**.

Base2Stay aims to offer four-star specs at budget prices. How? By stripping away money-sapping services like a bar and room service. With a fully equipped kitchenette and menus from upmarket delivery services, you won't miss them. Attention to detail in the comfortably minimalist, air-conditioned rooms is impressive – especially the chic limestone bathrooms with vigorous power showers. And as there are plans to roll out the brand in 2007, it's unlikely they'll jack up the prices any time soon.

Five Sumner Place

5 Sumner Place, Chelsea, SW7 3EE (7584 7586/www.sumnerplace.com). South Kensington tube. **££**.

Five Sumner Place is a smart address, and a convenient one too. The decor – the usual faux-period English – is pleasant enough; and the rooms are clean and comfortable. All have free wireless internet access and voicemail. Breakfast is served in a conservatory and is included in the price.

Halkin

Halkin Street, Belgravia, SW1X 7DJ (7333 1000/www.halkin.como.bz). Hyde Park Corner tube. **££££**.

Popular with affluent businessmen and publicity-shy Hollywood stars, the Halkin is a gracious, hype-free hideaway. You'd never guess the world's only Michelin-starred Thai restaurant, Nahm, is behind its discreet Georgian-style façade, down a Belgravia back street. A peaceful, unpretentious place to be cocooned in luxury and comfort.

ESSENTIALS

Pods you like

Yotel

Inspired by Japanese capsule hotels, a wave of pod-style accommodation is hitting London. Claustrophobia notwithstanding, capsule rooms can be a fine way to economise – particularly if you sit in the camp that sees a hotel more as a crashpad than a pamper fest. Those allergic to chintz will also be pleased to hear that capsule rooms tend towards a clean, minimalist style.

In summer 2006 a visionary solution to airport ennui arrived at Heathrow's Terminal 4 and Gatwick's South Terminal, when **Yotel** opened 40- and 50-cabin hotels. 'Cabins' can be booked overnight, or in four-hour blocks, and you get a clean, crisp room for your money, courtesy of Airbus designers Priestman Goode. For diversion, there's a monsoon shower, 'techno wall' with pull-down desk, flatscreen TV, free wired and Wi-Fi internet, and stacks of movies and CDs.

Of a less luxurious bent, central London budget favourite **Piccadilly Backpackers** took the plunge with dorm-style 'pods' in early 2006. The pods allow for more privacy (you get your own shelf and bed light!) than the old bunks, and have neat aesthetics. If you don't mind sharing a room with a bunch of backpackers, a pod can be yours for £17, including breakfast.

We're not quite sure at what point an extremely small budget hotel room becomes a more fashionably termed 'capsule' room, but central London's **easyHotel** is certainly a compact hotel option for compact wallets. When the website quotes you a room rate, take that literally – the 'small', 'very small' or 'tiny' rooms come with a bed, a bathroom and little more besides. That is to say there's no wardrobe, window (you can pay more for one), hairdryer, lift or breakfast. Rates, bookable online, start at £20 – but prices vary according to demand, and average nearer £40. To make savings, avoid extras like TV (£5) and housekeeping (£10). Check-in and check-out are at a less than generous 4pm and 10am.

■ www.yotel.com
■ Piccadilly Backpackers 12 Sherwood Street, W1F 7BR (7434 9009/www.piccadillyhotel.net)
■ easyHotel 14 Lexham Gardens, W8 5JE (www.easyhotel.com)

ESSENTIALS

Hotel 167

*167 Old Brompton Road, Chelsea, SW5
0AN (7373 0672/www.hotel167.com).
Gloucester Road or South Kensington
tube.* **££.**

It may be located in a Victorian townhouse, but this funky little hotel is no
period clone. Run by its affable Irish
owner for 30 years, the slightly
bohemian (yet well-kept) place has
been the subject of a song (an unre-
leased track by the Manic Street
Preachers) and a novel (*Hotel 167* by
Jane Solomons).

The Lanesborough

*Lanesborough Place, Hyde Park
Corner, Belgravia, SW1X 7TA (7259
5599/www.lanesborough.com). Hyde
Park Corner tube.* **££££.**

The Lanesborough epitomises discreet
luxury to a level barely dreamed about
by those not on supertax. As a
Victorian building remade into a hotel
in 1991, it offers a perfect combination
of historic handsomeness and modern
infrastructure and technology, with
endless thoughtful touches (including
personalised stationery). Obviously,
you pay a seriously hefty price for all
this, but, hey, personal butler service is
thrown in for free. Of the common facilities, the suave Library Bar is the
biggest asset.

myhotel Chelsea

*35 Ixworth Place, Chelsea, SW3 3QX
(7225 7500/www.myhotels.com). South
Kensington tube.* **£££.**

A boutique hotel that brings meaning
back to that degraded term: it's independently owned, individual and contemporary in decor, and offers a very
personal service, to charming effect.
There's pampering courtesy of Aveda
and a Cape Cod-styled bar.

New Linden

NEW *59 Leinster Square, Bayswater,
W2 4PS (7221 4321/www.mayflower-
group.co.uk). Bayswater tube.* **££.**

The brand new New Linden is a bit of
a budget showpiece. Rooms are simply
but pleasingly designed with wooden
floors and marble-tiled bathrooms
(some with deluge shower heads), and
flat-screen TVs and CD players come
as standard. The location – between
Notting Hill and Kensington Gardens
– is another pull.

Number Sixteen

*16 Sumner Place, Chelsea, SW7 3EG
(7589 5232/www.firmdale.com). South
Kensington tube.* **£££.**

Kit Kemp's most affordable hotel rubs
shoulders with budget establishments
in this row of white stucco townhouses.
The lower room rates at this gorgeous
B&B are presumably down to the lack
of bar, restaurant or big-hotel perks,
which leaves Kemp to get on with what
she does best: create beautiful rooms.
Breakfast is served in the conservatory or the lovely, large garden.

Trafalgar

*2 Spring Gardens, Westminster, SW1A
2TS (7870 2900/www.hilton.co.uk/
trafalgar). Charing Cross tube/rail.*
££££.

Part of the Hilton group, the Trafalgar
has dropped the branding in favour of
funky designer decor. The building is
imposing, but the mood inside is young
and dynamic. The rooms have a mas-
culine feel, but the bathtubs are made
for sharing; full-size aromatherapy-
based toiletries are a nice touch. The
location is its biggest draw: corner
rooms overlook Trafalgar square and
the small rooftop bar has lovely
panoramic views. Ground-level bar
Rockwell offers over 100 bourbons.

Windermere Hotel

*142-144 Warwick Way, Westminster,
SW1V 4JE (7834 5163/www.
windermere-hotel.co.uk). Victoria
tube/rail.* **££.**

The Windermere has a proud legacy:
London's first B&B opened on this site
in 1881. Surprise, surprise, the rooms
are done up in English chintz, but
they're well kept and not too frilly; the
bathrooms are clean and modern, with
power showers. The rustic Pimlico
restaurant – a rarity for a budget hotel
– has a sophisticated but reasonably
priced menu.

ESSENTIALS

Getting Around

Airports

Gatwick Airport

0870 000 2468/www.baa.co.uk/gatwick. About 30 miles (50km) south of central London, off the M23.

Of the three rail services that link Gatwick Airport to London, the quickest is the **Gatwick Express** (0845 850 1530, www.gatwick express.co.uk) to Victoria Station, which takes around 30 minutes and runs from 4.35am to 1.35am daily. Tickets cost £13 for a single, £13.20 for a day return (after 9.30am) and £24 for a period return (valid for 30 days). Under-16s travel half-price; under-5s go free. Note that this service is under threat.

Southern (08457 484950, www.southernrailway.com) also runs a rail service between Gatwick and Victoria, with trains around every 15 to 20 minutes (or around hourly 1-4am). It takes about 35 minutes, at £9 for a standard single, £9.30 for a day return (after 9.30am) and £18 for a period return (valid for one month). Under-16s get half-price tickets, and under-5s travel for free. The Thameslink service (08457 484950, www.thameslink.co.uk) stops at several central stations; journey times vary. Tickets to King's Cross are £10 (after 9.30am), £10.10 for an off-peak day return; £20.20 buys a 30-day return.

Hotelink (01293 532244, www.hotelink.co.uk) offers a shuttle service from airport to hotel at £22 each way (£20 if booked online). A taxi will cost about £100 and take forever unless it's the middle of the night.

Heathrow Airport

0870 000 0123/www.baa.co.uk/heathrow. About 15 miles (24km) west of central London, off the M4.

The **Heathrow Express** (0845 600 1515, www.heathrowexpress.co.uk) runs to Paddington every 15 minutes between 5.10am and 12.08am daily and takes 15-20 minutes. The train can be boarded at either of the airport's two tube stations. Tickets cost £14 single or £26 return; under-16s go half-price. Many airlines have check-in desks at Paddington.

A longer but considerably cheaper journey is by **tube**. Tickets for the 50- to 60-minute ride on the Piccadilly Line into central London cost £3.80 one way (£1.40 under-16s). Trains run every few minutes from about 5am to 11.45pm daily except Sunday, when they run 6am to 11pm.

National Express (08705 808080, www.nationalexpress.com) runs daily coach services to London Victoria between 5.35am and 9.35pm daily, leaving Heathrow Central bus terminal around every 30 minutes, depending on the time of day. For a 90-minute journey (traffic-dependent) to London, you'll pay £10 for a single or £15 (half-price for under-16s) for a return.

As at Gatwick, **Hotelink** offers a hand-holding service for £17 per person each way (£16 online). A taxi into town will cost roughly £100 and take an hour on average.

London City Airport

7646 0000/www.londoncityairport.com. About 9 miles (14km) east of central London.

The **Docklands Light Railway** (DLR) now includes a stop for London City Airport. The journey into central London takes around 20 minutes, and trains run 5.30am to 12.30am Monday to Friday and 7am to 11.30pm Sun.

Most people head to London on the blue **Shuttlebus**, a 25-minute ride to Liverpool Street Station via Canary Wharf. It leaves every 15 minutes from 6.30am to 9.30pm, when the terminal closes. Tickets to Liverpool

Street cost £6.50 one-way, or £3.50 to Canary Wharf. Have cash ready to pay the driver. A taxi costs around £20; less to the City.

Luton Airport

01582 405100/www.london-luton.com. About 30 miles (50km) north of central London, J10 off the M1.

Luton Airport Parkway Station is close to the airport, but not in it: there's a short shuttle-bus ride. The **Thameslink** service calls at many stations (King's Cross St Pancras among them) and has a journey time of 35 to 45 minutes. Trains leave around every 15 minutes, and cost £10.70 single and £19.70 return, or £10.90 for a cheap day return (after 9.30am Mon-Fri, weekends). The trip from Luton to Victoria takes 60 to 90 minutes by coach.

Green Line (0870 608 7261, www.greenline.co.uk) runs a 24-hour service every 30 minutes or so during peak times. A single fare is £10, £6.50 for under-16s, while returns cost £14 and £11. A taxi costs upwards of £50.

Stansted Airport

0870 0000 0303/www.stansted airport.com. About 35 miles (60km) north-east of central London, J8 off the M11.

The quickest way to get to London from Stansted is on the **Stansted Express** train (08457 484950) to Liverpool Street Station; journey time is 40 to 45 minutes. Trains leave every 15 to 45 minutes depending on the time of day, and tickets cost £14 for a single and £24 for an open period return; under-16s travel half-price, under-5s go free.

The **Airbus** (08705 808080, www.nationalexpress.com) coach service to Victoria takes at least an hour and 40 minutes and runs 24 hours. Coaches run roughly every 30 minutes, more frequently at peak times. An adult single costs £10 (£5 for under-16s), a return is £15 (£7.50 for under-16s). A taxi is about £80.

Arriving by rail

Eurostar

Waterloo International Terminal, SE1 (08705 186186/www.eurostar. com). Waterloo tube/rail.

Eurostar trains arrive at Waterloo Station, switching in November 2007 to St Pancras International.

Main line stations

For information on train times and ticket prices, call 08457 484950/ www.nationalrail.co.uk. You can get timetable and price information, and buy tickets, for any train operator in the UK via www.the trainline.com.

All London's major rail stations are served by the tube.

Arriving by coach

Eurolines

Victoria Coach Station, 164 Buckingham Palace Road, SW1W 9TQ (Eurolines 01582 404511/ www.eurolines.com).

Services to continental Europe from Victoria coach station.

Public transport

London's public transport – its tube, buses, Tramlink and the Docklands Light Railway – is run by Transport for London (TfL), whose **Travel Information Centres** provide maps and information. You can find them in the stations listed below. TfL's useful website is at www.tfl.gov.uk. It still also has a very efficient telephone service, on 7222 1234. Operators will advise you on the best way to get from A to B.

**Heathrow Airport Terminals
1, 2 & 3** *Underground station* **Open** *6.30am-10pm daily.*
Liverpool Street Open *7.15am-9pm Mon-Sat; 8.15am-8pm Sun.*
Victoria Open *7.15am-9pm Mon-Sat; 8.15am-8pm Sun.*

Oyster card

The Oyster card is a travel smart-card that you charge up with cash for single journeys and longer-period Travelards and bus passes. It costs £3 (refundable). You can use it on tubes, buses and limited local rail services. TfL is encouraging its use by charging less for one-off fares if you pay for them this way: a Zone 1 tube fare without an Oyster card is £3; with it, it comes down to £1.50. In addition, Oyster pay-as-you-go fares are capped at 50p less than the price of a Day Travelcard no matter how many journeys you make. For most visitors, Oyster is the cheapest way of getting around, so it makes sense to get hold of one. Oyster cards are available at tube stations, London travel information centres and and newsagents; UK residents can get them online at www.sales.oystercard.com and by calling 0845 330 9876. They can be topped up at the above outlets and at tube station ticket machines. London Transport has plans to turn Oyster into a more general cash card that you can 'spend' on small purchases at vending machines and supermarkets.

To pay by Oyster, pass your card over the circular yellow reader at tube station gates and bus entrances.

Travelcards

For most uses, the Oyster card has supplanted the Day Travelcard, but depending on your travel needs you might find it useful as Travelcards also cover National Rail services. Off-Peak Day Travelcards allow you to travel from 9.30am (Mon-Fri) and all day Saturday, Sunday and public holidays. They cost from £4.90 for Zones 1-2, rising to £6.30 for Zones 1-6 (children half-price).

Travelcards start to save you money with the three-day version, if you plan to be on the road a lot. The peak version, which is valid at any time, is available for £15.40 (Zones 1-2) or £37.20 (Zones 1-6), children half-price. Off-peak (9.30am Monday to Friday and all day on Saturday, Sunday and public holidays) is £18.90 Zones 1-6, children £6.

Day and three-day Travelards come as standard printed tickets that you insert into the slot in tube station entry gates or show to the bus driver.

For longer visits, a season ticket might save money: a seven-day Zone 1-2 version is £22.20. Seven-day and longer season tickets are issued to your Oyster card (no photocard is required).

Travelling with children

Under-16s travel free on the bus (though you may need to get them a photocard). Under-5s also go free on the tube and DLR, as do under-11s if they are travelling with an adult. Five- to 15-year-olds travelling on Oyster will pay no more than £1 for a day's off-peak tube and DLR travel; or they can get a £1 off-peak Day Traveland if an accompanying adult has any Travelcard. Sixteen- to 17-year-olds will need to show a 16-17 photocard to qualify for reduced fares.

London Underground

Though delays are common and rush-hour services overcrowded, the tube is still the quickest way to get around London. However, it's also the most expensive: a flat cash fare of £3 per journey applies across tube Travelard Zones 1-4 (£4 for Zones 1-5 or 1-6); customers save up to £1.50 with Oyster pay-

ESSENTIALS

as-you-go. Beware of £20 on-the-spot penalty fares issued to anyone caught without a ticket.

Using the system

An Oyster card is the best way to pay for your tube fare; otherwise, single or day tickets can be purchased from a ticket office or from self-service machines notoriously bereft of change.

Underground timetable

Tube trains run daily from around 5.30am (except Sunday, when they start an hour or two later). There is no service on Christmas Day. Generally, you won't have to wait more than ten minutes for a train, and during peak times services run every two or three minutes. Last trains from central stations leave at around 11.45pm to 12.30am daily except Sunday, when they are 30 minutes to an hour earlier.

Underground fares

The single fare for adults within Zone 1 is £3 (Oyster fare £1.50). For Zones 1-2 it's £3 (Oyster fare £2 or £1.50).

Buses

You musts now buy a ticket before boarding many buses, particularly in central London. Do so: there are inspectors about, who can fine you £20. You can buy a ticket (or a one-day Bus Pass) from pavement ticket machines, though they're often out of order and don't give change. Yellow signs on bus stops indicate where this is a requirement.

Using an Oyster card to pay as you go costs £1 or 80p depending on the time of day you travel. The most you will pay in one day will be £3. Paying cash costs £1.50 for a single trip. A one-day Bus Pass gives unlimited bus and tram travel at £3.50.

A book of six Saver tickets costs £6 from newsagents and tube station ticket offices.

Night buses

Many bus services run 24 hours a day. There are also some special night buses with an 'N' prefix to the route number, which operate from about 11pm to 6am. Most services run every 15 to 30 minutes, but many busier routes have a bus around every ten minutes.

Water transport

Thames Clippers (www.thamesclippers.com) runs a reliable commuter boat service. You can board the Clippers from the following piers: Savoy (near Embankment tube), Blackfriars, Bankside (for the Globe), London Bridge and St Katharine's (Tower Bridge). Frequency varies throughout the day and timetables vary with the season, so check online before planning a trip.

Taxis

Black cabs

If a taxi's yellow 'For Hire' sign is switched on, the cab can be hailed. If a taxi stops, the cabbie must take you to your destination, provided it's within seven miles. Expect to pay slightly higher rates after 8pm on weekdays and all weekend.

You can book black cabs in advance with **Radio Taxis** (7272 0272; credit cards only) and **Dial-a-Cab** (7253 5000). You'll pay a call-out fee in addition to the fare.

Minicabs

Minicabs (saloon cars) are generally cheaper than black cabs, but be sure to use only licensed firms (look for the yellow disc) and avoid minicab drivers who tout for

ESSENTIALS

business. They are likely to be unlicensed, expensive, unreliable and potentially dangerous.

Recommended licensed firms include **Lady Cabs** (7272 3300), which employs only women drivers, and **Addison Lee** (7387 8888).

Driving

Congestion charge

On 19 February 2007 London's congestion charging zone will extend westwards to take in Hyde Park, Notting Hill, Kensington and South Kensington. There are also other boundary changes elsewhere on the periphery. The congestion charging zone is prominently marked by road signs and red 'C' signs painted on the tarmac.

There is an £8 daily charge for driving or parking a vehicle within this zone between 7am and 6.30pm (6pm from 19 Feb 2007), Monday to Friday. You can register and pay online (www.cclondon.com) or by calling 0845 900 1234; passes can be bought from newsagents, garages and NCP car parks. You can pay any time during the day of entry, or, for an extra £2, up to midnight the next day. Expect a fine of £100 (£50 if paid in 14 days) if you fail to pay.

Parking

Parking on a single or double yellow line, a red line or in residents' parking areas during the day is illegal, and you may end up being fined, clamped (release fee £80) or towed. Always read the signs. However, in the evening and at various times at weekends, parking on single yellows is legal and free.

There is lots of meter parking in central London but it is expensive, often short-term and usually full.

NCP 24-hour car parks (0870 606 7050, www.ncp.co.uk) are numerous but expensive (£6 to £10 for two hours). Central ones include Arlington House, Arlington Street, St James's, W1; Upper Ground, Southwark, SE1; and 4-5 Denman Street, Soho, W1.

Vehicle removal

If your (illegally parked) car has mysteriously disappeared, chances are it's been taken to a car pound. Penalty and release fees are stiff. To find out where your car has been taken, call the Trace Service hotline (7747 4747, 24hrs daily). Take registration/rental documents with you when you collect.

Vehicle hire

EasyCar's online service, at www.easycar.com, offers competitive rates, just so long as you don't mind driving a branded car around town. Otherwise, try

Alamo
0870 400 4508/www.alamo.com.

Budget
0870 156 5656/www.gobudget.com.

Hertz
0870 599 6699/www.hertz.co.uk.

Sixt
08701 567 567/www.e-sixt.co.uk.
Sixt cars include environmentally friendly two-seaters.

Cycling

London Bicycle Tour Company
1A Gabriel's Wharf, 56 Upper Ground, South Bank, SE1 9PP (7928 6838/www.londonbicycle.com). Southwark tube/Blackfriars or Waterloo tube/rail. **Open** 10am-6pm daily. Deposit £100 cash or £1 by credit card.
Bike, tandem and rickshaw hire near bike-friendly South Bank; guided bicycle tours Sat, Sun.

Resources A-Z

Accident & emergency

Below are listed central London hospitals with 24-hour Accident & Emergency departments.

The UK's emergency number for police, fire and ambulance is 999.

Chelsea & Westminster Hospital *369 Fulham Road, Chelsea, SW10 9NH (8746 8000). South Kensington tube.*

Guy's Hospital *St Thomas Street (entrance Snowsfields), Bankside, SE1 9RT (7188 7188). London Bridge tube/rail.*

Royal London Hospital *Whitechapel Road, Whitechapel, E1 1BB (7377 7000). Whitechapel tube.*

St Mary's Hospital *Praed Street, Paddington, W2 1NY (7886 6666). Paddington tube/rail.*

St Thomas's Hospital *Lambeth Palace Road, Lambeth, SE1 7EH (7188 7188). Westminster tube/Waterloo tube/rail.*

University College Hospital *Grafton Way, Fitzrovia, WC1E 3BG (7387 9300). Euston Square or Warren Street tube.*

Credit card loss

American Express *01273 696933.*
Diners Club *01252 513500.*
JCB 7499 3000.
MasterCard/Eurocard
0800 964767.
Switch *0870 600 0459.*
Visa/Connect *0800 895082.*

Customs

For allowances, see www.hmrc.gov.

Electricity

The UK uses the standard European 220-240V, 50-cycle AC voltage via three-pin plugs.

Dental emergency

Dental Emergency Care Service
Guy's Hospital, St Thomas Street, Bankside, SE1 9RT (7188 0511). London Bridge tube/rail. **Open** 9am-5pm Mon-Fri.
Queues start forming at 8am; arrive by 11am if you're to be seen the same day.

Disabled

London is a difficult city for disabled visitors, though legislation is gradually improving access. The bus fleet is getting more wheelchair-accessible but the tube remains largely escalator-dependent. The Tube Access Guide is available free from ticket offices.

Access in London is an invaluable reference, available from www.accessproject-phsp.org.

Artsline
54 Chalton Street, Somers Town, NW1 1HS (tel/textphone 7388 2227/www.artslineonline.com). Information on disabled access to arts and entertainment events.

Embassies & consulates

American Embassy *24 Grosvenor Square, Mayfair, W1A 1AE (7499 9000/www.usembassy.org.uk). Bond Street or Marble Arch tube.*

Australian High Commission *Australia House, Strand, Holborn, WC2B 4LA (7379 4334/www.australia.org.uk).*

Canadian High Commission *38 Grosvenor Street, Mayfair, W1K 4AA (7258 6600/www.canada.org.uk). Bond Street or Oxford Circus tube.*

Irish Embassy *17 Grosvenor Place, Belgravia, SW1X 7HR (7235*

*2171/passports & visas 7225
7700/www.dfa.ie). Hyde Park
Corner tube.*
New Zealand High Commission
*New Zealand House, 80 Haymarket, St
James's, SW1Y 4YQ (7930 8422/www.
nzembassy.com). Piccadilly Circus tube.*
South African High Commission
*South Africa House, Trafalgar Square,
Westminster, WC2N 5DP (7451 7299/
www.southafricahouse.com). Charing
Cross tube/rail.*

Internet

There are lots of cybercafés around
town, including the easyEverything
chain as well as numerous smaller
ones. You'll also find terminals in
public libraries. For more, check
www.cybercafes.com. Wireless
access is just taking off here, but
usually for a fee. For locations,
check with your provider or visit
www.wi-fihotspotlist.com.

easyInternetCafé

*160-166 Kensington High Street, W8
7RG (www.easyeverything.com). High
Street Kensington tube.* **Open** 7am-
11pm daily. **Net access** from 50p.
Terminals 394.
Locations throughout the city.

Opening hours

Banks 9am-4.30pm (some close
at 3.30pm, some 5.30pm) Mon-Fri;
sometimes also Saturday mornings.
Businesses 9am-5pm Mon-Fri.
Shops 10am-6pm Mon-Sat; some
to 8pm. Many are also open on
Sunday, usually 11am to 5pm
or noon to 6pm.

Pharmacies

Britain's best-known pharmacy
chain is **Boots**, with ubiquitous
branches. Those on Oxford Street
are open until 8pm or 9pm Monday
to Saturday. **Bliss Pharmacy**, 5 &
6 Marble Arch (7723 6116), is open
until midnight daily.

Police stations

Look under 'Police' in the phone
book or call Directory Enquiries on
118 118/500/888 for more.
Charing Cross Police Station
*Agar Street, Covent Garden,
WC2N 4JP (7240 1212). Charing
Cross tube/rail.*
Marylebone Police Station
*1-9 Seymour Street, Marylebone, W1H
7BA (7486 1212). Baker Street tube/
Marylebone tube/rail.*
West End Central Police Station
*27 Savile Row, Mayfair, W1X 2DU
(7437 1212). Piccadilly Circus tube.*

Post

Post offices are usually open
9am to 5.30pm Monday-Friday
and 9am to noon Saturday, with
the exception of **Trafalgar
Square Post Office** (24-28
William IV Street, WC2N 4DL,
08457 223344, Charing Cross
tube/rail), which is open 8.30am
to 6.30pm Monday to Friday and
9am to 5.30pm on Saturday.

Smoking

From summer 2007 there will
be no smoking in any public
places in England, including bars,
restaurants and stations. Hotels
can still offer smoking rooms.

Telephones

London's dialling code is 020. If
you're calling from outside the UK,
dial your international access code,
then the UK code, 44, then the full
London number, omitting the first
0 from the code. To dial abroad
from the UK, first dial 00, then the
country code (Australia 61; Canada
1; Ireland 353; New Zealand 64;
South Africa 27; USA 1).

US mobile telephones will only
operate here if they are tri-band.

ESSENTIALS

Public phones

Public payphones take coins or credit cards (sometimes both). The minimum cost is 20p. International calling cards offering bargain minutes via a freephone number are widely available.

Time

London operates on Greenwich Mean Time (GMT), which is five hours ahead of the US's Eastern Standard Time. In spring (25 March 2007) the UK puts its clocks forward by one hour to British Summer Time. In autumn (28 October 2007) the clocks go back to GMT.

Safety

London is not a particularly dangerous city for visitors, but its crowded places – buses, busy streets, tube trains and stations – attract the usual complement of petty criminals. Keep your valuables in your hotel or room safe and make sure the cash and cards you carry with you are tucked and preferably zipped away in your bag.

Tipping

Tip in taxis, minicabs, restaurants, hotels, hairdressers and some bars (not pubs). Ten per cent is normal, with some restaurants adding as much as 15 per cent. Watch for places that include service, then leave the space for a gratuity on your credit card slip blank.

Tickets

With the exception of the major cultural institutions, which have in-house box offices and offer phone and web ticketing services at no significant premium, most venues subcontract their ticketing out to agencies. To find out which, consult the venue's website. Between them, Ticketmaster (www.ticketmaster.co.uk, 0870 534 4444, +44 161 385 3211 international) and TicketWeb (08700 600 100, ticketweb.co.uk), represent most venues.

tkts

Clocktower building, Leicester Square, WC2H 7NA (www.official londontheatre.co.uk). Leicester Square tube. **Open** 10am-7pm Mon-Sat; noon-3pm Sun.
A non-profit-making organisation selling reduced-price tickets for West End shows on a first-come, first-served basis on the day of the performance.

Tourist information

Visit London (7234 5800, www.visitlondon.com) is the city's official tourist information company. There are also tourist offices in Greenwich, Leicester Square, and by St Paul's Cathedral.
Britain & London Visitor Centre
1 Lower Regent Street, Piccadilly Circus, SW1Y 4XT (8846 9000/www.visitbritain.com). Piccadilly Circus tube.

Visas

EU citizens do not require a visa to visit the UK; citizens of the USA, Canada, Australia, South Africa and New Zealand need only a passport for tourist visits. Check current status on www.ukvisas. gov.uk well before you travel

What's on

Time Out magazine, available from central London newsagents on Tuesdays and containing a week's worth of listings, is the essential reference. For gay listings, also look out for *Boyz* magazine in venues.

ESSENTIALS

Index

ESSENTIALS

ESSENTIALS

Enjoy London
by river

Ask at central London piers
or visit tfl.gov.uk/river
for information about
London's river services

1/3 off for valid Travelcard holders*
*Show your Travelcard, or Oyster card loaded with a
valid Travelcard, when purchasing your ticket and get
1/3 off the normal Riverboat fare. Some restrictions
may apply.

**MAYOR
OF LONDON**

Transport for London

 RIVER